The Platoon

From the Library of

Frontispiece: bookplate with Joseph Johns Steward's signature. (*Family collection*)

The Platoon

An Infantryman on the Western Front 1916–1918

Joseph Johns Steward

Edited by
Andrew Robertshaw and Steve Roberts

Pen & Sword
MILITARY

First published in Great Britain in 2011 by
Pen & Sword Military
an imprint of
Pen & Sword Books Ltd
47 Church Street
Barnsley
South Yorkshire
S70 2AS

Copyright © The Platoon: the estate of Joseph Johns Steward
Copyright © Introductory text and notes: Andrew Robertshaw and Steve
Roberts

ISBN 978 1 84884 361 5

The right of Joseph Johns Steward, Andrew Robertshaw and Steve
Roberts to be identified as the Authors of this Work has been asserted by
them in accordance with the Copyright, Designs and Patents Act 1988.

Typeset in Ehrhardt by Phoenix Typesetting, Auldgirth, Dumfriesshire

Printed and bound in England by CPI UK

Pen & Sword Books Ltd incorporates the Imprints of Pen & Sword
Aviation, Pen & Sword Maritime, Pen & Sword Military, Wharncliffe
Local History, Pen and Sword Select, Pen and Sword Military Classics,
Leo Cooper, Remember When, Seaforth Publishing and Frontline
Publishing.

For a complete list of Pen & Sword titles please contact
PEN & SWORD BOOKS LIMITED
47 Church Street, Barnsley, South Yorkshire, S70 2AS, England
E-mail: enquiries@pen-and-sword.co.uk
Website: www.pen-and-sword.co.uk

Contents

Acknowledgements

The editors of *The Platoon* would like to express their thanks to all those without whom the book would not have been possible. The first is, of course, the author Joseph Johns Steward, a man whom we never met but now know so much about. We can only speculate as to the circumstances in which he wrote this book, but his personal account of warfare on the Western Front is war from the point of view of the 'PBI', the Poor Bleeding Infantryman. It is a frank, factual and moving account that on his death was nearly thrown away as rubbish. The fact that it was not lost was due to the intervention of Joan Gray, who rescued the folder from the house in Croydon and passed it on to her daughter-in-law Jean Gray. Jean brought the typescript to the attention of Julian Waltho from Kent College, who suggested that Andy Robertshaw might like to look at it.

The rest, as they say, is history, but the publication would not have been possible without the support of our long-time publisher at Pen & Sword, Rupert Harding. He saw the potential of *The Platoon* and freely admits that his attitude to the value of the book improved with every version we sent him. This process of editing would have been rather delayed had it not been for the skills of Lesley Wood, who retyped the entire book. (The editors would still be typing now, had it been left to them.)

Thanks must also go to Colin Lattimore, Chairman of the Book Plate Society, for his assistance in dating the original book plate and subsequently enabling the editors to establish an approximate time frame for the writing of the manuscript, and to Bruce Harling, who, despite residing in Nice, illustrated the ease with which information from the United Kingdom census records could be accessed.

We are also grateful to Major Chris Carling, whose friendship, companionship, opinions and map reading expertise were much appreciated while we were attempting to follow the movements of 'The Platoon' around northern France.

We would also like to thank the staff at the Imperial War Museum and the National Archives for all their assistance in tracing various individual and unit records and images. We must also thank Barbara Levy for allowing us to reproduce 'Twelve Months After' by Siegfried Sassoon.

Finally we want to thank Joanna and Russell Gray, Jean's son and daughter, for allowing us to publish the book, and Jean's relative Laurence Hawkins for providing vital family history and some of the photographs we have used. Without the assistance of Jean's extended family, we would have no photographs of the author at all.

Andy Robertshaw and Steve Roberts
March 2011

Abbreviations

7 RIF	7th (Service) Battalion, Royal Irish Fusiliers
8 Middx	8th (Service) Battalion, Middlesex Regiment
10 A&SH	10th (Service) Battalion, Argyll and Sutherland Highlanders
10 E.Yorks	10th (Service) Battalion, East Yorkshire Regiment
12 Manchester	12th (Service) Battalion, Manchester Regiment
13 London	13th (Kensington) Battalion, London Regiment
14 London	14th (London Scottish) Battalion, London Regiment
15 London	15th (Civil Service Rifles) Battalion, London Regiment
16 London	16th (Queens Westminster Rifles) Battalion, London Regiment
20 London	20th (Blackheath and Woolwich) Battalion, London Regiment
22 London	22nd (The Queens) Battalion, London Regiment
AFB103	Army Form B103, Casualty Form Active Service
AFZ21	Army Form Z21, Certificate of Transfer to the Reserve on Demobilisation
AMOT	Army Museums Ogilby Trust
ASC	Army Service Corps
BEF	British Expeditionary Force
BWD	Battalion War Diary
CCS	Casualty Clearing Station
CO	Commanding Officer
COP	Close Observation Patrol
CSM	Company Sergeant Major (Warrant Officer Class II)
CWGC	Commonwealth War Graves Commission
DCM	Distinguished Conduct Medal
FGCM	Field General Courts-Martial
FMO	Full Marching Order
FSMO	Full Service Marching Order
IWM	Imperial War Museum
MC	Military Cross

MDS	Main Dressing Station
MIC	Medal Index Card
MM	Military Medal
MO	Medical Officer
NCO	Non Commissioned Officer
OC	Officer Commanding
QM	Quartermaster
RAMC	Royal Army Medical Corps
RAP	Regimental Aid Post
RASC	Royal Army Service Corps
RE	Royal Engineers
RFC	Royal Flying Corps
RMO	Regimental Medical Officer
RSM	Regimental Sergeant Major (Warrant Officer Class I)
SB	Stretcher Bearer
SDGW	Soldiers Died in the Great War
TNA	The National Archives
VC	Victoria Cross
WO	War Office (Series classification at The National Archives)

Preface

It is true to say that people are interested in other people's lives. Whether this is based on events in the headlines, the strange domestic activities of 'celebrities' or the virtual lives of actors in television dramas makes no difference. As a result there is a profusion of magazines dedicated to revealing the minutiae of other people's daily lives, human frailties and indiscretions. For many of us, however, it is our own families and ancestors that remain a subject of fascination, surprise and revelation. Whether the connection is genealogical, biological, via marriage or other relationship, 'family' history compels tens of thousands of people to spend hours of their leisure time in pursuit of facts about 'their' relatives' past lives. The success of family history magazines, television programmes and spin-off events such as 'Who Do You Think You Are? Live', held annually at Olympia, demonstrate that this interest is no longer the preserve of antiquarians or specialist societies. Web-based genealogy sources such as 'Ancestry' and 'Find my Past' have been created to both foster and feed this passion for information. The number of magazines dedicated to family history may not quite rival the profusion of those concerning celebrities, yet the availability of family history magazines in supermarkets indicates a clear trend. Membership of the Society of Genealogists and the Family History Society has rocketed over the past twenty years, as have groups dedicated to family names and local history. In consequence, the numbers of people using the resources of Somerset House, local archives and The National Archives (TNA) have grown dramatically in the same period. Any visitor to TNA in Kew, on even a gloomy winter day, cannot be unaware that the majority of people searching the records are not authors and academics. They are on the hunt for family members who, frequently, they had never met and were totally unaware had ever existed until they 'caught the family history bug'.

Steve and Andy are frequent visitors to Kew, and what always strikes them is the number of people who are researching their Great War ancestors. Despite the passage of over ninety-five years since the guns fell silent on 11 November 1918, people are drawn back to that conflict to try to understand what their family members experienced, and perhaps wanting to 'close the book' by discovering how or why an individual was killed. Both Steve and Andy receive a large number of letters and e-mails from people who are keen to discover the fate of a family member who saw military service and gain some insight into their experience. It is, therefore, no coincidence that some of the most compelling episodes in the series 'Who Do You Think You Are?' are those concerning military history. This is partly due to the drama of any involvement of a family member in world events, but it is also linked to the way in which the War Office at the time had the fortunate habit of keeping records about both events and individuals. As a result, it is possible to research not only what was happening generally on a specific day during a war, but also where an individual may have been at that time. By comparison, the records for contemporary civilians are frequently at best sketchy and may only cover the basics of birth, marriage and death. One result of this interest was the BBC series 'My Family at War', first broadcast in November 2008, which examined the Great War military careers of the relatives of various celebrities. A wide variety of sources was used and although only a limited number of careers could be explored, these and other programmes indicated to the public what information could be available about their family members.

Steve and Andy have both met people who began to research their Great War ancestors because the potential of unlocking military records was revealed by this type of television. However, a large number of people remain deterred by the apparent complexity of military records, the language used and their own lack of knowledge of military service. This book is not intended to be a guide to the many sources available, but rather it is a case study on how someone with little or no experience can use those resources for themselves. Rather than providing a simple systematic 'how to' guide, which might lack interest for the reader, it has been based around an original account of the experience of the war written by one of its participants, Joseph Johns Steward. He was a member of a small military sub-unit, a platoon, and his story reveals much about the experiences common to most servicemen in the war. His account has allowed Andy and Steve to demonstrate what information is available, where to find it and how to use it to reconstruct the experience of the war for yourself. Where necessary, it has indicated the limitations of research and, it is hoped, demonstrated that mistakes can be made by jumping to conclusions or not understanding the sources. Further, it explains the slang and terminology used by soldiers and provides some context to the world-changing events in which the men of Steward's platoon participated. Many of those men did not come home, but the majority did and 'The Platoon' was written by a veteran of the Great War before the mass-market appeal of memoirs about the period between 1914 and 1918. It was not until the 1960s that memoirs by 'Other Ranks', rather than officers, were published in large numbers and there is nothing to suggest that the author ever tried submitting his type-script to a publishing house.

The author clearly wanted to convey something of his experience to another generation; he could not have imagined that his book would finally be in print nearly a hundred years after the events it describes. Steve and Andy hope that they have done the author justice and that his work will help readers to understand the experiences of their own family members. And that it will show, too, how an amateur historian can link up the fragmentary records they left behind and ultimately walk their battlefields, whether in reality during a tour of France or Belgium, or from the safety and comfort of desk and computer, which is where most of this work is done.

Timeline

1914
August
4 August   **War declared**
5 August   **13th (Kensington) Battalion, London**
                      Regiment [13 London] mobilised
23 August   Battle of Mons
                      Retreat from Mons
26 August   Battle of Le Cateau

September
5 September   Battle of the Marne
13 September   Battle of the Aisne

October
10 October   Fall of Antwerp
19 October   First Battle of Ypres commences

November
4 November   **13 London arrives in France**
22 November   First Battle of Ypres concludes
                      Establishment of fixed trench lines along the
                      Western Front

December
16 December   Bombardment of Scarborough by German Navy
                      Unofficial Christmas truce reported in some areas
                      of the Western Front

1915
January
19 January   First Zeppelin raids on the United Kingdom at
                      Great Yarmouth
24 January   Naval action at Battle of Dogger Bank

February

18 February   German Navy commences submarine blockade of
                   United Kingdom

March

10 March   Battle of Neuve Chapelle

April

22 April   Second Battle of Ypres commences
22 April   First use of gas as a weapon on the Western Front
                   by German Army
25 April   Allied landings commence in Dardanelles
                   (Gallipoli)

May

7 May   *Lusitania* sunk by German submarine *U20* in the
                   Atlantic
9 May   Battle of Aubers Ridge
15 May   Battle of Festubert
25 May   Second Battle of Ypres concludes
31 May   First Zeppelin raid on London

June

                   Formation of a coalition government in the United
                   Kingdom

July

29 July   First use of flamethrowers by the Germans at
                   Hooge

August

15 August   National Register completed in the United
                   Kingdom

September

25 September   Battle of Loos commences

October

5 October   British and French troops land in Salonika

8 October	Battle of Loos concludes
12 October	Nurse Edith Cavell executed as a spy by German Army

November   British forces begin their advance on Baghdad

December

19 December	Sir Douglas Haig replaces Sir John French as Commander in Chief of the British Expeditionary Force on the Western Front
19 December	Evacuation of forces in Gallipoli commences

1916
January

4 January	**Joseph Johns Steward enlists in 15th (Civil Service Rifles) Battalion, London Regiment [15 London]**

February

	Military Service Act introduces conscription for unmarried men aged 18–41
21 February	Battle of Verdun commences

March

	Actions around The Bluff and St Eloi areas south of Ypres

April

24 April	Start of the Easter Uprising in Ireland
25 April	German naval bombardment of Yarmouth and Lowestoft

May

21 May	Introduction of British Summer Time
25 May	Military Service Act amended and conscription introduced for married men
31 May	Battle of Jutland: naval engagement in the North Sea

June

5 June   Lord Kitchener dies when HMS *Hampshire* sunk
                   by mine en route to Russia

**12 June   Private Joseph Johns Steward arrives in
                   France with draft for 15 London**

July

1 July   Battle of Somme commences (60,000 casualties
                   including 20,000 dead on first day)
                   **In the evening Private Joseph Johns Steward
                   arrives at front with draft for 15 London and
                   is transferred to 13 London as one of the
                   replacements for the battalion's 300-plus
                   casualties**

August

                   Battle of the Somme continues with attacks on
                   Pozières and Delville Wood

28 August   Italy declares war on Germany

September

                   Battle of the Somme continues with attacks on
                   Guillemont and Ginchy

9 September   13 London take part in attack on Leuze Wood

15 September   First use of tanks during the attacks on the villages
                   of Flers and Courcelette on the Somme

23 September   Joseph Johns Steward to hospital

27 September   Joseph Johns Steward rejoins battalion

October

                   Battle of the Somme continues with attacks on
                   Transloy Ridge and Ancre Heights

November

13 November   Battle of the Somme concludes with attacks along
                   the River Ancre and at Beaumont Hamel

28 November   First bombing raids by aircraft on London

December	Herbert Asquith resigns as Prime Minister and is replaced by David Lloyd George Battle of Verdun concludes
1917 **January** 19 January	Explosion at TNT processing factory in Silvertown, London **13 London in the line near Neuve Chapelle (as part of 56 Infantry Division)**
February	Germany declares unrestricted submarine warfare **13 London inspected by Sir Douglas Haig**
March	German Army withdraws to pre-prepared defensive positions on the Hindenburg Line **56 Division withdrawn from the line to prepare for the Battle of Arras**
April 6 April	United States of America declares war on Germany
9 April	Easter Monday: first day of the Battle of Arras. **13 London in the first wave attacking the village of Neuville Vitasse southeast of Arras**
16 April	French launch their offensive on the Chemin des Dames under General Nivelle
17 April	First reports of mutinies in the French Army
May 15 May	Marshal Petain appointed as French Commander in Chief
25 May	First heavy bomber raid on Folkestone **13 London spend the month alternating between periods in the line and rest periods in Arras**

June

7 June	Battle of Messines opens with the exploding of nineteen mines under the German lines along the ridge
13 June	First heavy bomber raids on London
19 June	British royal family becomes the House of Windsor
	13 London remain on the Arras front, alternating between periods in the line and at rest in Arras, billeted in Schramm Barracks

July

	13 London remain on Arras front
31 July	Opening day of the Third Battles of Ypres, more commonly referred to as the Battle of Passchendaele

August

5 August	**Battalion moves north from Arras and arrives in the Ypres area. Major V. Flower assumes command**
11 August	**13 London remain in reserve, located near Ouderdom**
15 August	**13 London move forward in preparation for an attack on Glencorse Wood. During the preparations the CO, Major Flower, killed by shellfire and replaced by Captain, Acting Lieutenant Colonel, R.E.F. Shaw**
16 August	**13 London in reserve during an unsuccessful attack on Glencorse Wood. At nightfall 56th Division is withdrawn from the line**
24 August	**56th Division withdrawn from the Ypres salient to St Omer**
31 August	**56th Division relocated to the Somme area**

September

	Third Battle of Ypres continues with actions at Langemark, Menin Road and Polygon Wood
	13 London move to the Cambrai front in the area of Lagnicourt

October

Third Battle of Ypres continues with actions at Broodseinde, Poelcapelle and Passchendaele

13 London remain in Lagnicourt area

7 October
Joseph Johns Steward proceeds on leave to the UK

13 October
Rescue of Australian pilot who crash-landed in no man's land opposite the battalion lines

17 October
Joseph Johns Steward returns from leave

November

6 November
Canadian troops capture Passchendaele village

10 November
Third Battle of Ypres concludes

16 November
Clemenceau becomes French Prime Minister

20 November
Battle of Cambrai commences with the first use of massed tanks in the war. **The 56th Division is deployed in a diversionary role on the left flank of the attack. During this period 13 London remain in reserve**

24 November
13 London engaged in attack on Tadpole Copse

30 November
13 London heavily engaged together with the rest of 56th Division against a surprise German counter-attack on the Cambrai front

December

1 December
56th Division withdrawn to Arras area for rest and refitting, and then move into the line between Oppy and Gavrelle with 13 London responsible for the Oppy sector

9 December
British troops capture Jerusalem

15 December
Armistice signed between Russian Bolsheviks and the Central Powers

23–28 December
13 London out of the line, in billets at Roclincourt

1918
January

> **13 London spend the month in reserve, resting at Wakefield Camp and Magnicourt**

February
14 February

> **13 London moves back into the area of Roclincourt**
> At this point the British Army restructured from four infantry battalions per brigade to three. This resulted in 13 London receiving a draft of three officers and 150 extra men

March
3 March

> Treaty of Brest–Litovsk between Russia and Germany ends the war on the Eastern Front and releases large numbers of German forces for the Western Front
> **13 London reports an increase in enemy raiding and gas shelling on the Oppy front**

21 March

> German Army launches the first of a series of offensives designed to break the Anglo–French lines prior to the arrival of large numbers of American troops. The first stage of the offensive is directed at British and French troops on the Somme
> **13 London remain in the Roclincourt area**

28 March

> The second stage of the German offensive is launched against the Arras front with five German divisions attacking the 56th and 4th Divisions.
> **13 London in support near Oppy**

29 March

> **13 London withdrawn from the line into rest at Mont St Eloi**

April
1 April

> Formation of the Royal Air Force (amalgamation of Royal Flying Corps and Royal Naval Air Service)

6 April	**13 London move into line in the Tilloy/Beaurains sector opposite Neuville Vitasse**
9 April	Germans launch third stage of offensive in the valley of the River Lys south of Armentières
14 April	Marshal Foch becomes Allied Supreme Commander
21 April	**While in reserve 13 London supplies 500 men to working parties**
23 April	Raid by Royal Navy on Belgian port of Zeebrugge The American Expeditionary Force begins to arrive in France and Belgium
May	
	13 London remain in the line in Arras sector, alternating between periods in the line and at rest in Arras. During this time the battalion was able to use St Saveur's Caves as a shelter. During periods in the line the battalion conducted an active programme of raids against the enemy lines
28 May	Germans launch offensive against British and French troops on the River Aisne
June	
	13 London continue to hold the line in Arras sector
16 June	**13 London hold church parade and medal award ceremony**
July	
	The 56th Division (and with it 13 London) spend the month out of the line. On 18 July they move to Chateau de la Haie, where they spend the rest of the month training and taking part in sports
16 July	Murder of Tsar Nicholas and his family by Bolsheviks
31 July	**13 London move back into the line near Tilloy**

August

3 August	British forces land in northern Russia
8 August	Allied advances commence with the Battle of Amiens. This was the start of the final hundred days of the war and was described by the German High Command as 'The Blackest Day of the German Army'
4–12 August	**13 London located in Schramm Barracks, Arras**
22 August	**13 London involved in attack on the village of Boyelles. During the day the CO, Acting Lieutenant Colonel R.E.F. Shaw, is killed**
26–30 August	Battle of the Scarpe

September

12 September	American forces engaged in attacks at St Mihael
12 September	Start of attacks on Hindenburg Line
27 September	British forces successfully break the Hindenburg Line defences on the Canal du Nord
	During this period 13 London alternate between periods in rest in the area of Vis en Artois and their turn in the line. The advance moves along the Arras–Cambrai Road and turns north along the Canal du Nord
28 September	**D Company advances through Mill Copse towards the canal. It is at this point that the author's account ends**

October

	Battle of St Quentin Canal
	Battle of Beaurevoir
	Battle of Cambrai
	Pursuit to the Selle
14 October	**13 London withdrawn from the line to Arras**
20 October	**Joseph Johns Steward proceeds to UK on leave**
27 October	**Joseph Johns Steward promoted from private to lance corporal**

November
4 November   Battle of the Sambre
**3 November   Joseph Johns Steward returns from UK and
                    rejoins unit**
**11 November   Armistice comes into effect at 11am on the
                    Western Front
                    13 London engaged in repairing roads**

December
14 December   British General Election

1919
January
18 January   Opening of Peace Conference in Paris

February
5 February   Joseph Johns Steward returns to the UK

March
**8 March   Joseph Johns Steward demobilised to the
                    Army Reserve and returns to civilian life**

Introduction and Methodology

In 2009 Andy Robertshaw gave a presentation to a group of history students studying the Great War at Kent College near Canterbury. After the session was over the teacher, Julian Waltho, showed him a photocopied version of a typescript that belonged to a colleague at the school, geography teacher Jean Gray. The original, rather battered, black quarto-sized ring binder, bursting at the seams, contained a typewritten novel entitled 'The Platoon'. There were 211 pages, typed on one side with double-spaced lines, so it was physically easy to read, although the style was rather limited and as a novel it was not a page-turner. At the front of the file was a bookplate bearing the name of the author, Joseph Johns Steward, and a very interesting map of northern France with over fifty places underlined in ink, from Mons in the northeast, to near Amiens in the southwest, with the obvious southern boundary being the Somme. When Joseph died, the folder was very nearly thrown away. Fortunately Joan Gray, Joseph's niece, rescued it and later passed it to Jean, her daughter-in-law.

Jean eventually passed the folder on to her children Joanna and Russell, but, although they all looked at it, it remained forgotten on a bookshelf for several years. They could not think of anyone who might be interested in it, but just could not bring themselves to throw it away as the author had obviously poured so much energy into it. The children left home and moved into flats with limited space and so 'The Platoon' stayed on Jean's bookshelf, leaving her pondering the question of what to do with it.

In 2009 Jean, a geography teacher, accompanied the history department visit with Year 9 pupils to the Ypres salient, and in a quiet moment had told Julian Waltho about the dilemma with 'The Platoon'. Julian was immediately very interested and said that he might have a solution as he knew that Andy Robertshaw, who would be coming in to school to give a lecture to Year 9 about the trenches, might be interested and would certainly be able to tell her the best course of action.

Andy's initial thought, based on a scan of the content, was that it was probably written by a participant in the war who had served as an officer in one of the battalions of the London Regiment. It described service on the Western Front from the Somme in July 1916 to the eve of victory in the autumn of 1918. This coincided with the same period as that of his own grandfather, John Andrew Robertshaw, who served as a private in the Manchester Regiment and later the East Yorkshire Regiment. Critically Andy did not recognise the content of the typescript, which suggested that it had, indeed, not been published and could be a rare find. It is not every day that there is an opportunity to read a document about the Great War which has not been seen by anyone other than the author and his family. Although it was late when he returned home, armed with the typescript, Andy carried out an Internet search for both a book called *The Platoon* and the name of the author. To his relief there was nothing available with the same or a similar title, and Joseph Steward's name did not produce any results either. The next morning, with a copy of the typescript in hand, Andy arrived early at the Royal Logistic Corps Museum, at which he is Director. His plan was to search the archive before the working day started. (There are advantages to working in a museum!) A search of the Army List for 1916, which contains the details of all serving officers, proved fruitless. There was no officer called Joseph Johns Steward, or J.J. Steward, listed in that year or any other year of the war. This was an early lesson in not jumping to conclusions. You do not have to be an officer to write a book.

An on-line search of the Medal Index Cards [MIC][1] available from TNA at Kew demonstrated what Andy should have done first. In the case of Joseph Steward, the details were surprising, to say the least. The document confirmed Andy's suspicion that the author was in the 13th (Kensington) Battalion, London Regiment [13 London], and noted the detail that his regimental number had changed at some point from 7515 to 493489. He was eligible for just two service medals, the 'Victory' and 'British War'. This indicated that he had not served overseas before 1916, and fitted with the typescript, in which 'The Platoon' is described as arriving in France during the summer of 1916. The information the MIC provides is limited but incredibly useful as it records an individual's eligibility for service and gallantry medals, together with details of rank and unit. In some cases it provides additional information such as the fate of the individual, when and where they first served overseas and, in rare cases, details of post-war home addresses. Critically it provides the regimental number for all other ranks. Officers did not receive numbers until 1920, when the old method of allocating a regimental number was scrapped for new recruits and a system of army numbers was adopted.[2]

Armed with this information, there was a chance of finding Steward's service record at TNA. Without this vital detail, it would be a great deal harder, not exactly like looking for a needle in a haystack, but still time-consuming. The archives listed eight Joseph Stewards, although only one of them was in the London Regiment. The next step was to discover whether his service record was among those lost in the Second World War. Once again, Andy relied on the Internet but the news was not good. It appeared that Steward's record was among the 65 per cent of British military service records that had been destroyed by enemy action during the Blitz in September 1940.[3]

The records that did survive were fire- or water-damaged and were placed on microfilm to protect the already fragile documents. These are the so-called 'Burnt records', which are now available via TNA, although they represent only about a quarter of the original archive. Following a partnership between TNA and Ancestry.co.uk, the records are available through Ancestry.co.uk and consist of both 'the Burnt records' (WO/363) and surviving 'Pension Records' (WO/364).[4] As a final complication, the records of soldiers, or other ranks, who continued to serve after April 1920 are not held by TNA but are still retained by the Ministry of Defence in Glasgow.

On a pleasant spring morning in 2010 Andy set off to Kew to search the records. The result of a morning's work was, to say the least, satisfactory. It transpired that Joseph's records had not been destroyed or even damaged and armed with his combined TNA Reader's Ticket and charge card, Andy was able to print off twelve A3-sized pages of information about Joseph's military career.[5] These pages were a treasure trove of information, providing details of his service including early service in the 15th (Civil Service Rifles) Battalion, London Regiment [15 London] as Private 7532. The service record also contained dates of home leave, his height and chest measurements in 1916, his home address on enlistment and, importantly, confirmation of the units in which he served. What was most remarkable was that some of the early detail provided in 'The Platoon' was echoed by the information in the service record. In the typescript the draft of soldiers leave Winchester in mid-June and arrive at Southampton to *'board the boat waiting to take them to Le Havre'*. Army Form B.103 Casualty Form Active Service [AFB103],[6] contained in Joseph's service record, indicates that he left

Southampton on 12 June 1916 and arrived at Le Havre the following day. Later in 'The Platoon' the soldiers arrive at the front in the evening of 1 July 1916, the first day of the Battle of the Somme. This seemed unlikely and Andy uncharitably thought that the author had picked this date for dramatic effect. However, there in the record it states that Private Joseph Johns Steward joined the 13 London on the evening of 1 July 1916. This demonstrated that 'The Platoon' was clearly based on Joseph's personal experiences. How much more was autobiographical and what insights could the typescript give into the life and experiences of Joseph himself and the characters that populate his account?

Andy's first thought was to discuss the prospect of turning 'The Platoon' into a published book, which was clearly what the author had intended, with Steve Roberts. Steve is an expert on the archives of the Great War and had worked with Andy on a number of television programmes about the archaeology of the Western Front. Importantly, Steve and Andy had already worked together, with Alastair Fraser, on a book about filming the Battle of the Somme in 1916, *Ghosts on the Somme*.[7] This had proved a model of how a source can be forensically investigated and Steve Roberts, with his background in the Metropolitan Police, had provided ideas for new forms of historical detective work. Importantly, Andy was aware that Steve relished a challenge and knew his way round the records and sources. In a brief meeting, during which Andy provided copies of what research was already available, Steve said 'yes' to the project and, with the support of Rupert Harding of Pen & Sword Books, work began. After years on shelves and in cupboards, Joseph Johns Steward's book was going to be published.

It was decided to use Joseph's semi-fictionalised account to both tell the story of 'The Platoon' and to demonstrate how the sources used to find out the facts behind the fiction and to complete the biographical and military details could be accessed by any family historian. Having worked for more than twenty-five years in museums, Andy was aware how daunting many researchers find military sources. Steve was on the verge of establishing a business that carried out that sort of research for those people to whom the prospect seems difficult, if not impossible. *The Platoon* was not going to be a dry-as-dust 'how to do it' guide book. It was, instead, intended to show how anyone can do their own research, even if they are beginners who, whilst engaged in research, find that they have a relative who served in the Great War. With over five million service men and women in Britain's forces by 1918, few families do not have at least one soldier, sailor or airman in their family tree.

Using the Sources

The first step in investigating an ancestor from the Great War is establishing a name. As with all forms of family history research, it helps if the name is uncommon. There are, for example, at TNA 16,372 records relating to soldiers named George Clarke who served in the Great War. Finding which one is yours would be virtually impossible without other information. The survival of evidence about family members is often random and may well be very limited. Clues can be easy to find if you are lucky! The typescript of 'The Platoon' was almost put out with the rubbish after the death of the author.

In the case of the author of 'The Platoon, the first clues came from his first name, family name and initials, in addition to a few references in the typescript. Using the MIC, on-line via TNA website, it was possible to establish that a Joseph J. Steward was a member of 13 London with two different regimental numbers – 7515 followed by 493489. It is important to note that the birthplace or home address of a man does not necessarily mean that he would join, or be conscripted into, a local regiment. In this case it was likely and the evidence of the account placed him in a London battalion.

Once the unit in which the man served has been identified, it is possible to use two other sources of information. The first of these are the Operational Records or War Diaries kept by units on active service throughout the war. These records are mainly in the series WO95 at TNA and provide a daily record of significant events for all units in the British Expeditionary Force [BEF].[8] The information recorded includes the location of units, the main events, casualties, officers, often by name, and other ranks by number, and in some cases maps and diagrams. They were, however, compiled by an officer of the unit and the content can sometimes reflect that officer's attitude to what must have seemed a dull and laborious task at times. Some of the maps have been removed to WO153 and some confidential information is in WO154. Establishing which regiment, or better still which battalion, your relative served in will make finding the correct War Diary much easier, but there is a way of relating his unit to a brigade or division, both successively higher formations.

The 'bible' for this process is either a search of the Internet, which may have the information, or better still the book by Brigadier E.A. James, *British Regiments, 1914–1918* (Samson Books, 1978).[9] This volume covers every cavalry regiment and infantry battalion that served in the Great War. Once you know the regiment or battalion, you can use the index to cross-reference this information with the brigades and divisions that unit served with during the war. Usefully, the book also tells you where the unit was at the outbreak of war or when it was raised, when it went overseas and its location at the end of hostilities. For example, the entry for 13 London records the following detail:

1/13th (County of London) Battalion (Kensington)
(Army Order 408 of October 1914 changed the title to 13th (County of London) Princess Louise's Kensington Battalion)
4.8.14 Iverna Gardens, Kensington, W.: 4th London Bde. 2nd London Div. Aug to Abbots Langley, Herts. Nov 1914 left 2nd London Div and went to France landing at Havre on 4.11.14. 13.11.14 to 25th Bde. 8th Div. 20.5.15 to G.H.Q. Troops and 11.8.15 formed a composite Bn with 1/5th and 1/12th Bns for works on the L. of C. 11.2.16 to 168th Bde. 56th Div. forming in Hallencourt area. 11.11.18 168th Bde. 56th Div. Belgium; Blaregnies north of Maubeuge.[10]

Armed with this information, you can go further still by using the *Order of Battle of Divisions,* originally produced by Major A.F. Becke in the 1920s. This multiple volume work covers all formations within the BEF from divisional level to general headquarters. They are now available in facsimile and are essential for searching the composition, senior officers, movements and battles of the respective division.[11] The entry for the 56th Division, for example, appears as:

56th (1st LONDON) DIVISION
On 7th January 1916 the Army Council authorised the re-formation in France, as soon as circumstances would allow, of the 56th (1st London) Division; and on the 5th February 1916 the division began to assemble around Hallencourt, in the Third Army area. Seven of the original battalions returned and the artillery rejoined . . .
By the 21st February the bulk of the division had been assembled.

For the remainder of the Great War the 56th Division served on the Western Front in France and Belgium, and was engaged in the following operations:-

1916
BATTLE OF THE SOMME

1 July	**Gommecourt** [VII. Corps, Third Army]
9 Sept.	**Battle of Ginchy** [XIV. Corps, Fourth Army]
15-22 Sept.	**Battle of Flers-Courcelette** [XIV. Corps, Fourth Army]
25-27 Sept.	**Battle of Morval** [XIV. Corps, Fourth Army]
1–9 Oct.	**Battle of Transloy Ridges** [XIV. Corps, Fourth Army]

1917

14 March–5 April	**German Retreat to the Hindenburg Line** [VII. Corps, Third Army]

BATTLE OF ARRAS

9–14 April	**First Battle of the Scarpe Line** [VII. Corps, Third Army]
3 and 4 May	**Third Battle of the Scarpe Line** [VI. Corps, Third Army]

BATTLE OF YPRES

16 and 17 Aug.	**Battle of Langemarck** [II. Corps, Fifth Army]

BATTLE OF CAMBRAI

21 Nov.	**Capture of Tadpole Copse** [IV. Corps, Third Army]
23–28 Nov.	**Capture of Bourlon Wood** [IV. Corps, until m/n. 24/11; then VI. Corps, Third Army]

1918
FIRST BATTLE OF THE SOMME

28 March	**First Battle of Arras** [XIII. Corps, First Army]

THE ADVANCE TO VICTORY

SECOND BATTLE OF THE SOMME

23 Aug.	**Battle of Albert** [VI. Corps, Third Army]

SECOND BATTLE OF ARRAS

26–30 Aug.	**Battle of the Scarpe** [XVIII. Corps, Third Army]

BATTLES OF THE HINDENBURG LINE

27 Sept.–1 Oct.	**Battle of the Canal du Nord** [XXII Corps, First Army]
8 and 9 Oct.	**Battle of Cambrai** [XXII Corps, First Army]
9–12 Oct.	**Pursuit to the Selle** [XXII Corps until 5pm, 11/10; then Cdn. Corps, First Army]

THE FINAL ADVANCE IN PICARDY

| 4 Nov. | **Battle of the Sambre** [XXII Corps, First Army] |
| 5-7 Nov. | **Passage of the Grande Honnelle** [XXII Corps, First Army] |

By m/n. on the 10th November the division was relieved in the front line and drawn back into support to the XXII Corps, but the 56th Division Artillery remained in action until the 'Cease Fire' sounded at 11a.m. on the 11th November. At that time, the leading infantry brigade of the 56th Division (advancing between Maubeuge and Mons) had reached Harveng.

During the 1,010 days of its existence (since its reformation) the division spent 330 days in rest, (The divisional artillery was frequently left in the line after the withdrawal of the infantry of the division.[12]) 195 days in a quiet sector of the Western Front, 385 days in an active sector, and 100 days in active operations.

Of course this kind of information can be supplemented, often with far more detail, by the use of printed regimental, battalion and formation histories, such as O.F. Bailey and H.M. Hollier, *The Kensingtons: 13th London Regiment* (London, Regimental Old Comrades Association, 1936) and Major C.H. Dudley Ward, *The Fifty-Sixth Division, 1st London Territorial Division 1914–1918* (Naval & Military Press, repr. edn, 1921). Sadly, not all battalions or larger units produced such histories, so it may be necessary to check with the regimental or corps museum, if such an institution still exists. One way to do this is to use the website of the Army Museum Ogilby Trust [AMOT] (www.army-museums.org.uk). Regimental and corps museums will usually hold printed histories from the Great War relating to their unit and some may have copies of war diaries, referred to above. Many have archives, which contain photographs, letters, memoirs and sub-unit histories that may not be available elsewhere. Traditionally, regiments have produced regular journals, which can be a useful source of information on wartime and peacetime careers of long-serving soldiers.[13] With the exception of those within the Household Division, regiments generally did not retain individual service records, so do not expect a miracle if your relative's service record was lost in the Blitz. Regimental museums are also under increasing constraints of time and money, so be aware that there may be a charge for research or for using the archive. This money funds the care and preservation of these collections, without which we would have even more gaps in our knowledge of events in the Great War.

Some of this work can be avoided if the original medals are available. Medals include those for service in addition to those issued for gallantry. Service medals relate to a soldier's service either in the United Kingdom or overseas, and were issued to all who served in a variety of combinations. Although millions of them were issued during and after the Great War, each one was engraved with the service man, or woman's family name, initials, rank, number and unit of the recipient, even if the award of the medal was posthumous. On some medals the information is engraved on the back. On others it is in small script around the edge of the medal's rim. Establishing a soldier's number at an early stage is very helpful, as it will enable you to locate records more effectively. Although officers did not have numbers in the Great War, their records are better preserved and, because there are fewer of them, they are easier to research.

In researching the Great War there are two types of medals that may provide information, if available. The first of these are the more common service medals, the British War and Victory medals. Additionally, if a man served in a theatre of war between 5 August and 22 November 1914 he was entitled to the 1914 Star, frequently referred to as the 'Mons Star'. Men who served after this date but before 31 December 1915 were entitled to the 1915 Star. It was apparent from the account that the author had joined the army in 1916, so would only get the standard two medals. Had he been serving in the Territorial Army in 1914, he would have been eligible for the Territorial Forces War Medal. Soldiers who were disabled and discharged received the Silver War Badge to wear with civilian clothes to indicate that they had previously served, if the nature of their disability did not make this obvious.

Relatively few soldiers receive gallantry medals and for some, such as the Victoria Cross [VC], of which 634 were awarded in the Great War, there is a good deal of information both in published accounts and on the internet. Some medals, including the Distinguished Service Order [DSO] and Military Cross [MC], were awarded to officers, and these awards are registered by date in the *London Gazette*. A copy of this is held in series WO390, with additional information in WO389, at TNA. Gazette entries are also available on the internet via www.gazettes-online.co.uk. This information can then be supplemented with details from the battalion or unit war diaries [BWD]. The Distinguished Conduct Medal [DCM] was more generally awarded and the *Gazettes* for these are in WO391, with more information available from the MIC.[14] Other awards, which include a Mention in Dispatches [MiD], the Military Medal [MM], the Meritorious Service Medal [MSM] and others, are noted in the MIC and mentioned, by date, in the *London Gazette*.

If you have access to medals, you will be able to obtain a great deal of valuable information, but if not, an alternative source can be letters sent to or from service men or women. Although there was no postal address as such for service men and women on active service, mail could be addressed to the unit name and region of service. For example, a letter from the comrades of John Andrew Robertshaw was addressed to 14 Platoon, D Company, 12 Manchester Regt., BEF, France.

This kind of information can also be found on postcards – one of the most common souvenirs of the Great War to survive in many families. In a period before the telephone or the internet, they provided a cheap and relatively quick way for a soldier to communicate with his family. The result is that millions of cards were sent from training camps and the front to families all over the United Kingdom and Empire. Obviously the written information, if it was passed by the military censor, can be useful in providing all sorts of clues as to location and unit, but it is frequently the front of the card that is most useful. Although photographs and embroidered pictures of places in France and Belgium can suggest where the sender had been located, either shortly before or at the time the card was sent, photographs of people are also useful.

Although general cards were available, perhaps the most famous being those produced by the *Daily Mail*,[15] others were more personal. As photographic equipment was expensive, cameras were a rare item in training camps and were officially banned by the military authorities, even for officers on active service. In consequence, studio photographs of soldiers and family members taken while they were training or before embarkation are common. So, too, are photographs taken by commercial photographers who came to the training camps in the United Kingdom or who set up behind the lines to record the appearance of individuals or small groups of soldiers on active service.

All of these photographs are packed full of information, which may include the sitter's unit, from his cap badge or shoulder title, his rank, from the insignia on shoulder or cuff, his medal entitlement, as worn on the left side of the chest, and even how often he had been wounded, based on the wound stripe, worn late in the war, on the lower left arm. Add to this the service stripes, which tell a trained observer how long the man had been overseas, and it is easy to see why picture postcards are a gold-mine for family historians. One of the best sources for information explaining how to decipher this profusion of potential information is any of the series of books produced by the Federation of Family History Societies, such as *Identifying Your World War 1 Soldier from Badges and Photographs.*[16]

In the case of Andy's grandfather, and potentially many others, this information was also supplemented by other documents that had been retained by his family. These included the single letter referred to above and a series of official notifications, relating to his three wounds, between 1917 and 1918. All this provides his regimental numbers, confirms his unit and his transfer in 1918 from 12 Manchester to 10th (Service) Battalion, East Yorkshire Regiment [10 E.Yorks], and also indicates where he was medically treated. The most useful document is, however, Army Form Z.21 [AFZ21], his Certificate of Transfer to Reserve on Demobilisation. This gives details of when he was demobilised (18 March 1919), his medical grade ('A') and even his year of birth. Critically, it confirms his final rank (private) and his service in both the Manchester and East Yorkshire Regiments, and provides the additional information that he first served with the North Staffordshire Regiment. All of this helps to reconstruct his career, although there is no additional detail because, like so many others, his service records were destroyed in the Blitz. Because of this destruction, for many people the MIC is the only surviving record available from TNA. This is frustrating and can be very much a dead end.

Tragic though it may seem, if a service man or woman was killed or died in service, this greatly increases the possibility of finding additional information about them. About 700,000 British officers and men died and information about them was recorded in a variety of ways. The most obvious is the Commonwealth War Graves Commission [CWGC] which maintains the Debt of Honour Register, which can be found at www.cwgc.org. This is a quick and easy way to find information, but you will need to have the basics, such as name and initials; further information, such as branch of service and year of death, is useful if available. Once again an unusual name can save a great deal of searching. Information available from the records normally includes the regiment or unit, date of death and place of burial or commemoration. Supplementary information relating to age, details of family members and home address may sometimes be provided. Additional details are also available from the register *Soldiers Died in the Great War* [SDGW]. Based on a series of books produced in the 1920s, the entire series is now available on CD or on-line at www.military-geneaology.com. This can supplement other information and, although not exhaustive, can provide valuable information,[17] as can local war memorials and the rolls of honour often listed in local churches.

Another source is newspapers. During the Great War the details of many men who were killed or wounded on active service were published in local and sometimes, depending upon status, national newspapers. These are worth consulting and can, in addition to family details, provide photographs not available anywhere else.

It is the intention of the editors to illustrate, using 'The Platoon', how these sources can be used to support this manuscript or perhaps validate a family story passed down through generations. As will be seen, the sources when used properly can either substantiate or disprove facts as presented. In respect of 'The Platoon', the work of Joseph Johns Steward appears as per his original manuscript. It has been reproduced in full, with only minor alterations to correct obvious misspellings, and references to locations and individuals have remained unaltered. The principal amendment undertaken by the editors to the narrative is the use of chapters. These have allowed each chronological phase of the narrative to be examined individually, and enabled each chapter to be separately noted. The explanatory notes are intended to enhance the reader's understanding of the story. They demonstrate the types of information that can be gleaned from the manuscript, the sources used to support them, and the path by which the reader could undertake similar research. Where relevant, the notes indicate the sources used to provide the information, using items such as battalion war diaries [BWD], CWGC, SDGW and TNA.

Notes

1. The Medal Index Cards, originally held on microfiche at TNA under the classification WO372, are, as described, an index system for the Medal Rolls. These are a series of ledgers which record regiment by regiment an individual's medal awards. They are sequentially listed by regimental number, not alphabetically. These ledgers are retained at TNA in class WO329. MIC searches can now be undertaken both online via the TNA at www.nationalarchives.gov.uk and at www.Ancestry.co.uk.
2. This amendment to the army numbering system was instituted by Army Order 338, 1920.
3. A curiosity of this situation is that these records do not relate to men who served in the Household Cavalry or the Foot Guards, whose records were retained by the respective regiment and, in the case of the Foot Guards, can be sourced by writing to the Adjutant of the Guards regiment in question via Bird Cage Walk. The Household Cavalry records have now been relocated to TNA under catalogue WO400.
4. These references link directly to the catalogue system employed by TNA. Electronic searches of these classes are still possible at TNA but the relevant microfilms have now been removed and placed in long-term storage. Searches undertaken at TNA will direct the reader via the catalogue to a link with Ancestry.co.uk.
5. The service record of Joseph Johns Steward was located in WO363/S2335.
6. AFB103 is an extremely useful form within a serviceman's record. It details not only any incidents of ill health or wounds, but records movements between units, periods of leave, promotions, etc.
7. A. Fraser, S. Roberts and A. Robertshaw, *Ghosts on the Somme, Filming the Battle, June–July 1916* (Pen & Sword, 2009).
8. TNA are currently conducting a programme of digitisation regarding war diaries, intended to preserve the fragile documents while still making them available to researchers.
9. James, E.A., *British Regiments, 1914–1918* (Samson Books, 1978).
10. The entry relating to 13 London records both the brigade and division to which the battalion belonged. An infantry brigade between 1914 and 1918 consisted of four infantry battalions, supported by a field ambulance of the Royal Army Medical Corps [RAMC], and by late 1916 a brigade trench mortar battery and machine gun company. The controlling element for the brigade was the division. The division contained three infantry brigades with their supporting elements, and in addition divisional engineer, signal and artillery units.
11. Becke, A.F., *Order of Battle of Divisions, Part 1, The Regular British Divisions* (Naval & Military Press Ltd, 2007).
12. Becke, A.F., *Order of Battle of Divisions, Part 2a, The Territorial Force Mounted Divisions and The 1st-Line Territorial Force Divisions 42–56* (Naval & Military Press Ltd, 2007), pp. 146–7.
13. Using *The Snapper*, the regimental journal of the East Yorkshire Regiment, allowed Steve to follow the antics of his paternal grandfather, who enlisted in the regiment in 1907. Despite the fact that the service record had not survived, it was possible to trace his grandfather's career with entries relating to the awards of good conduct stripes and qualification as a regimental signaller in the journal. In 1913 Private Roberts came thirteenth in the battalion cross-country race at Kamptee, India.
14. Walker, R.W., *Recipients of the DCM, 1914–1920* (Midland Records, 1981).
15. During the Great War a number of newspaper publishers produced images of the troops and battlefields, normally reproduced from their daily news sheets and then

sold as individual images to the general public. Some of the most popular of these were a series of 176 images made available as postcards by the *Daily Mail*. Still available today at specialist postcard fairs, these cards are now highly sought-after by collectors.

16. Swinnerton, I., *Identifying Your World War 1 Soldier from Badges and Photographs* (Federation of Family History Societies, 2000).

17. Whereas CWGC searches locate individuals, SDGW, in addition to searching for individuals, allows a researcher to examine a unit's casualties on a daily, monthly or yearly period, thus offering an idea of the unit's activities on a given day.

Joseph Johns Steward: A Biography

Joseph Johns Steward was born into a working class family, the second son of William Johns Steward and Sarah Ann, in Balham, London, on 17 October 1885.

The 1891 census shows that by this time the family was living at 8 Balfern Street in Battersea.[1] His father is listed as a leather cutter, having been born in Chelsea, just north of where the family was then resident. He and Sarah Ann had seven children, two boys and five girls, although others may have died in infancy. The eldest, Frederick, was fourteen and already working as a messenger boy, and the youngest, Ethel Elsea, had been born that year.

Judging from where the children were born, the family had lived in Islington between around 1877 and 1883.[2] Very little is known about Joseph's early life, but judging by the expectations of the period he would have left school when he was fourteen years old or a little younger if he could pass his school certificate at thirteen. Certainly his elder brother was in full-time employment at this age. In 1901, when Joseph was fifteen, he was boarding at 35 High Street, Marlow, in Buckinghamshire.[3] According to the 1901 census the head of the household was Harriet Anthony, and she had eight people aged between fourteen and twenty-eight living in her house. One is listed as a domestic servant and another is her niece; the others are, apparently, boarders. These boarders are from all over England and all are male, apart from Nellie Hicks. The young men are all 'outfitters' or 'drapers', and Nellie is listed as a 'milliner'. The number of people all in the same trade suggests that they are employed by a single business. Joseph is listed as a 'draper's clerk', which perhaps confirms that he worked with the others and this was his first job.[4] This snap-shot does not tell us how long Joseph stayed in Marlow, but we do know from later evidence that he moved closer to home in the intervening period.

Ten years later the 1911 census shows him as a boarder with Mr and Mrs May at 23 Queens Road, Feltham.[5] We cannot be certain where he was working at this time but his occupation is listed as 'book keeper'. By the time he joined the army in 1916 he was working as a clerk in the motor trade at the Chesham Supply Company in Kennington and gave his next of kin as his father, then residing at 119 Speke Road in Balham.[6]

Joseph's enlistment date is not without significance. On 27 January 1916 the Military Service Act introduced conscription into Britain for the first time in its history. Under the act, every British male who was over the age of nineteen but not yet forty-one and was unmarried or a widower without dependant children was eligible to serve. There were other exemptions but Joseph did not qualify for any of these. Before the act came into force it was possible to register as a volunteer prior to 15 December 1915 through the so-called 'Derby Scheme' established by Lord Derby, the Director-General of Recruiting. If the individual did so, he was regarded as having voluntarily 'attested' with the obligation to serve when called up. As a volunteer, a man could request to serve in a local regiment of his choice rather than being allocated to a unit by the War Office. The Derby Scheme was not a great success, despite the offer of a war pension, and voluntary attestation was reopened on 10 January 1916. It was against this backdrop of a move to universal conscription that Joseph enlisted as private 5372 in the 15 London.[7] This battalion was regarded as being socially elite, perhaps reflecting his social aspirations. The battalion's headquarters were at Somerset House in Westminster, and it is here he would have reported on 4 January 1916.

Joseph's Attestation Form states that he had enlisted for 'Four Years' Service in the United Kingdom'. However, on the same day, and with the same countersigning officer, A.C. Bull, he also completed the Imperial Service Obligation form in which he agreed to serve 'in any place outside the United Kingdom'. The Medical Inspection Report provides some vital information about Joseph that is not available elsewhere. He was 5ft 6½in tall (169cm) with a chest expansion of 32½in (82.5cm). He was small by modern standards for a man of thirty-one but well above the regulation minimum and it is worth noting that the doctor who conducted his medical noted his development as 'fair'.[8] His Attestation Form provides the additional information that his employer was the Chesham Supply Company of 27–43 Walnut Tree Walk, Kennington, and that his home address was 119 Speke Road, Balham, London.[9]

With the battalion already at the front, there was no question as to where the new private would be sent. The only question was when? After a little more than six months' training in the United Kingdom, Joseph arrived by troopship from Southampton in Le Havre on 12 June

1916.[10] Three weeks of further training in the Le Havre base camp followed to prepare him and his comrades for trench warfare. Late on 1 July 1916 he arrived with a draft of a hundred casualty replacements for the 13 London. Joseph and the rest of the draft were transferred permanently to this battalion on 30 July 1916 and served with it until the end of the war. He was issued a new Regimental number of 7515 at this point.[11]

There is no evidence that Joseph was ever wounded, although he spent a period of time from 23 September 1916 in XIV Corps' Rest Station suffering from neuralgia.[12] His Military History sheet, part of his service papers, indicate that he served on the continent from 12 June 1916 and returned to the United Kingdom at the end of hostilities on 4 February 1919. During this time he had ten days' leave from 7 to 17 October 1917, and almost exactly a year later he enjoyed a fourteen-day leave from 20 October to 3 November 1918. On his return to his unit he would have discovered that, on 27 October 1918, he had been promoted to lance corporal.[13] He returned to his battalion just in time for its last battle of the war near Valenciennes on 6 November 1918. The battalion was in billets at Rieu-de-Bury, just inside the Belgian frontier and on the route to Mons, when the Armistice was announced at 11.00am on 11 November 1918.[14] Despite having received recent leave, Joseph's occupation meant that he was classified in a group earmarked for an earlier return to civilian life. After three years and sixty-four days' service he was demobilised in London on 8 March 1919, and returned to civilian life at 119 Speke Road. As a Territorial, this was not, however, the end of his military commitment and with a new number, 493489, he was retained in the 13 London and recorded as medical category A, the highest category, indicating full fitness. His specialist military qualification was as a second-class shot.[15] His father's home address had not changed during the war and he was still resident at 119 Speke Road. At the end of his war service he was eligible for two medals, the British War and Victory Medals.[16] When he left the Territorial Army is not clear, as it is not recorded in his service record, although there is no evidence that he prolonged his relationship with military service.

He appears to have prospered in the post-war world and became a manager in Balham. He married Emily Olive Garrard, who was ten years younger, on 14 October 1922 in Wandsworth. At this time he was living at 10 Laitwood Road, Balham, and she a few doors away at no. 18.[17] In 1931, when his father died, Joseph was listed as a coachbuilder.[18] Their only child, Eric Johns Steward,[19] was born in 1924 but sadly died in early childhood, aged just eight, in 1933.[20] What happened to them in the Second World War is not known but as Londoners they would have been witnesses to the Blitz. Unfortunately, Joseph also endured the common wartime experience of being 'bombed-out' when a firebomb gutted the family home. Although he was fifty-five in 1940 Joseph was eligible for service in the Home Guard. A wartime photograph shows him with the rank of corporal, one rank higher than he achieved in the Great War.[21] Emily died in 1971[22] and Joseph just three years later in Croydon, aged eighty-nine.[23]

Notes

1. 1891 census, www.ancestry.co.uk.
2. 1891 census, www.ancestry.co.uk.
3. 1901 census www.ancestry.co.uk.
4. 1901 census www.ancestry.co.uk.
5. 1911 census, TNA.
6. Service Record, Attestation Form of Joseph Johns Steward, WO363/S2335, TNA.
7. Service Record, Imperial Service Obligation Form of Joseph Johns Steward, WO363/S2335, TNA.
8. Service Record, Medical Inspection Report of Joseph Johns Steward, WO363/S2335, TNA.
9. Service Record, Attestation Form, WO363/S2335, TNA.
10. Service Record, AFB103 of Joseph Johns Steward, WO363/S2335, TNA.
11. Service Record, AFB103 of Joseph Johns Steward, WO363/S2335, TNA.
12. Neuralgia is classified as a pain that follows the path of a nerve. Treatment is complicated and may be prolonged.
13. Service Record, AFB103 of Joseph Johns Steward, WO363/S2335, TNA.
14. O.F. Bailey and H.M. Hollier, *The Kensingtons: 13th London Regiment* (London, Regimental Old Comrades Association, 1936), pp. 196–9.
15. Service Record, Protection Certificate and Certificate of Identity of Joseph Johns Steward, WO363/S2335, TNA.
16. MIC of Joseph J. Steward, www.ancestry.co.uk.
17. Marriage certificate. Supplied by family.
18. Probate of William Johns Steward. Supplied by family.
19. There is only evidence for Eric J., but based on his father's name Joseph would almost certainly have used the Johns middle name.
20. Death certificate of Eric J. Steward. Supplied by family.
21. Information from Lawrence Hawkins.
22. Death certificate. Supplied by family.
23. Death certificate. Supplied by family.

The Platoon in the Great War

The Regiment

During the Great War, although a British soldier was a member of a regiment with a common cap badge and history, he served as a member of a battalion, which was a sub-unit of that regiment, for example, the 12th Battalion, Manchester Regiment or the 1st Battalion, Lancashire Fusiliers. The individual battalions served as both a fighting and an administrative unit. It prepared the members of the battalion for combat, fed and uniformed them, arranged pay and leave, and even organised their recreation. In peacetime there were a limited number of Regular and Territorial battalions in every regiment and the number of these depended upon the ability of the regiment to recruit volunteers and maintain their strength. Typically regiments drawn from urban areas with high populations had more battalions than those from rural areas. Joseph volunteered for the London Regiment, which, following the creation of the Territorial Force in 1908, was entirely Territorial and hence liable for service at home rather than overseas. In 1914 it consisted of twenty-eight battalions. These were numbered as fractions and named after existing regiments, districts of the capital, regions of the United Kingdom or employers. The 1/1st, for example, was the (City of London) Battalion (Royal Fusiliers), the 1/13th the (County of London) Battalion (Kensington) and the 1/15th the (County of London) Battalion (Prince of Wales's Own Civil Service Rifles). On the outbreak of war the number of battalions expanded in line with recruitment and some regiments expanded to many times their original size. During the Great War the Liverpool Regiment, for example, had forty-nine battalions, the Durham Light Infantry forty-two and the London Regiment eighty-eight. The consequence of this was that the army expanded to many times its peacetime strength but each battalion retained its links to the common history of a pre-existing regiment. 'Cap badge loyalty' – the connection between soldiers, their regimental history and membership of the 'regimental family' – was, and remains, a key feature of the British Army.

The Obligation to Serve

At the time of the outbreak of war, unlike Britain's European allies and enemies, the soldiers who made up the BEF that served in France and Flanders were all volunteers. As a result of the civil wars of the mid-seventeenth century, successive British governments did not favour large standing armies and relied for defence on the Royal Navy. As there was no conscription or other obligation to serve, British men had a choice about going into the military or remaining civilians. In consequence Britain's Regular Army was small in comparison with those of Europe, numbering around 247,500 men, compared to the millions France and Germany could mobilise. In 1914 the BEF was smaller than the armies of either Belgium, whose invasion by Germany had led to Britain's declaration of war, or even neutral Switzerland. To bolster the Regular Army on the outbreak of war Reservists were also mobilised. The Reserve, which numbered about 200,000 men, was made up from those who had completed their Regular service and returned to civilian life, the Army Reserve, those who had undergone a period of training on the understanding that they would be called up in the event of war, and the Special Reserve. This was both a means of bolstering the strength of the army and providing some much-needed experience to units that had never been in action before.

The Territorial Force did not form an additional reserve for the Regular Army and its members did not have an obligation to serve abroad until 1916, although it was clear on the outbreak of war that their services would be required overseas if the war showed no signs of being 'over by Christmas'. In consequence members of the Territorials were asked to sign an Imperial Service Form, which made them eligible for overseas service. Not all members of the force agreed to this and many remained in the United Kingdom while other units signed en-bloc. The first Territorial battalion to arrive on the Western Front was the 14th (London Scottish) Battalion, London Regiment [14 London], which arrived at Le Havre on 16 September 1914. It is worth adding that Lord Kitchener, who in 1914 was Secretary of State for War, had little enthusiasm for the Territorial Army but also foresaw that the 'European War' could last until at least 1917. In consequence, within days of the outbreak of war Parliament had agreed to the expansion of the army to half a million men and Kitchener had called for 100,000 volunteers. Although far more men than had originally been called for flocked 'to the colours', these volunteers of 1914 would not be able to take the field until they were at least partially trained; they did not arrive on the continent until 1915 and were largely committed to action in 1916. By this stage in the war the number of men prepared to volunteer had greatly diminished and there was evidence that those who continued to 'join up' were from the skilled and well educated male population. Faced by a potential postwar skills-shortage and a wartime manpower shortage, Parliament, reluctantly, introduced conscription in January 1916. Those called up from 1916 onwards form the final group of British soldiers who served in the Great War, the first being the Regulars and Reservists of August 1914, followed by the Territorials during the autumn of that year. These trained, if not experienced, soldiers were joined by the Kitchener Volunteers of 1915 and early 1916 who were enthusiastic and willing, if under-trained. Finally, from the middle of 1916, the army was supplemented by conscripts, who would ultimately provide half its manpower.

The Battalion

In 1914 a British infantry battalion at full establishment consisted of 1,007 other ranks and thirty officers. It was organised into a battalion headquarters and four companies usually lettered A to D. These were subdivided into sixteen platoons and sixty-four sections. The battalion was usually commanded by a lieutenant colonel with a major as second-in-command. The headquarters included an adjutant, responsible for administration, the quartermaster [QM], who dealt with stores, and a transport officer responsible for the horse-drawn wagons and carts that supported the battalion. In 1914 every battalion included a machine gun section armed with two Vickers or Vickers-Maxim medium machine guns. This section was commanded by a lieutenant and had a strength of seventeen, providing six-man detachments of machine-gunners and ammunition carriers. Attached to the battalion was a regimental medical officer [RMO], from the Royal Army Medical Corps [RAMC], who had a small staff of six orderlies and sixteen stretcher-bearers drawn from the battalion. Also part of the headquarters was the regimental sergeant major [RSM], the most senior non-commissioned officer, fifteen signallers, ten pioneers, and eleven transport drivers. Other specialists included an armourer, cooks, clerks, officer's servants, musicians (who often functioned as stretcher-bearers in action) and a shoemaker.

The Company

In late 1913 the battalion was reorganised into four companies from the previous eight, as this simplified the command structure and provided larger units of firepower.[1] Each company consisted of six officers and 221 other ranks and was commanded by a major, or more commonly a captain, with a junior officer as second-in-command. Like the battalion, the company had a headquarters element, which included a company sergeant-major [CSM], a company quartermaster sergeant [CQMS], two soldier servants and three drivers, in addition to the company cook.[2]

The Platoon

The battalion's four companies were each subdivided into four platoons, numbered consecutively from 1 to 16 (A Company's platoons were numbered 1 to 4, B Company's 5 to 8, and so on). Each platoon was commanded by a lieutenant or second lieutenant (subaltern) and included a platoon sergeant as second-in-command and at least four corporals, one for each section. The platoon was subdivided into four sections, each of up to sixteen men early in the war, later reduced to nine men under an NCO. It was the platoon that eventually became the tactical sub-unit of the war. It consisted of around forty men who trained, lived and served together. This meant that in most circumstances the members of the platoon knew each other by name. The platoon members identified their place in the battalion and mail sent home includes details of a soldier's battalion, company letter and platoon number. If wearing a specific cap badge could engender pride deriving from previous battles often dating back hundreds of years, it was through his platoon that the individual soldier identified his place in the battalion. There could be many 'number one sections' but only one 'B Company number six platoon'. Fierce competition reinforced by competitive sports and training regimes meant that the men 'knew' their own platoon was the best in the regiment and they would protect its reputation with their fists against fellow soldiers if needed.

The final building block was the section, originally of around a dozen men. This number relates to civilian organisations such as football and cricket teams but also represents the number of close friends many people have in their address book or mobile phone. Historically this number of men in a military organisation equates to the *conturbenium* of eight men in the Roman army or the squad in the Second World War. A section shared a tent or barrack space, drilled together and in the trenches held the same piece of line. Men might be detached for duties or sent on leave but they always returned to the same section of men, who were their friends and comrades. On the field of battle this meant that men went 'over the top' not necessarily for the love of King and Country, but because they were going to show everyone else who was best in the regiment. This meant sticking with your mates, and the bond of comradeship was a crucial element in allowing the men to see through danger and hardship.

The characteristics of an infantry platoon and the bond of comradeship within the small group of men are epitomised in the poem 'Twelve Months After' by Siegfried Sassoon, who served as a platoon commander in the Royal Welsh Fusiliers. The poem sums up the strong bonds that existed within the platoon in the Great War. The officer in command is familiar with the men, even after an absence, and there is an affection for their strengths and frailties. The language used would have been familiar to the men of the Great War but today requires some deciphering.

Twelve Months After

Hullo! Here's my platoon, the lot I had last year.[A]
'The war'll be over soon.'
'What 'opes?'
'No bloody fear!'
Then, 'Number Seven, shun![B] All present and correct'[C]
They're standing in the sun, impassive and erect.
Young Gibson with his grin[D] and Morgan, tired and white;
Jordan, who's out to win a DCM some night;[E]
And Hughes that's keen on wiring;[F] and Davies '79,[G]
Who always must be firing at the Boche front line.[H]
'Old soldiers never die, they simply fide a-why!'[I]
That's what they used to sing along the roads last spring;
That's what they used to say before the push began;
That's where they are today, knocked over to a man.[J]

Arms and Equipment

In 1914 a British infantryman was armed with a rifle, usually the Short Magazine Lee Enfield [SMLE], and bayonet. He carried up to 150 .303 rounds (bullets), usually 120 for Territorials, in addition to his personal equipment. This included a water bottle, rations, mess tins for cooking, a groundsheet and limited spare and warm clothing. Early in the war headgear consisted of a stiff peaked cap with a regimental badge worn on the front. No protective equipment was provided other than an entrenching tool or pick-mattock that a soldier could use to dig a shallow scrape to protect himself from rifle or artillery fire if caught 'in the open'. The Boer War (1899–1902) demonstrated that the accuracy of British infantry in shooting up to 400 yards (380m) was poor. As this was the distance at which an enemy attack would need to be stopped to prevent them getting to close quarters, great emphasis was put on 'musketry' training in the post-Boer War period. The SMLE was a short, handy rifle capable of a high rate of fire. However, rather than relying on pure weight of fire, it was decided that the fire should also be accurate. An infantryman had to be capable of firing fifteen rounds per minute and most of them could put all their shots into a two-foot (61cm) target from a set distance. Many of the best shots could achieve twice this accurate rate of fire and a pre-Great War instructor who fired thirty-seven rounds in one minute achieved a record. Although the principal weapon of the infantryman was the rifle, and at close quarters the bayonet, he had the support of two Vickers or Vickers Maxim machine guns per battalion. These fired the same .303 ammunition as the rifle, but with a far greater rate of fire. In theory a machine gun could fire over 500 rounds in a minute, but a slower rate of sustained fire was usually employed. This was the equivalent of more than thirty riflemen but presenting the target of just one. Over-heating presented a potential problem but this was solved by means of a water-jacket around the barrel which contained seven pints of water. This would begin to boil after 1,000 rounds so a tube was fitted that took the water vapour to a water-proof fabric bag or empty petrol tin where it could be cooled and condensed back into water. The machine gun was heavy, at 50lb (23kg), partly because of the water-cooling but also because of the heavy tripod that provided stability and allowed the weapon to be accurately aimed. Elevation was achieved by turning an elevating wheel below the breech, and traversing, moving left and right, was done by 'taps' with the palm of the gunner's hand. This meant that a far higher level of sustained accuracy was possible and, importantly, machine guns could fire over woods and over cover and could be used at night, in smoke or fog firing on pre-selected 'fixed lines'. Machine-gun tactics, like all others, became more sophisticated and technical as the war progressed.

By the time the author joined up the straightforward tactics of 1914 had been adapted to deal with the circumstances of trench warfare and the new weapons that had been developed by science and industry in the technical frenzy of total war. Some developments were apparently simple, while others reflected a new sophistication that had not been envisaged at the outbreak of war. Experience from the opening months of the conflict demonstrated that more practical digging tools were required than the simple pick–mattock or 'entrenching tool' carried by infantrymen. Shovels and pick-axes were increasingly carried when going into action or were made available as 'trench stores'. Although trenches provided protection from weapons such as rifles and machine guns, the use of gas by the German Army at Ypres in May 1915 meant that soldiers had to carry a respirator or gas mask from this date. These were initially quite simple and light but by the autumn of 1916 the Small Box Respirator had to be worn high up on the chest so that it could be fitted quickly and correctly. One consequence of the efficient manufacture of respirators by the British was the relatively low level of fatal casualties caused by gas, although it remained a constant threat until the end of the war. The move from open warfare to trench stalemate resulted in an increase in head injuries. This was the area of the body most likely to be accidentally exposed when a soldier worked or moved about in a trench system, or to be struck by shell splinters or shrapnel. Head injuries were frequently made worse by fragments of dirty cloth caps being driven into the wound. As a result, the RAMC recommended the issue of steel helmets to provide some protection and reduce the chance of infection. Helmets began to be issued in late 1915 and were virtually universal by 1 July 1916. One unexpected effect of their issue was that the number of reported head injuries went up, although the proportion of fatalities went down. This was because soldiers believed the helmets could offer more protection than was realistic. The editors have both come across accounts of sceptical soldiers on both sides shooting at 'spare' helmets to test their resistance. In most cases they were not impressed. Helmets, shovels, grenades, leather jerkins and respirators all added to the weight carried by the soldiers, and this would continue to increase throughout the war. One weary soldier home on leave was asked by his son, 'What is a soldier?' His response was 'Something to hang things on, son.'

Unlike the British Army, the German Army made extensive use of grenades from the beginning of the war. This is because the Germans were aware that the invasion of Belgium and France would involve the

assault of fortresses. However, once the trench system had been established, the British Army needed a means of retaliation. The first
grenades, called bombs in British service, were improvised from empty
tins filled with scrap iron and explosives and ignited by means of a fuse
and lit cigarette. By the middle of 1916, when the author arrived in
France and had his first experience of 'bomb' training, the standard
hand grenade was the No. 5 Mills pattern. This cast-iron weapon was
fused before use and could be carried in a pocket or special haversack.
Once the safety pin was removed and the bomb thrown in an over-arm
'bowling action', five seconds elapsed before the weapon exploded.
Range was limited and it was critical that the bomb was thrown either
from a trench into the open or vice versa as the lethal fragments could fly
further than a soldier could throw. In an emergency all soldiers could use
grenades, but the specialist title of 'bomber' was introduced into the
battalion. These soldiers had a sleeve badge to indicate their specialism
and carried their bombs in adapted haversacks or special 'vests', which
could carry up to twenty.

The limitations of a hand-thrown bomb were obvious and various
types of grenade-thrower were developed. By 1916 the standard 'rifle
bomb' was the No. 23, which was projected by means of a powerful
blank rifle cartridge. The grenade was fitted with a metal rod that was
put into the muzzle of the rifle while the bomb itself sat in a cage
attached to the fore end of the weapon by means of a fixed bayonet. Once
the pin was removed and the grenade lever was released against the side
of the cage the weapon could be fired. As the bomb left the muzzle the
lever flew off and the grenade travelled towards its target, exploding
after seven-and-a-half seconds. The rifle grenade required another
specialist skill and this led to the creation of 'rifle bombers', who once
again had special equipment and insignia.

On the outbreak of war it was clear that the number of machine guns
available was going to be critical and the British Army looked for
weapons with which to equip troops in the trenches. The number of
Vickers machine guns was rapidly increased but the weight of the
weapon made it difficult to move, even in trench warfare. In consequence, the army adopted a new machine gun for infantry use, the Lewis
gun, which was capable of being carried and fired by one man. Classified
as an 'automatic rifle', it fired the same .303 cartridge common to other
British rifles and machine guns. As the weapon was air-cooled, it was
lighter than the Vickers at just 28lb (12.7kg). It was equipped with a

circular forty-seven round magazine and, in theory, could fire 550 rounds per minute. The restricting factors were the number of rounds in the magazine and the risk of over-heating. As an emergency back-up, the section leader carried a revolver while all the other members of the section carried rifles. First ordered by the army at the outbreak of war, the Lewis gun became increasingly numerous and by October 1915 the Vickers machine guns were withdrawn for infantry battalions and grouped into the newly formed Machine Gun Corps. The 'Lewis gunners' had their own specialist badges and, although a section had only one firer, 'the number one', the other members of the section were trained in its use and carried the ammunition required. By 1917 the battalion had sixteen Lewis guns split evenly between the companies.

The Platoon in 1917

In February 1917, based on the experience of the Somme battle of the previous year, it was decided to reorganise the battalion into a number of tactical units based on the platoon.[3] Each platoon would in future have a headquarters section of just one officer and four other ranks, and would contain four specialist sections each made up of roughly ten men equipped and trained to use weapons with differing characteristics. These were (1) the Lewis gun section equipped with one or more light machine guns; (2) the bombing section; (3) the rifle section, which contained the best shots, bayonet men and scouts; and finally (4) the rifle bombers section. The theory was that each platoon contained its own machine gun to provide covering fire and had rifle bombers to deal with enemy even if they were out of sight in a trench; the manual calls the rifle bomb 'the "howitzer" of the Infantry'.[4] To discover or clear an enemy position the platoon made use of the rifle section backed up by the bombers, who could clear trenches or dugouts. As is made clear in *The Platoon*, British infantrymen spent an immense amount of time training in these new tactics during the spring of 1917. The tactical advantage that this training provided became clear during the battle of Arras and subsequent operations. By 1918 the process had become virtually second nature to the experienced soldier. With the collapse of static German defences and the end of trench warfare in the late summer and autumn of 1918, the training also proved to be ideally suited to 'Open Warfare'.

Notes

1. General Staff, *Infantry Training (4-Company Organisation)* (War Office, 1914).
2. F. Myatt, *The British Infantry 1660–1945: the Evolution of a Fighting Force* (Blandford Press, 1983), pp. 163–4.

'Twelve Months After'

A. 'My platoon' – this poem is written from the point of view of an officer who has returned to command the same platoon after an absence. He would be a lieutenant or second lieutenant.
B. 'Number Seven shun!' – a shortening of the command 'Number Seven Platoon, B Company, Attention!'
C. 'All present and correct' – the report made by the platoon sergeant to inform the officer that all the members of the platoon are on parade.
D. 'Gibson with his grin' – a soldier with an indefatigable sense of humour has always been a valuable asset to British units. The ability to make light of the worst situations can make an otherwise poor soldier a useful comrade and a 'pal'.
E. 'win a DCM some night' – this soldier is keen to get a Distinguished Conduct Medal for gallantry on a night raid or other exploit.
F. 'keen on wiring' – wiring refers to putting out barbed wire – an unusual activity to be keen on, but all soldiers have different skills and Hughes clearly enjoyed the process of erecting barbed wire in the dark. He would have been a valuable asset to the platoon.
G. 'Davies '79' – Siegfried Sassoon served in the Royal Welsh Fusiliers, in which there would have been several men with the same surname, perhaps Jones or Davies. To distinguish between men with the same name and rank, the final two digits of an individual's regimental number are used. This was and still is common practice.
H. 'firing at the Boche front line' – being keen on firing at the German trenches could be seen as either foolhardy or a useful military attribute. As the risk was greatest to the firer, it is likely that the men of the platoon tolerated Davies' dangerous exploits.
I. 'Old soldiers never die' – a well known soldier's parody of a nineteenth-century gospel hymn, 'Kind Words Can Never Die'.
J. 'knocked over' – soldiers' slang indicating wounded or absent, rather than all dead.

3. General Staff, *SS 143 Instructions for the Training of Platoons for Offensive Action 1917* (HMSO, February 1917).
4. F. Myatt, *The British Infantry 1660–1945: the Evolution of a Fighting Force* (Blandford Press, 1983), p. 7.

The Platoon

Chapter One

The Bull Ring

A detachment of troops from a London training battalion swung singing along a sunny Hampshire road in mid June on its way to join Kitchener's army in France.[1] The sergeant in charge swore they were the sauciest lot he had ever handled. On the previous evening, the men had had a jovial supper together at a Winchester hotel, gone to see a revue, and at the end, the amorous ones raided the stage and kissed all the girls in farewell. Now, as they marched along behind the band, bandying jokes to each other, a youthful tear-away named Snipe took off his cap, pulled out the regimental wire stiffener and tossed it into the hedge.[2] Yesterday he had smashed windows in their hut, being, as he said, his way of getting even with the Army against the mythical 'barrack damages'[3] that had been deducted from their meagre pay.[4] As the draft[5] entered Winchester on its way to the railway station, and passed the tall statue of Alfred the Great, many people turned out to shake hands and wish the men God-speed. On reaching Southampton, they joined more troops, to board the boat waiting to take them to Le Havre.[6] Each man was ordered to go below, fasten himself inside one of the dirty life jackets, and remain there. They were packed so close that very soon the air became dense with tobacco smoke and sweaty exhalations.[7] It was six hours before the little boat weighed anchor and slipped out. Not a light showed: piquets[8] were posted to keep the men below decks. It was hard on those scared of being seasick; they sat on the companion way[9] with their heads between their knees, longing for morning and the French coast.

In the faint light of early dawn the boat slid along-side the quay at Le Havre.[10] Here a nonchalant soldier of France patrolled, with rifle and bayonet casually slung on shoulder. The troops quickly disembarked, then the Winchester draft detached itself, formed column of fours[11] and began to march the five miles to Havre Central Training Camp.[12] On their way, they passed a dock full of captured German vessels, then on through slum land. Small urchins kept pace with the men, soliciting in shrill voices 'bully-bee-ef, beeskeets?'[13] A cockney lad named Smart told them to scarper, and was laughed at when the saucy kids swore at him in his own vulgar tongue. One of them offered (in broken English) to swap his sister's virginity for a tin of bully.[14]

"Clear off, you dirty little brat", yelled the sergeant.

The camp the draft reached was of enormous dimensions, so large that it was sub-divided into several lesser camps, each having its own commandant. Our draft was conducted to its own particular parade ground and told to listen to standing orders for the day, 13th June, 1916.

After dumping their equipments in bell tents[15] the men were again paraded. Each was handed a groundsheet, a short Lee-Enfield rifle smothered in package grease and a pungent-smelling flannel hood with a protruding mouthpiece and goggles called a gas-respirator.[16] Then they were ushered into a large marquee for a medical inspection. The M.O.[17] wasted no time, for, coming to a man whose big toenail was loose, he gripped it with thumb and forefinger and quickly ripped it off.

Afterwards they went into a large eating hut, where, taking their rations, they sat at one of the trestle tables littered with discarded potato peelings, scraps of meat and bits of bread. One of the draft named Peter Knight sat with Smart. The former ate without zest, for his palate had been depraved by six months' army rations[18] but the paucity and poorness of the meal did not worry young Smart.[19]

"What's your Christian name, chum?" enquired Knight.

"Sam".

"Well, come on, Sam, let's make way for the others."

They went out past a long queue of waiting men. When they reached their tent they learned to their relief that parades were finished for the day: but were told darkly that tomorrow they would 'Start going through it'.[20]

In the evening Knight took a walk around the camp; it was teeming with troops. There were hundreds of rows of tents for thousands of men. The Y.M.C.A. had provided recreation huts and shops, as had all the churches, and there was a large cinema.[21] But the sight that intrigued Knight was when he stood watching a group of men squatting in circles around a chap who stood in the centre chanting in loud monotonous tones a queer mixture of words and numbers. The heads of all the men were bent over squared and numbered cards that were being covered with buttons, bits of paper or small stones.

"Legs eleven", entoned the master of ceremonies. "Kelly's eye". "Blind forty". "Clickerty click," and so on.

"Alas! Regardless of their doom, the little victims play" a quiet voice whispered into Knight's ear. The speaker, a quick-witted, urban scholar named Blake had, months before, forsaken his books for the battlefield.

"What sort of game is this?" he enquired.

"You'll see in a minute."

Suddenly one of the squatters yelled out "ouse". The M.C.[22] abruptly stopped; an accessory went and checked the shouter's card and gave him the prize money minus a goodly balance for the promoters.[23]

"Who'll 'ave a card?" sang the touts; the players stumped up again; the M.C. resumed his chanting, and clickerty flourished once more. As they turned to leave Blake remarked:

"That's a childish short of pastime."

"It's only one for money the Army permits," replied Knight.

Meanwhile, Snipe was strolling around with Frane, (another of the draft) who told him how he had seen the Guards marching off to the Boer War.

"Get away; you wasn't born then."

"I was; I was fourteen. They were marching down the Chelsea Bridge Road.[24] I remember it because one chap was half-sozzled, singing some sort of devil-may-care chorus." (Frane had joined up on his thirtieth birthday,[25] and trained with the others at Hazeley Down Camp.[26])

"Were you still at school when you saw the Guards?" asked Snipe.

"Yes, but I left soon after, and took a job at a big outfitter's in Lambeth, where all the staff lived in."[27]

"What was it like?"

"It was rotten; I got five shillings a week and worked to half past nine at night. But they had to let me off on Saturday evenings, as they weren't allowed to work me more than seventy-four hours a week."

"What kind of work did you do?"

"What an inquisitive bloke you are" said Frane. "I was a cashier: I sat in a big open box like a pulpit, and raked in the money – umpteen sovereigns of it."

"Gosh; for five bob a week!"[28].

"Plus the living-in, such as it was," continued the other. "The grub was poor; the men had to buy their own jam."

Frane made an impatient gesture. "Let's talk about something else," he said.

"No, go on," urged Snipe.

"Well, we all slept in a long bedroom above the store rooms. It was unfurnished except for a row of iron bedsteads with lockers opposite. When I got there the walls were all bare."

"What, no pin-ups?"

Frane laughed: "No, you young rake: the room had been fumigated; there'd been an infectious disease. The walls were still bare when I left a year later. The dining room was on the floor below: it had a long table for meals, with chairs to seat each batch of shop assistants – nothing else."

"What about easy chairs?" queried Snipe.

"There weren't any; the only easy chairs were our beds upstairs."

By now the two had reached their tent. Frane put his hand on Snipe's shoulder: "That's enough about me" he said, "they're going to start putting us all through it tomorrow."

Early next morning the vast camp presented a scene of lively activity: men in all stages of undress hurried about or stood outside their tents cleaning up, then went to the ablution sheds, each to wait in queue until his turn came to grab a bowl, turn a tap and get a wash. Private Calder saw Smart trying to shave. Sam had managed to hang a small piece of mirror outside a shed in jeopardy from bustling men.

"How are you getting on, Sam?"

"Wers'n[29] Petticoat Lane a Sunday morning".[30]

The serious work of the day began after breakfast, the men parading in full marching order.[31] Before they left, baskets containing lumps of bread and cheese were passed between the ranks, each man helping himself and placing the food in a white calico ration bag.[32] The parade was then called to attention, and with sloped arms climbed up a steep hillside to the Camp. When they reached the top, the troops were divided into small parties, each marching to its allotted line on the parade ground. The officers in charge then reported all present to the Commandant.

At a signal, a waiting crowd of sergeant-instructors dispersed amongst the men. Each led his 'scholars' to a section of ground set apart for his particular subject. They wore yellow armlets, so the troops nicknamed them 'canaries'. Most had been in the early battles and had been sent to the school for a rest.[33] During the morning, all the men assembled in a large wooden amphitheatre and listened to the Chief Medical Officer, who stood in the centre of the great space giving hints on the preservation of health and showing how wounds could be tended with field dressings.[34] After a break for consumption of the bread and cheese ration, the troops were lectured by the Camp Adjutant. (A captain risen from the ranks.) His subject was Hate. He had stock stories of fiendishness that, according to him, had been perpetrated by the enemy. He followed by a demonstration of bayonet fighting tricks, with contortions of face fearful to behold.[35]

After that, the Regimental-sergeant-major entered the arena. His discourse on Hate was even more hateful than the previous turn. On sex, he warned his hearers to be wary of wanton women who spied for the Germans. Blake remembered the bible story of Samson:

"And when Delilah saw that he had told her all his heart, she sent and called for the lords of the Philistines."

The R.S.M. then turned to a livelier subject, esprit-de-corps and regimental pride.[36] At the conclusion of the day's training all forgathered on the wide parade ground and, led by pipers, marched off between an avenue of 'canaries', who busied themselves 'correcting the slope' of men's rifles and bellowing out diatribes on deportment. Some used their canes for stinging the fingers of fellows who were not holding their rifles in the approved fashion. Blake and company treated the tactics of these old sweats with stoical disdain; whilst little Smart mocked and swore at them under his breath in the swirl of the bagpipes as he marched along.[37] On reaching the camp and being dismissed, the men scurried to their tents, dumped their equipments and made for the 'dining hall', where they avidly consumed the rich fare of potatoes and meat. After that, the time was their own to roam the place. Knight and his pal Blake went to the cinema; Smart squatted and played housey-housey. The June weather was mild and fine, so most kept out of doors until close on lights out.

The draft worked hard for seventeen days at this training camp, increasing their knowledge of the martial arts learnt during their six months' training in England, with plenty of bayonet fighting on the assault course. The routine consisted of a climb out of the deep assembly trench, a run over No-Mans-Land, a jump into another trench in whose unknown depths the line of attackers plunged, sticking their bayonets into the prostrate bags of straw deputising for the enemy; out again, another run, a yelling charge at the line of swinging dummies, then on, a leap, over a deep wide trench, another sprint, then down into the last trench, the final objective. Sometimes, through excitement or clumsiness, men were killed or wounded. The exercise was not without its occasional comedy; one day a little chap with short legs hesitated at the open mouth of the gaping wide trench and stopped. The instructor ordered him to go back and try again; again, he lost courage. The sergeant, seeing that his repeated shouts and adurations were in vain, sought to shame him:

"Women in England are looping the loop, yet you can't do a simple thing like that!"[38]

He was determined to have his man over, so stood him several paces back, then ordered him to run forward. Just as the poor chap drew level with the dreaded gap and was about to hesitate the sergeant let loose a blood-curdling yell into his ear, which sent him flying across. Thus another pupil qualified at this school of death.

On the bombing ground Smart, who always liked to keep close to Knight, was being taught how to manipulate and chuck a Mills bomb from a trench.[39] The sergeant-instructor held one of the deadly eggs in his right hand to demonstrate:

"You 'old it like this 'ere and keep your fingers pressed down on this 'ere lever. Then with the other 'and you stick your finger through this 'ere ring and pull the pin out, still keeping your 'and over the lever. Nah, you look over the trench and fro it out for all your worth; the lever springs up and the bomb goes off, right in Jerry's face – we 'ope. Any questions?"

"Yes sergeant" says Smart, looking innocent, "wot 'appens if I drop it?"

The canary's face turned purple. "You bloody fool, you <u>don't</u> drop it, or we'll all be blown to 'ell".

Knight smiled; he suspected that Sam was trying to take the mickey out of the sergeant.

The lad held the bomb lightly in his right hand and rocked it gently, and then he stretched out his other arm in a theatrical gesture and slowly brought his finger down to the pin, grinning all the time. The sergeant would fain have snapped out "Git on with it" but he daren't speak. Knight stood fascinated by the antics of this cockney boy. At length Smart pulled out the pin, drew his arm back cricket-wise, bowled the bomb well out, and ducked. The sergeant's face relaxed and the watching men breathed again.

The rifle range was the happiest place, more congenial, more civilised. The officer in charge, an elderly Scottish major, liked to have a few men around him during intervals, for informal talks. Once he spoke of pluck and endurance. "Never give in; fight it out, boys, if you're badly cornered, and, with your British grit, by God, you'll get through".

There was no parade for the 'pimple' next morning. Instead, the day was to be devoted to interior economy. (By the way, 'The Pimple' was the troops' name for the notorious training ground on top of the hill). Weltering in an orgy of washing of clothes, of bodies, etcetera, the troops beguiled the hours interior-economising, intercepted by the medical officer who waded in to pursue his study of the nude.

"Wot's the idea of 'im telling some of the chaps to stand a'oneside?" queried Smart during the short-arm inspection.[40]

"I think he suspects they've been consorting too freely with the mademoiselles outside the camp" said Blake, drily.

"Wot, on a bob a day!" ejaculated the boy.[41]

The next day, being Sunday, training was suspended and, apart from church parade in the big cinema hut, all except the lucky few possessing passes had perforce to make do with the dubious blandishments of the camp. By now, the draft had worked hard for a fortnight and the time had come for the final test. So, on Monday morning they manned a model trench system, had mock gas attacks and sudden stand-to's, trying to imagine that the enemy was just across the way.

They carried on like that for more than thirteen hours; and as it was raining all the time, they had a slight foretaste of the arduous days ahead. The Army, having now satisfied itself that it had produced crack warriors, again subjected them to the tender caresses of the M.O. who duly pronounced them fit for armageddon. The next day the draft hung about until the evening, when they were inspected in full marching order by the Camp Commandant. They quickly found that the martinets had not done with them, for this man, having inspected the packs on their backs, walked to their front and barked out that they were incorrectly dressed because the right-hand strap crossed the left ditto instead of vice versa.[42]

"I don't care if it <u>was</u> the rule in your battalion" he said, "I want it my way, so take off your packs and change the straps over".

As they marched away out of the camp Calder exploded "I'm glad we've got shot of those cursed base-wallahs".[43]

"Well, corse 'e 'ad to find sumfink to grouse about" said little Smart.

"You know, we can't fight if our pack straps aren't on right", mocked Blake.

Someone said that would make a good line for a chorus. Smart seized on it, singing:

"We carn't fight if our pack-straps aint on rite".

The others took it up, chanting the words as they marched on the way to Havre station. The refrain swept along the column of fours, stabbing the air with its derision and scorn – scorn of the little man they had left behind.

Notes
1. The men from 1914 and early 1915 who responded to Lord Kitchener's appeal for volunteers were collectively known as 'Kitchener's Army'. Lord Kitchener died on his way to Russia when HMS *Hampshire* was sunk by a mine on 5 June 1916.
2. The khaki service dress cap issued to British soldiers early in the war had a distinctive flat top created by the use of a circle of wire. By 1916 it had become common, if not the fashion, to remove these stiffeners, giving the wearer the look of someone with experience at the front. This practice was officially disapproved of and could result in the culprit being charged with having committed a military crime.
3. Soldiers were collectively charged for any article, real or fictional, missing or damaged in the barracks they left. In this case Snipe had taken the decision that as he was to be fined anyway it might as well be for real damage.
4. Private soldiers received one shilling a day before any deductions. This compared unfavourably with an agricultural labourer of the time who was earning one shilling and four pence per day. Military pay was, however, certain all year round and food and clothing was provided, which explains why many men volunteered in 1914.
5. A draft was a group of soldiers selected from a depot to be sent as reinforcements for a unit in the line. On arrival at their destination, the members of the draft would be split up and sent to where they were required. Whereas experienced soldiers were cynical and depressed by the process, new soldiers were excited and curious.
6. Although the general perception is that men serving on the Western Front arrived in France via Calais or Boulogne, harbours as far away as Brittany were used as ports of arrival to avoid the U-boat threat and make better use of the French railway network.
7. During the Great War the word 'frowsty' was coined to describe these conditions or those found in packed dugouts. It implied a combination of unwashed bodies, candle fumes and cigarette smoke.
8. Piquets were sentries in army terminology, but also the supports for barbed wire as they stood like men on guard duty.
9. The ship's stairways.
10. The author's service record indicates that he embarked at Southampton on 12 June 1916 and arrived at Le Havre the next morning. AFB103 (WO363/S2335, TNA).
11. British infantry units marched four abreast. By the eve of the Second World War the increase in fast motor transport made a narrower three-wide column advisable.
12. All the major ports of arrival were linked with a training camp. The best known and most notorious was that at Etaples, near Bolougne, known as the 'Bull Ring'. Here soldiers who were about to have their first experience of life at the front and those returning after recovering from wounds were 'put through their paces' by instructors. AFB103 indicates that the author arrived at the camp on 13 June 1916. (WO363/S2335, TNA.)
13. In French corned beef is 'boeuf bouilli', which means boiled beef, hence the common name Bully Beef. It formed an important part of the soldier's diet. In camp

or in the line it could be cooked as stew but it was also issued as part of emergency 'Iron Rations'. The tins were heavy and the taste, without relish, not always popular. Ration biscuits were also unpalatable and often easy to dispense with. As a result, kind-hearted British soldiers gave both to children. This resulted in frequent appeals by children to passing columns of British soldiers, as described here.

14. Soldiers in their more private memoirs frequently mention the nature and language used in this conversation.

15. Bell tents were named after their inventor rather than their shape.

16. The groundsheet of 1916 was made from rubberised fabric with reinforced metal eyelets around the edge. It could be worn as a waterproof coat in the trenches or on the march or made into a sleeping shelter with the use of a few sticks, bits of string and pegs. The Short Magazine Lee Enfield [SMLE] was introduced in 1908 and remained in short supply for the early part of the war. The result was that many soldiers trained with older model rifles and were issued with their personal SMLE on their arrival with the BEF. The gas respirator of mid-1916 was the Phenate Hexamine [PH] Hood made from grey flannel and provided with two eyepieces and a non-return valve held in the teeth to breathe out through. Known as the 'Boogey-eyed monster with a tit', the respirator was claustrophobic and unpleasant to wear but offered protection against most forms of gas.

17. The MOs of the RAMC were never referred to as doctors. They were either 'Doc' or 'The MO'. Many had an unenviable reputation for brutality, as here, or for being too soft, in which case it was possible to take advantage of their character by faking illness.

18. The reference to the time in training is identical to that of the author.

19. Rations, even in training camps, were not luxurious but they were plentiful and for many soldiers it was the first time in their lives that they had experienced three meals a day. The result was that many soldiers put on weight and even grew taller in a few months of training. Soldiers from more privileged backgrounds could afford to be suspicious about the rations they received.

20. This expression was used in these circumstances to indicate that whatever had been experienced by the soldiers up to this point was nothing compared to what training, action or hard work would follow. It came with the suggestion of dark foreboding and dread.

21. The YMCA – Young Men's Christian Association, often called the Y M or Y Emma from the phonetic military alphabet – ran a range of recreation huts and stalls for the benefit of soldiers when they were out of the line.

22. 'MC' – Master of Ceremonies.

23. This game, now called 'Bingo', was a favourite gambling game in the Great War in both the army and the navy and was called 'House' from the winner having a full house. The call for players to join the game was 'Housey Housey'.

24. This reference may not be a coincidence. Joseph's father was born in Chelsea, then not a fashionable area of London, and he, Joseph, would certainly have known Chelsea Barracks, which housed the Guards.

25. This reference to an underage volunteer should not be a surprise. In an era in which young people left school at thirteen to enter the world of work, a soldier of this age would not be as surprising as it is today. Any soldier who was underage had to lie to get into the forces and many did so not because of misplaced patriotism, but to put clothes on their back and food on the table.

26. This reference is a useful clue to where the author trained. Hazeley Down Camp is located near Winchester and in 1915 became an infantry training centre for reserve

battalions of the London Regiment. These included 14 London, 15 London, 16th (The Queens Westminster) Battalion, [16 London] and the 20th (Blackheath and Woolwich) Battalion [20 London]. We can conclude that the fictional Snipe damaged the windows in one of the many huts that made up the camp. One wonders whether Joseph saw this happen or participated in the event before the march to Winchester. Information about the camp came, initially, from the Internet following a Google search for Hazeley Down Camp. We were unaware of the connection between the camp and the training of men from London until this point. We took the time to cross-reference this 'fact' with other sources, but it demonstrates the value of both the internet and searching round your main line of enquiry. Further references to the camp, maps of the layout and photographs were located in file WO161/117 at TNA.

27. This description may well be based on the author's experience of working in the outfitters in Marlow.
28. A 'bob' was one shilling.
29. 'Wers'n' – worse than.
30. A reference to the crowds at the Sunday market in Petticoat Lane, held there since medieval times. The market was well known to Londoners and at the time of the Great War the area was predominantly Jewish.
31. Full marching order [FMO], or more properly full service marching order [FSMO] consisted of everything the soldier took from one location to another, but not into the line. It consisted of rifle and bayonet, a full set of webbing or leather equipment, a full haversack, full water bottle, his valise or large pack containing an overcoat in winter, a respirator, groundsheet, iron rations, entrenching tools and other articles either personal or issue. Total weight was in the region of 80lb (36.2kg).
32. These rectangular bags, with a sewn-in tie cord, known in army terms as 'bag, unconsumed portion of day's rations', frequently appear in photographs of British soldiers of the period usually tied to a haversack or other item of equipment. They sometime appear triangular because they have been tied by one corner to a buckle or strap.
33. Instructors at the training camp at Etaples received the unenviable nickname of 'Canaries' and this spread to other camps. They were distinguished by an armband and known to the troops for their brutal methods. In their defence many had indeed been at the front and realised that whatever rough treatment they put the men through was likely to be nothing compared to what they would endure at the front.
34. Every British soldier had an internal pocket in the lower right-hand front skirt of his tunic. This was designed to take a 'first field dressing' so that every man knew where it was if he was wounded. The dressing consisted of an outer cover with instructions, which no one read, an inner waterproof jacket and two sterile bandages, each with a pad and safety pins. In the event that a soldier was wounded he, or a comrade, was meant to tear open the outer covers and use the dressings to cover the wound or wounds, reducing blood loss and helping to prevent the wound from being infected with contaminated soil, which could lead to gangrene. The dressings were issued before soldiers went into action for the first time.
35. Bayonet training was regarded as very important for men going into action and a variety of techniques were used to encourage soldiers to close with the enemy and engage in hand-to-hand combat. The most famous bayonet instructor and exponent of a variety of fighting techniques was Lieutenant Colonel R.B. Campbell of the Gordon Highlanders, who was an army instructor in bayonet fighting. His method included blood-curdling and thrilling descriptions of hand-to-hand fighting and was

intended to inspire troops with the necessary 'hate' prior to meeting the Boche. The 1917 Training Manual, *SS 143 Instructions for the Training of Platoons for Offensive Action*, indicates that 'Bayonet fighting produces lust for blood; much may be accomplished in billets in wet weather!' Perhaps not everyone was convinced but it is significant that the instructor at Le Havre is described as being a 'captain risen from the ranks'. Despite the somewhat stereotypical view held by many today, it was common for other ranks to become officers. Although they may have been 'temporary gentlemen', a massively expanded British Army needed their experience and they played a key part in securing victory in 1918. Men who were promoted as officers were posted to another unit, so that they would not be commanding men with whom they had previously been friends. This explains why the service records of many promoted soldiers indicate that they went to another regiment or battalion.

36. The regimental sergeant major [RSM] was the senior warrant officer [WO] in a battalion and as such was responsible for discipline and the reputation of the battalion.

37. Manuals of the period emphasise the importance of a 'ceremonial' and competition at the conclusion of training.

38. A reference to women in Britain who were learning to fly aircraft and hence were able to carry out this acrobatic manoeuvre.

39. The Mills Company manufactured the most common British grenade, known for most of the war as a 'bomb', rather than a grenade. Introduced in 1915, the Mills bomb was fused before use and was safe until the pin was removed. Even with the pin removed, the thrower was able to prevent an instant explosion by holding down the striker lever on the side of the bomb's casing with his right hand. Once this was released, the thrower had five seconds before detonation.

40. 'A short-arm inspection' was an army euphemism for an inspection by the MO of the soldiers' genitals to check for signs of venereal disease. Rifles were classified as 'long arms', hence the humour.

41. A private soldier was paid one shilling – 'a bob' – a day. That compared very badly with many civilian workers on the Home Front, and even with Australian and Canadian soldiers who faced the same dangers but were paid far more than the British 'Tommy'.

42. The correct way to cross the straps on the 08 Pattern Webbing equipment, as illustrated in the manual of 1913, is, indeed, right over left when viewed from the rear, but it is doubtful whether soldiers followed this rule unless it was by chance. The point where the straps cross is hidden by the pack or haversack so we must assume that the Camp Commandant had 'swallowed the rule book'. *The Pattern 1908 Web Infantry Equipment* (War Office, 1913), Plates I and III.

43. 'Base wallah' – soldiers' slang for anyone living in the comfort and safety of a base. Wallah is originally a Hindustani word meaning 'chap' or 'fellow'. A surprising amount of military slang in the Great War originated in India.

Chapter Two

Into Action

At the station, with an officer in charge, the draft kicked their heels until a train took them away at 1.30 a.m. next morning. The men travelled all night until they reached Rouen.[1] Knight thought he might have the pleasure of marching down the picturesque streets of Old Town and perhaps seeing some of the fine churches; but he was disappointed; the troops were not allowed to leave the station. So they made for the refreshment room, a large buffet put there for the men, and graced by smiling British girls busily serving cups of tea. Late in the afternoon the train steamed in. So, with an ominous issue of dry rations in their haversacks, the lads resumed their odyssey. At times, the train just crawled along, so the chaps got out and walked alongside. At one of the frequent stops, Frane met Snipe who was carrying his mess-tin steaming with tea.

"How did you get that?" he queried.

"Scrounged hot water from the engine driver".

"Trust you to have an eye on the main chance; you'll go far".

"Not in this blooming crawler".

"Don't you be in such a hurry, my lad; we shall probably have more than we bargain for when we get there".

So, the tardy train trundled on, bearing its curious cargo. As darkness crept, the pontoon players packed up, the strategists stopped arguing, the singers subsided, the scholar slumbered, and a poet dreamed his dreams. Hour after hour through the night, then into the daylight. Parks craned out to ascertain their whereabouts; evidently, they were travelling north. At last the train pulled up at a small town east of Doullens named Halloy.[2] They had been travelling seventeen hours.

It was nine o'clock of the morning of July the First in the year of our Lord and of Europe's paranoia, nineteen hundred and sixteen.[3] The draft detrained and lined up in the little country lane outside the station. Before the men moved off the officer in charge said:

"I shall be leaving you after I have handed over at the reinforcement camp, so I will say good-bye now. You're a good stout team, so I know you will pull your weight. Good-bye and jolly good luck". Hot, stiff and hungry as they were, they returned the compliment.

A few minutes walk brought the draft to a cantonment of low wooden huts. The Commandant inspected them and gave them a cheery little speech, telling them they were to remain there until called for: "It might be several days or a few hours".

Emergency rations were issued (a bag of tiny biscuits, a tin of bully beef and a small tin containing tea and sugar).[4] Any man whose rifle was defective was required to have it attended to immediately.

But their first urge was to have a good wash, so after dumping their equipment in the huts they took soap and towels from haversacks, drew water and, at ablution benches in a field, removed two-days accretion from their bodies. After tea, some explored the village, but others rested in case of marching orders. The order came suddenly, at five o'clock. It was to be a forced march; the need was desperate. A few minutes later the whole draft, with a corporal, was making its way through fields of corn and poppies under a fierce midsummer sun.[5] They slogged on, mile after mile, on into the dusk, through the night, then with the dawn.

Once they ran against a convoy on the high road, racing to succour and support the fighting troops – heavy lorries, limbers, guns, horses, mules, staff cars. The fields en route were chockfull of war material. Then they passed some artillerymen who told them of fierce fighting that morning;-

"You going to join the Londoners? Poor devils! Your chaps have been cut up", they said.

"Cheerful blighters" muttered Blake.

Long lines of red-cross ambulances carrying the pathetic debris of the battlefield met them. The draft left the road and headed eastward towards the fighting line. By this time little Smart was lagging behind, Knight limped with two raw heels, Blake's humour had dried up. But they had another fifteen miles to go. Eventually the men halted at a village called Sailly au Bois, close behind the Hebuterne – Gommecourt front. Here the corporal sought out their battalion quartermaster. Whilst waiting in the street for orders they were told the truth. All day long, the battalion had taken part in a fierce battle for the Gommecourt salient.[6]

In a gloomy barnyard, the men were given steel helmets and were told to get into battle order, by fastening their haversacks on their backs in place of their packs, which were left behind.[7] Then, with an officer in charge, they went on. They seemed to wander interminably; but at last, drawing near the firing line, they saw for the first time shrapnel bursting and heard the deafening detonations of the guns. It was past midnight; they were so tired that they swayed like drunken men as they walked. Finally, the draft arrived at a point behind the front line, where they met the shaken remnant of their battalion.[8] The survivors had just been relieved and were given hot meat extract and rum.[9] Quickly, in the darkness, the draft was divided amongst the four companies of the battalion, and friends who had kept close found themselves together in one platoon.[10] All the men were ordered to lie still in narrow slit trenches to deceive the enemy airmen hovering above. They stayed thus until the afternoon, when, harried by the argus-eyed Boche[11] gunners. The battered regiment tramped down the hot dusty road towards a field in Souastre village.[12]

The newcomers were visibly moved at the sight of these men, who bore all the marks of the hell's torment through which they had passed – one of the most terrific bombardments ever suffered by British troops. Their eyes, which had looked upon Death in horrid form, were wild and staring. Wisps of dank hair hung over their grimy foreheads. Their faces were wrinkled with the utter fatigue of their superhuman exertions, their shoulders bent. They had grown old in a day. Their clothes were ripped and torn, and as they dragged their feet along, they looked like men released from purgatory. Suddenly one fell senseless, face downwards, upon the road. His companions continued their tramp, whilst a sergeant lifted him on to a small iron frame on wheels drawn by a horse that a French peasant was leading. A little later, they passed a sentry, who stood rigidly at the 'present arms' until every man had gone by.[13] The officer in charge returned the salute but refrained from ordering his weary followers to slope arms as was customary.[14] Knight thought that if he were an artist he would like to paint that picture: the parched fields, the white road, the midsummer sky, and the silent, statuesque sentry proudly saluting his bedraggled comrades as they scuffled slowly past, followed by the exhausted lad drawn by his four-footed rescuer led by the old Frenchman.

The Battalion's destination was a field in Souastre village. The cooks had hot food ready waiting for the men, who ate it from their mess-tins, squatting upon the grass.[15] Next, word went round from the medical officer advising all to remove puttees and boots and stay so for an hour or two to ease feet, as they would be going again into the trenches that evening. The M.O. had his aid post[16] in a corner of the field, whither Knight repaired to have his sore heels dressed. Here the sick were being dosed with number nines and the lame with iodine.[17] On that Sunday evening, while the people at home were bubbling over with excitement at the good news of the previous day's battle, the new platoon quietly fell in with the others and turned their faces toward the trenches. Their path led across the cornfields. There was a lull in the firing, the birds had returned and were sending their sweet vespers to the blue heavens. A quiet breeze stirred the myriad golden wheat-wands, revealing the vivid red of the poppies and restful blue of the cornflowers. Blake asked himself why men were forever ravaging the fair earth to satisfy their insensate ambitions. The bells of the village church gave no answer; the little building was in ruins, save where a broken remnant of wall still upheld the lone figure of a tortured man.[18]

It was twilight when the Company reached the communication trench; a channel of deep mud; and waded to the front line. The 4th Lincolns they had come to relieve left quietly as they exchanged places.[19] This line which, before the bombardment had been a series of fire-bays and traverses made to reduce casualties, was now a desolation of erupted earth, shell holes and mud, littered with broken rifles and torn equipment. Most of the dead and wounded had been taken away during the previous night. The men were told to space out, pump out the water and try to build up some sort of parapet, which pairs of sentries could man. Calder was posted on sentry with one of the original platoon, a tall, fair, strong Londoner named Godfrey, who appears to have survived the savage gruelling better than most of his fellows. There was very little shelling; both sides were exhausted by yesterday's fierce struggle.

Godfrey was depressed and frustrated over the collapse of their offensive. He told Calder that he had tried to get across No-Mans-Land with a party carrying bombs to reinforce, but all, with the exception of himself, had been wiped out. "The charge of the Light Brigade was a walk-over in comparison", he added. "Now we're back where we started – what's left of us – and the Germans still hold Gommecourt". As the two watched the dark battleground facing them Calder felt that his fellow sentry was at that moment re-enacting in his mind his vain struggle in that raging inferno of fire; so, to break the tension, he enquired:

"What part of the line are we in now?"

"We're about a mile north of Gommecourt; the village we just came through is Foncquevillers". After a pause: "The're asking for runners to take the place of the casualties; our platoon lost twenty men out of thirty-five".

"What's a runner?"

"A chap who takes messages; it's a chancy job when there's hot stuff flying about; but I'd be excused all fatigues – that suits me – so I'm going to apply".

A sergeant came along to warn them to avoid hasty action, as a patrol and a burying party were out in front.[20]

"That's our new platoon sergeant" said Godfrey. "Sergeant Ross was killed, the Platoon officer was killed too".[21] They stood on guard for two hours, after which their relief took over.[22] Then they worked in the trench until their time came again. Just before dawn, at 3 o'clock, everyone stood to arms, scanning the ground in front and wondering whether a sudden crash of enemy guns would presage the emergence through the mist of grey-clad figures advancing towards them. Sgt. Alex thought it was improbable so soon after Saturday's upheaval. With the coming of daylight, all 'stood down' and were ordered to clean rifles.[23]

Dry rations for twenty-four hours came up in sandbags. Lance corporal Love served his section: a round loaf was divided amongst four men, and each received a small piece of cheese, a fraction of butter and a little jam. The bread and cheese were put into a calico ration bag; the butter and jam found temporary accommodation in a small tin, which in happier times had housed fifty cigarettes. Lastly, the corporal extracted some dubious rissoles, smelling of sandbag, and tossed one to each of his section. Private Barnet sat on the fire step picking hairs from his rissole.[24] He surmised that Fritz was engaged in a similar operation, excepting perhaps that his sustenance was a sausage. Hence the lull in the firing. The unsavoury state of the meal did not worry Private Barnet, he being one of the hardened original platoon. It seemed that the violent shocks of the last few days had failed to pierce the simple armour of his youthful spirit. Through all he had managed to keep a bright eye, a shiny nose, a cheerful countenance. Whilst contending with the muddy trench the platoon was enfiladed; a shell splinter 'blooded' Calder, cutting his hand. Suddenly a little dog jumped into the trench, trembling with fright. The poor mongrel was in a pitiable condition; somehow it had got through from the German lines. Snipe held it against his muddy puttees and began to feed it with bits of army biscuit, stroking it as he sang the verse of a cockney song:

"'arf a nicker wouldn't buy that tyke, But there's one fing abaht 'im aint for sale, it's a kind of a sort of 'ome sweet 'ome in the wagging of the ol' dog's tail".

Godfrey had his wish and became a runner. One dark night as he splashed his muddy way down the long communication trench that led to Battalion Headquarters, he heard a movement on the top, and an insidious voice said: "Good evening; Tommy: we want you". He looked up and saw a pair of mocking eyes under a German round army cap. Before the man could bend down to get him he darted forward, when a second Boche grabbed his epaulet to haul him up. Godfrey drew his breath then shot a mouthful of saliva and chewing gum straight into his adversary's face. The man incontinently let go and fell back; whereupon Godfrey broke the runner's record. After delivering his message to B.Hq.[25] he reported the incident and described how he had got away. The Regimental-Sergeant-major smiled; "Unarmed combat, eh, well, you won't find them about when you go back, they're too crafty." Nonetheless, Godfrey kept his loaded rifle at the ready and his eyes skinned on the way back.

On the third day of the platoon's turn the Adjutant brought a Lewis gun into Knight's fire bay, shot off several pans of ammunition and departed. Whereupon one of the nerve-racked survivors of Saturday's battle blurted out: "Stone me! Why the hell did he want to do that? It's been quiet all the morning; now we shall get the shit over".[26] A few minutes later a fury of whizz-bangs crashed on the parapet.[27] Next evening the Company was relieved and went into supports, a few paces from the communication trench.[28] The platoon's temporary resting place was a sort of shed built against a high bank covered with a thick layer of earth. The interior was dark, and fitted with a wooden frame-work of bunks covered with chicken wire extending from floor to ceiling. To the tired men this was a palace compared with their water-logged gutter in the earth, without shelter from the heavy rains, hardly any sleep, constant work, and the unnerving activities of the Boche gunners.

Sam Smart ecstatically flung himself down on a bunk. But he was quickly disenchanted by the sergeant-majors command, 'stand-to'. So they all stood-to outside the shed in common with the men in the front line. After stand-down the platoon took spades to the comm. trench, spread out, and were told to scoop out the mud and throw it to the top. The heavy rains had joined with devil himself to badger them. Godfrey's fond hope of being excused fatigues had faded.[29] The acute shortage of men had forced him to join in the work of mud removing. He achieved his objective by brute force and native pugnacity: with every throw of the stubborn stuff he ejaculated "Get up there, blast you", oblivious of ducking heads and protesting shouts around him. He stuck his tool into the glutinous muck, and after twists managed to get a spade full. With a backward and forward sweep he flung it up to the top, only to watch it slither down the sloping wall of the trench to land at his feet.[30]

Next day the whole Company marched the three miles back to Souastre. On the way the rain clouds disappeared, and the hot sun baked the crusts of grime on unshaven faces.

Mr. Summers, the new platoon commander, led his men to their billet, a barn in the village, then took up his quarters in the farm house facing, thirty yards away. A big round heap of muck lay festering in the centre of the yard awaiting the farmer's decision to have the stuff removed when it became too ripe to be tolerated.[31] In the afternoon the platoon paraded for baths.[32] The men marched to a shell-torn stable where they stripped and dropped their clothes among the horses' hoofs. In a field nearby six long baths stood in a row, to reach which each man shuffled along clad only in his identity disc[33] and boots, over a narrow greasy plank athwart a stream, past a hedge whose nettles administered a stinging rebuke to all that nakedness passing by. Mr. Summers stood and watched his men, telling any having serious blemishes on their bodies to report sick. Some of the chaps' legs were covered with septic sores caused by scratching at the trench lice that had tormented them under their uniforms in the firing line.

Back in the evening the officer treated his platoon by sending across a franc per man.[34] A nice lad, with a pink complexion like a girl's, he used to look in just before lights-out to see that everyone was all right. One evening he sat outside his billet scribbling on a writing pad when a crowd of his lads who happened to be pottering about on their side of the muck heap, struck up a song beginning with "Just a letter I am writing, Kitty, dear" pretending not to look at him. A sly glance discovered him endeavouring to smother a smile. Among orders that were read out that night was the King's message of congratulations on the 'success' of the Somme offensive. The next morning, being Sunday, the battalion held a church parade in a big barn. The service took the form of a memorial for those who fell in the battle eight days ago. As he stood listening to the chaplain's elegy, Barnet's thoughts went back to that stricken Gommecourt field, to Smokey and the others. Smokey, pitching forward and spewing blood in his death agony. Scot, the argumentative bloke, so generous to his mates with his food parcels; Peter, the gentle lad who wore a tiny silver cross with his identity disc round his neck; Corporal Double, the Casanova in khaki, who went down as the savage cartridge tore through the love-letters near his heart.

In the afternoon, half the Brigade was inspected by the Third Army Commander, General Allenby, and the Corps Commander, General Snow. This done, the troops in their turn had the satisfaction of sizing up the two brass-hats[35] who had sent them into battle, and now stood facing them. Gen. Allenby, a heavily built old soldier, was the first to address them.

"Now for the soft soap", muttered Private Godfrey. Then Gen. Snow, more voluble, took up the theme.

"Gentlemen", said he, "I call you gentlemen because if any of you did not enjoy that title before July the First your conduct on that day earned it for you".

He went on to tell them that the Division's role had been a diversionary one, because the very determined attack of the British on this sector had held large forces of the enemy at their front, thus enabling their comrades farther south to break through and hold their gains. This was small comfort for the poor devils that had no gains to show for their sacrifice – the bitterest feeling a British soldier can have. At the end of that disastrous July day, this 56th London Division had nothing to show for its valour but its 4749 casualties and a handful of shell-shocked prisoners who somehow had got through their own fierce barrage in No-Mans-Land.[36] As the platoon marched off, Blake, the sardonic one, ejaculated "Some diversion! Good God!"

Its five days' break having ended, the Company left Souastre next afternoon and arrived at Hebuterne, south of Gommecourt, in the evening. It was their turn to be here for a while, supporting the other Companies in the line. They found Hebuterne a village of blackened waters, blasted trees and neglected vegetation. It had been lost and recaptured several times. Not one of its inhabitants remained. The doors of its tiny shrine were lying amongst the debris at the foot of the broken altar; whilst, at the other end of a once-verdant avenue of tall trees, stood the remains of the church: just two portions of wall, as it were beseeching hands stretched out to heaven from the mangled form that lay upon the sore ground. A few paces off a great cross stood, the suffering Christ looking down upon this abomination of desolation wrought by 'Christian' hands. The platoon went in sections to bits of houses, sheds and stables. One section was billeted in a barn sans door, sans roof, sans nearly everything[37] except a thick collection of ancient straw and dirt which housed a world of insect life so forbidding that the men unanimously decided to leave it undisturbed lest loosed terrors assaulted the five senses. So they covered their spaces with ground-sheets, using overcoats as bedspreads. Although it was summer, the nights were cold; but they consoled themselves with the thought that it was better than the trenches; and they could look up through the open roof to the starry firmament when the rain left off.

Barnet did sentry-go in the ghostly village, where German spies dressed in British khaki were known to lurk, and sudden showers of machine gun bullets rattled upon his beat.

Communication trenches led direct to the support and front lines. Three companies would go into the trenches, while the fourth remained in the village. After three days, the order was changed, the men in the village relieving some of their comrades, so that in time everyone was served alike – except battalion headquarters, which stayed in the rear. There the cooks had their field-kitchens; and it was one of the duties of the men stationed in the village to take hot meals to their pals in the trenches. So one day Parks and Smart carried a dixie[38] of stew up the narrow communication trench. Suddenly Sam's lively chatter died in his throat as with a vicious hiss a shell crashed down outside, tossing up chunks of mud and splinters of iron, one of which fell a few feet from Parks. Almost immediately, another dropped in the trench about fifty yards to the rear. Involuntarily they hunched their shoulders, Parks stumbled against the sooty side of the dixie, the lid slithered off and little pieces of floating fat bespattered Smart's tunic; grimly clutching their precious charge they pushed on, Sam grumbling all the while: "It'll take 'ours to scrape off this grease". "Stop grumbling and hang on to the dixie" said the older man. At length, by dint of alternate spurts and stops, they reached their goal. There the corporal took the food, blandly commenting "Jerry had you properly taped this time".[39]

Meanwhile, others of the platoon were engaged in a fascinating fatigue clearing water, mud and the beastliest ordure from an old German trench near their billet so that it could be used in an emergency should the village be heavily shelled. It was a vile job; the stench was nauseating, necessitating frequent exits to the top for gulps of fresh air. Godfrey was luckier; being an occasional runner, he could deviate somewhat, passing through the orchard where red cherries and currants hung in defiance of black death. Once he sat on a bit of broken wall to watch dancing butterflies and listen to the sweet birds sing. He strayed into a cottage garden and lighted upon a brave little rose bush. He stretched out his hand to pluck a pink blossom, then changed his mind and left it there. A few paces from the garden, on a grey mound by the roadside, stood a crude wooden cross upon which was scribbled 'An unknown German soldier'. This was the very trench from which the Battalion had begun its share of the 'big push' a fortnight ago.[40]

Blake asked Jack Lawley, a survivor, what his feelings were as he waited in that assembly trench to go over the top.

"All mixed up; one minute I'd be wondering what I would meet when we went over; the next I'd say to myself, it can't be that bad; we've been pulverising them for days. The waiting was the worst. I kept fidgeting with my equipment. I wanted to put an end to the uncertainty. An hour before we went over the Germans sent heavy stuff – they knew we were coming. We were packed close together: some of the chaps near me were jumpy and smoking fag after fag. Barnet was trying to talk above the crashes, but his mouth was dry and he gave it up. One or two were leaning against the side with their eyes shut – praying perhaps. Then the order was passed along: 'fix bayonets' and my heart gave a jump. Suddenly the guns stopped, and I thought; now we're for it".

"What went wrong?" asked Blake.

"What went wrong? Everything. A lot of Jerry's wire wasn't shot away nor his trenches flattened out or his dugouts smashed in. He had deep underground dugouts and kept down there until our barrage lifted and fell to his rear then ran up with his machine-guns – they had them every few yards – it was murder; with their big guns joining in."

During that spell in the trenches a night bombing raid was carried out by another company, who rehearsed back at Halloy. To stimulate the enthusiasm of the raiding party the instigators of the project concocted a crafty scheme: they fed the men with juicy joints, treated them to three or four pay parades, took them to army concert parties, gave them strawberry jam in lieu of the plebeian plum and apple, and generally petted them. Before the raid, Corporal Green took four men from the platoon to spy out the lie of the land and take a look at the German barbed wire.

A little before midnight the raiders came up and crept near their wire, spread themselves out, laid on their bellies and waited. Suddenly the guns in the rear broke into a fury of thunder and the shells whizzed over the heads and in front of the crouching bombers, on to the German wire and trench, then lifted. The raiders rushed in, slinging their bombs; one laid about him with a heavy knobbly-headed cosh.

'All you've got to do,' the back-room boys had said, 'is to nip in, snatch one or two prisoners, and nip back again' – unmindful of the probability that their ballistic overture would give away the show. So, it came about that the raiders found their opponents ready waiting for them and about to drop a barrage on No Man's Land to baulk their getaway.[41] 'Parapet Percy' got busy spraying the ground with his machine-gun. (This chap was the successor of 'Parapet Pete', another gunner cursed but admired by Tommy for his smart shooting and cleverness in sweeping the dust from the parapets: he was killed on July the First. Rumor said that the troops who stormed his stronghold found him chained to his gun. [42]) After the raid, Corporal Green again took his men out on patrol. They did not relish the job, as the Germans had now got the wind up and were feverishly shooting up Verey lights.[43] In the interim Snipe whispered to his leader "Look Corp, two Jerries". Green crept towards the crouching figures, and then a star shell shot up and revealed them; their own medical officer and the chaplain, looking for wounded and dead.[44]

Notes

1. Although it is only a total distance of fifty-six miles (ninety kilometres) from Le Havre to Rouen the French trains were notoriously slow. The cattle wagons used to transport soldiers were marked 'Hommes [Men] 40 or Chevaux [Horses] 8'.
2. The village of Halloy les Pernois is ten miles (sixteen kilometres) southwest of Doullens. A railhead for some of the war, it later became the location of a casualty clearing station [CCS] and cemetery.
3. This date is significant because it is that of the attack made by the BEF and French Army astride the River Somme. Called at the time 'The Battle of Albert' or 'The Big Push', it is now known as the Battle of the Somme. The fighting would last until November.
4. Emergency rations were referred to as iron rations.
5. The weather on 1 July 1916 was famously clear and hot following a period of cold wet weather, which had delayed the start of the battle for two days.
6. Together with a hundred men from his regiment, he was sent forward as part of a reinforcement draft for the 13 London. The battalion formed part of 168 Brigade, 56th (London) Division, and had been in France since November 1914. In addition to the 13 London, the brigade consisted of the 4th (Royal Fusiliers) Battalion, London Regiment [4 London], the 12th (The Rangers) Battalion, London Regiment

[12 London] and the 14 London. Steward's draft arrived at the battalion late on 1 July 1916, shortly after it had been withdrawn from the line to the village of Sailly au Bois having taken part in the diversionary attack by the 56th (London) and 46th (North Midland) Divisions on the Gommecourt salient. O.F. Bailey and H.M. Hollier, *The Kensingtons: 13th London Regiment* (London, Regimental Old Comrades Association, 1936), pp. 72–9. This is also confirmed by the BWD of the 13 London, WO95/2955, TNA.

7. Battle Order was developed early in the war when it was realised that in trenches and in the attack the large pack containing the soldier's greatcoat and other spare clothing was, largely, unnecessary.

8. According to the Regimental History, during their attack on 1 July 1916 the 13 London suffered the loss of sixteen officers and 300 other ranks killed and wounded.

9. In cold and wet weather the unit MO could issue rum before an attack and, as here, as an antidote to shock for men coming out of battle. The meat extract was probably Oxo, the most common brand of beef extract issued as rations.

10. The BWD reports the arrival of the draft at about midnight on 1 July 1916. A number of references within the narrative, when checked against the diary and other sources, support the suggestion that Steward was posted to the battalion's D Company. These sources will be referred to at the appropriate point within this comparison. Contained in the document archive of the Imperial War Museum [IWM] is a set of papers relating to 5367 Private Percival Dillon Mundy, a resident of Boscombe, Bournemouth. Like Steward, Mundy originally enlisted in the 15 London and formed part of the draft which joined the 13 London on 1 July 1916. His uncle published in a local newspaper a letter sent by Mundy, in which he describes his arrival at the front: 'We spent the night in some reserve trenches where we joined up with the Battalion to which we had been transferred, much to our disappointment' (Box 80/43/1, IWM). The timing of the draft's arrival was clearly intended to replace the anticipated casualties that would be the inevitable result of the day's fighting. It is worth noting that the groups of friends make a point of staying together to ensure that they are posted to the same platoon. Sticking with mates was important as being alone among strangers made a newly arrived member of a draft vulnerable and friendless.

11. The use of the word 'Boche' by the author is quite revealing. Other ranks more frequently used the term 'Hun', while the French term 'Boche' was used more often by officers. It was also increasingly used after the war.

12. Souastre village was used as a rest area for the 56th Division.

13. In the drill movement 'Present Arms', a stationary soldier holds his rifle vertically in front of his body to pay a military compliment to an officer or other unit.

14. 'Sloping arms' was a drill movement used by soldiers when marching smartly. On this occasion the officer lets his exhausted men march 'easy'.

15. Each company had a two-wheeled, horse-drawn cooker in which the cooks could prepare meals and keep water hot even on the march.

16. Every battalion had a regimental medical officer [RMO] attached from the RAMC. He and a small team of orderlies acted as a general practitioner for the men and provided initial medical care for those wounded in action. In the trenches the RMO's home was the regimental aid post [RAP].

17. 'Number Nines', which were freely administered to soldiers who reported to the MO, were believed by the troops to be laxative pills. Iodine was the favoured antiseptic of choice on boils, blisters or wounds.

18. Roadside Calvaries were a new experience for the soldiers of the BEF and deeply

perplexing to Indian soldiers serving on the Western Front. Many of them believed that the figure of Christ actually represented an executed criminal and was a warning to the French to avoid breaking the law.

19. Relieving a unit in the front line was a process, usually carried out under the cover of darkness, in which outgoing troops were gradually replaced by an incoming formation. Trenches, periscopes and tools were handed over and signed for and breaks in the wire, damaged trenches or vulnerable spots were pointed out to the newcomers of the relief who were rarely as truly relieved as the men leaving the trenches for a period of rest or at least time spent in relative safety. The timing of this process and the relieving unit is confirmed by the Regimental History as occurring on 2 July 1916. O.F. Bailey and H.M. Hollier, *The Kensingtons: 13th London Regiment* (London, Regimental Old Comrades Association, 1936), p. 79.

20. All too frequently nervous and inexperienced soldiers opened fire on such parties and a warning that British soldiers were in no man's land would have been very timely. No record was kept of the number of men killed by 'friendly fire', as we call it today, and witnesses rarely told family members how a man had died if it was an accident.

21. According to SDGW the battalion lost only one sergeant on 1 July 1916, 1227 Sergeant Thomas Aikman. There were, however, four second lieutenants killed: N. Mackenzie, W. Mager, H. Pilgrim and C. Sach. Of these, the BWD account places Second Lieutenant Mager as serving with D Company and it is likely therefore that he is the platoon officer referred to in this account.

    According to the CWGC Sergeant Aikman is buried in Hebuterne Military Cemetery (Plot IV, M, 45), as is Second Lieutenant Mager (Plot IV, M, 51). Their proximity in the cemetery may indicate that they were recovered from the same area on the battlefield, and certainly supports the suggestion that both men were in the same company and possibly the same platoon.

22. Soldiers in the trenches were rarely expected to be on guard duty for more than two hours. At night this meant standing on the fire step with head and shoulders above the parapet staring into no man's land ready for any movement that might indicate enemy action.

23. The routine of trench warfare called for all the men in the front line to 'stand to' at both dawn and dusk, the most likely times for an enemy attack.

24. The company cook and his assistants working behind the lines would have divided up the rations and sent them forward in sandbags, hence the smell and hairs.

25. 'B.Hq' – Battalion Headquarters.

26. Any usual firing or activity from the trenches could attract retaliation and activities such as the firing of machine guns by men who could then withdraw, leaving the occupants of the trench to receive the incoming return fire, and potential casualties, was resented.

27. Whizz-Bang was the nickname used by British soldiers to describe light shells fired at high velocity from enemy guns. There was little warning before the bang.

28. 'Supports' were the supporting trenches behind the front line. These were slightly safer than the front-line trenches.

29. 'Fatigue' – a pre-war army term related to any manual work.

30. Any digging, especially in wet weather or under fire, was backbreaking and frequently dispiriting. Not all soldiers were used to heavy physical activity and while farm labourers or coal miners would be familiar with the rhythm of this type of work, clerical workers could be reduced to tears of exhaustion by a night spent entrenching.

31. British soldiers frequently comment on the manure heaps on French and Belgian farms. The chief remarks concerned the proximity of the pile to the farmhouse and the 'agricultural' smell that resulted. This was not a surprise to soldiers from farming areas but was a new experience for city dwellers.

32. Baths were a crucial part of the arrangements for all units out of the line. Operated by the Army Service Corps [ASC], they offered the possibility of baths or showers for the men and clean underwear and uniforms. One forgotten aspect of the Great War is that up to half of the BEF never went into the trenches because their jobs did not call for them to do so. Tens of thousands of men drove lorries, cared for pigeons or operated bath units.

33. We have an example here of just how accurate the author's memory of events was, even nearly twenty years later when we believe that he wrote this book. Until around September 1916 British soldiers wore a single, red, heat-treated fibre identity disc, not called a 'dog tag' until the arrival of American soldiers in 1917. This tag was stamped with the wearer's name, rank, regimental number, religion and unit. In the aftermath of the first day of the Somme, when so many men were killed and their tags recovered without their bodies, it was clear that many would be unidentifiable. In consequence, a second greeny/grey octagonal tag was issued from September 1916 so that one tag, the red one, could be recovered from a body and the other left to identify the man for subsequent burial. The failure of this system, especially in the early phase of the battle, is demonstrated by the monument to the 'missing' of the Somme at Thiepval, which bears the names of more than 72,000 British soldiers. Their 'missing' status does not indicate that their bodies were not found, rather that they were not identified during the wartime and postwar battlefield clearances.

34. The rate of exchange in 1916 suggests that a franc was worth around five old pence, less than half a day's pay for a private soldier. It was enough for a drink or two, but not much more.

35. The term 'Brass hats' is frequently used as to refer to senior officers and is a comment on the amount of gold braid worn on their caps. The two officers were indeed the relevant army and corps commanders at this time and there can be no doubt that the author heard the speeches.

36. This is based on the figures given in the history of the 56th Division published in 1921. This indicates that 182 officers and 4,567 other ranks became casualties. The total, 4,749, matches the figures quoted by the author. He must have been writing with this book to hand. Major C.H. Dudley Ward, *The Fifty-Sixth Division, 1st London Territorial Division 1914–1918* (Naval & Military Press, repr. edn, 1921), p. 47.

37. 'Sans' – French for 'without'.

38. A dixie is an oval metal container with a cover and handle used for cooking and carrying food.

39. 'Jerry' – German, in the singular or plural. It was used alongside 'Hun', although 'Jerry' indicated a level of familiarity.

40. The attack on the Somme was frequently referred to by the press as 'The Big Push'.

41. The BWD places this raid on the night of 16 July 1916, when a party of fifty men led by Lieutenant Leigh, Lieutenant Shaw and Second Lieutenant Jones raided the enemy trenches, killing one man and wounding six others. They had previously rehearsed the raid on practice trenches at Halloy.

42. The German machine gun, the MG08, was heavier than the British Vickers or Maxim machine guns. In consequence, German gunners had straps that were

clipped to the weapon to take the weight over their shoulders. To a British soldier this looked as if the gunner had been chained to the weapon, and it is often commented upon in contemporary memoirs.

43. Verey or Very Lights were a form of flare fired from a pistol to either illuminate an area at night or, by use of colours, to convey a simple message.

44. The BWD also referred to the RMO and Padre searching no man's land for wounded. The RMO at this point was Captain T. Fox, RAMC. He was replaced on 22 July 1916 by Captain H. Stranger, RAMC, who in turn was relieved on 24 July 1916 by Lieutenant Davidson, RAMC. The battalion Padre at the time was the Reverend Captain J. Rees.

Chapter Three

The Somme

Next morning the Battalion was relieved by another of the Brigade and the platoon went back to Sailly au Bois.[1] The village had been subject to systematic bombardment, which had driven away the population save one courageous old dame who, like her counterpart in the deserted village, refused to leave her house. Although the battalion was not holding the line and had a limited degree of comfort in sundry barns, the men worked a great deal in and about the trenches. They went up on the night of their relief to fill in the remains of a trench at Hebuterne from which an attack was launched on July 1st. The trench had been pulverised by enemy guns; here and there it was manned by dead men. Parties were detailed to bury the bodies of British and Boche lying in No Man's Land. When possible, any private papers found were taken away so that they could be sent to next of kin.[2] Calder was shown a picture post card depicting a little German girl kneeling in prayer for her father's safety. When the men were halfway through their job they were rumbled by Boche sentries who fired Verey lights. Then the strafe began.[3]

"'Ullo, 'ere comes their 'im of 'ate!" exclaimed Barnet. Shrapnel and minnies[4] began to drop, machine gun fire and four-twos were shot at them, wounding and killing – for they were filling in their own cover. Then the bright moon shone behind them, turning them into targets. A shell splinter tore a big gash in Savage's shoulder. The stretcher-bearers took him off and his pals carried on. Later, as the strafe showed no signs of abating, orders to pack up were issued, so no more work was done that night.

Next night the work was resumed, and, to everyone's surprise, the men were allowed to finish it, the enemy having discovered during the day that the trench was being filled in.

Sailly au Bois was now known as a 'quiet sector', but occasionally the guns opposite barked out a sudden bombardment, as though a host of indignant monsters had been rudely awakened from slumber. Their

target was an anti-aircraft gun, which had been placed close to the
platoon's billet in the village. Last Sunday evening, when Barnet and
Snipe were occupying their brief leisure playing cards, Sgt Williams
burst in shouting "Get equipment on; stand by; attack expected". In the
midst of the hustle Gawkey Rudd, whose big army boots had a habit of
knocking against each other as he walked, lurched on to Snipe and sent
him sprawling, scattering his hand of cards and sending the king and
queen gliding around the barn. The men had scarcely got inside their
equipment when the shells tore in, savaging their first victims. Calls for
stretcher-bearers were intermingled with yells from the sergeant "Take
cover in the cellars". Forty of the men scrambled down into a dark
noisome hole, reeking in long decay.[5] Someone produced and lit a bit of
candle, but it petered out, loath to live in that noxious atmosphere. One
or two tried to talk and speculate on the hazard of the company holding
the line, but they spluttered and choked so much that they had to stop;
then clambered back up the broken stairs, electing, as Blake said, to "take
their chance to die clean in the fresh air rather than suffocate in that
stinking sepulchre".

There was no attack; the bombardment slackened then grew intermit-
tent. Later in the day Bobby Thomas met Lawley emerging from a
cellar.

"Hello Jack, been trying to find a 'better 'ole'?"[6] "Well, in a way; one
or two of us have been helping the padre make some sort of a chapel".

"A what?"

"He scrounged around until he found this cellar; miles better than the
hole we were in this morning".

"I should hope so".

"Come and have a look".

These two liked to share each other's company whenever the exigen-
cies of their service permitted, in or out of the trenches. They had
trained together in England and gone through the fires in France.
Lawley was short, dark, with a round good-natured nose, Thomas tall,
red, with sharp captious nose. But how sadly their faces bore the cruel
war's impress! The two friends went down. The small cellar had been
cleaned, patched up and tidied. An oil lamp hanging from the low ceiling
cast a subdued light on a little altar upon which had been laid a fair linen
cloth, a tiny brass cross, and some daisies and speedwell.

"All very nice; but not for me", said Thomas. "Here you're forced to
do your worship underground, forced by other Christians. That Jerry

we saw lying out in No Man's Land the other night, staring up at nothing, had on his belt 'Got mit uns'. What mockery; both sides say the same thing: God with us".

"We are fighting the forces of evil", said Lawley, the fiends responsible for the atrocities against the women and children of little Belgium and the blinding of Canadians at Ypres with gas. "What other devilishness will they think up unless we crush them?"

"True", said Thomas, "but you know our fight is with the whole German people. For years their writers, their professors and some of their parsons have made them believe they are super people. The Kaiser told them that they were the salt of the earth. They're jealous of us, and they won't be satisfied until they've beaten and bossed us".

The 7th Yorkshire Division was on its way to effect a relief.[7] The platoon pessimist, fearful that he might be done for before they arrived, groused so frequently that he was told to "put a sock in it". At length, soaked through, the troops answered the usual questions[8] when handing over, then marched to Bayencourt, a village three miles back. That night the relief of the whole Division was completed and it went out to 'rest'. It was a warm, bright sunny evening as the platoon tramped along the countryside, watching the exquisite colours of the great unseen artist glide across the sky-canvas. They marched through villages that had not known the blasting breath of battle, and felt how good it was to be in civilisation again after so many weeks in the infernal regions. The battalion halted at Halloy near midnight. Next day was given over to inspection of equipment and men's clothes (exterior!). Early the following day they were off again for a march to Doullons railway station. So as not to be late, the men were got there with best part of five hours to spare. Eventually the train crawled in and took them to St. Ricquier. From thence, another march got them to Millencourt, their destination, late at night. They had reached the Abbeville area.

Without loss of time, rehearsals for attacks commenced: watched by the Generals who trotted around on their chargers, convulsing the troops and putting the wind up some of the subalterns. The weather was variable; sometimes sharp showers caught the whole concourse in the midst of its manoeuvres: but most of the time tropical, when the early September sun scorched the men during route marches. They would return to billets perspiring freely, hurriedly discard their packs and take their mess tins to an adjoining farmhouse to purchase a pint of cool fresh milk from the dear old lady within. Every night before lights-out the orderly-sergeant went around with his book to read the orders of the day. Demanding silence by a loud "Pay attention to orders", he would proceed to read out the programme for the next day's work. One evening he read a letter from the Corps Commander, bidding good-bye to the Division upon its withdrawal from his Army Corps, thanking it for its work in repairing the system of trenches lately occupied and paying it the compliment that he hoped to welcome it back at some other time. (Ironical cheers.) Another item headed 'Honours and Awards', published the names of officers, warrant-officers, N.C.O.s and men who were to be decorated. Blake said the only decoration he wanted was a whole skin and joie de vivre at the finish of the ghastly business. The sergeant moved on, after announcing that Italy had declared war on Germany, and Russia on Austria.[9] On the last day of their stay in the region of Abbeville the whole Brigade marched to a fresh area and rehearsed attacks upon a system of newly-dug trenches. A big metal contrivance of curious design, fitted with long tractor wheels, stood in the field taken over by the platoon. Knight thought it was some sort of ingenious implement that the French farmers had thought up. But as the troops commenced to advance to the 'attack', the contraption, manned by a khaki-clad crew, moved with it. It lumbered on until it reached the belt of barbed wire and crushed it down, then went on serenely to demolish the model trenches. It dawned on everyone that a new and fearsome engine of war had been evolved (as Frane said) "by some brainy blokes in blighty".[10]

At the finish of the manoeuvres the seventeen hundred odd men sat closely packed on the grass and listened while Major (Strafer) Campbell demonstrated all the up-to-date tricks of hand-to-hand fighting. Here nature had provided him with a high bank for a platform. Armed with a rifle and bayonet, he showed his skill, with the co-operation of a staff-sergeant-major, similarly armed, who played up to him with fiendish dexterity. He told his (cynical) audience that although they might feel a certain repugnance at plunging their sharp weapons into the soft flesh of their opponents, after the first thrust they would see red and get busy. This bloodthirsty talk was relieved by anecdotes of humorous Tommies he had known; and the entertainment terminated with a round of applause – although the chaps were saying to each other 'that means we're for it, mate, over the top at the tout'.[11] On the way back to Millencourt, Parks and Godfrey, who were marching together, talked about the bellicose Major Campbell. Said Godfrey: "It's easy for him to go motoring round the back areas talking to units about pig-sticking; most of the fighting nowadays is done with high explosives and machine-guns; thousands of the chaps are knocked out before they ever see a German."

"Not to mention the poison gas", added Parks.

The platoon reached its billet wearied with the day's work and ready for a long night's rest. But an unpleasant rumour of an early move went round; and was confirmed when the orderly-sergeant read out that reveille would be at 2.30 am next morning. Darkness and silence brooded over the French village; the cocks had not yet begun their crowing; all the sleepers in the barn lay quiet, save an agitated dreamer and the champion snorer. An occasional rat rustled the straw. Suddenly the door flew open, and with a cheerful "wake up, my lucky lads", the sergeant unceremoniously summoned his platoon of civilian soldiers to face the hazards of another day. The first man to move was the unfortunate chap by the door; he got a crack on the head as the sergeant burst in. Someone produced a bit of candle and stuck it on a piece of wood. Yawning, stretching, rubbing their eyes and scratching their heads, they slowly realised that they had got to get going: the war had come back to them. Godfrey reached to his tunic for a lucifer to light his fag,[12] Gawkey Rudd floundered and swore in an endeavour to retrieve his small kit from the thievish, secretive straw. Outside, the pump did its best to satisfy the demands of a dozen clamouring lads. And over all, the insistent, maddening: "Git a move on there".

All the hullabaloo was unnecessary. For an unconscionable time the Battalion stood in the street, minus officers.

"I wish they'd finish their blithering pow-wow," said Thomas.

"P'aps the C.O.'s gorn to arsk 'aig simfink", Smart suggested.[13]

At last the officers appeared: the parade was brought to attention, and with arms sloped the column of fours left the hospitable village for the St. Ricquier railway station.

Somehow or other a dixie of the oval sort had been foisted on the platoon, and each man had to take a turn at carrying it. When Tubby Steel took over, the thing behaved reasonably well – until it began to object to its manner of transit: it bumped its sooty side against Tubby's bow legs, tried to dislodge his rifle, then jerked off the lid with a clatter as they marched along.

Now, unlike this disgusting pot, Tubby had a very equable temper. He had been nurtured by staid, sober, church-going parents, so scorned to use the cusswords current among his fellows: he thought the purity of the English language should not be debased by such crapulence. But that was in tranquil moments. Now the thing was doing its damnest to infuriate the little man. He shook it at arms-length, and got out of step in doing so. Then the floodgates burst: a torrent of curses interspersed with umpteen bloodies, followed by the whole army catalogue of bawdy adjectives shot from his virginal lips.

Thomas was laughing.

Smart, for once bereft of words, could only ejaculate "Cor!"

"Give me the bloody thing," said Taylor, taking over.

"I'm sorry," said Tubby, straightening his tin hat.

"Forget it, mate; I could see you was out of sorts this morning".

"Yes, I felt rotten".

The Battalion reached St. Ricquier with more than two hours to spare, so the men piled rifles along the platform and sat on their packs. Some beguiled the time singing choruses; while one browned-off group rendered 'We are Fred Carno's army' to the tune of 'The church's one foundation'.[14] The train took them thirty-odd miles to Corbie, and from thence, they marched to Sailly le Sec, a little village by the river Somme, where they stayed the night.[15] Before retiring, Lawley and Thomas strolled round the village as the setting sun shed its last golden beams and the western sky glowed with translucent colour.

Their conversation veered round to Tubby Steel's astonishing explosion of adjectival fireworks on the march that morning. Recollecting it, Thomas laughed and said, "I'm afraid he blotted his copy-book".

"I don't know", replied Lawley, "probably his recording angel laughed too".

They turned in early in anticipation of possible sudden marching orders; and slept on a curious wooden platform complete with ladder.

At two o'clock next afternoon the Battalion was given fifteen minutes' notice to pack up and march. The roads were alive with hurrying troops and transport – something big was going on. The Battalion halted for the night at a tented field a mile and a half north of Bray-sur-Somme, and about five miles from Albert. The tents were few and the troops many. Knight found himself and twenty-four others in a tent made to accommodate seven: with their boots off, there were fifty human feet clustered around the centre pole. Knight was tired and dozed off, only to dream that he was in a dungeon in the Tower of London having his feet screwed into one of the engines of torture. He felt the cruel screws pressing against his raw heels that had been abraided by so much marching in his ill-fitting army boots. He awoke, to find his feet held by that fleshy vice at the pole. With a mighty effort he extricated them and placed them on top of the pile, but quickly they were submerged again. After repeating the struggle several times he gave in, so sat up and dozed until dawn. Being a keen observer of homo sapiens, he got some entertainment listening to the groans and grunts of his fellow lodgers as they struggled in their sleep to free their 'plates of meat' and turn over.

The collection of letters had been stopped and field cards substituted.[16] Just before the move Barnet with five others was sent to a dump where they were loaded with drums of Lewis gun ammunition. On rejoining the platoon the ammunition was distributed, to be carried during the march. The troops tramped across the open country then came out upon the main road leading to Bapaume with its avenue of tall sad trees. The whole length was choked with British and French guns, limbers and troops travelling in both directions. This congestion was the cause of frequent halts, during which a man would ease the weight of the pack on his shoulders by using his rifle as a prop behind him. At one point they passed a group of Poilus[17] resting at the roadside, and as they went one called out: "Give 'em a —— good hiding, boys".

They lost all time, as darkness usurped the daylight. Still they went on. The rhythm had long since gone out of their stride, as the sixty-six pounds of equipment weighed them down.[18] Now they were passing motor ambulances loaded with stretchers of broken men, under the incessant thunder of gunfire. At length the platoon was halted on a muddy road and told to get into battle order. This meant taking off webbing equipment, detaching pack from the back and buckling the smaller haversack in its place. Then the packs were piled together for transport to the rear.

"Do you expect to find your pack if you come out of this show?" enquired Corporal Green of Snipe.

"I hope so".

"Then you'd better write your name and identity on the back or you'll be unlucky".

Snipe pulled a stub of copying-ink pencil from his pocket, licked it and started laboriously to print his name.

"Here give it to me", said the corporal. Snatching it, he hurriedly wrote in capitals Snipe's name, number and platoon on the canvas, dipping his pencil in an adjacent puddle from time to time to bring out the violet lettering.[19]

Large quantities of petrol cans full of water, tins of biscuits, bully beef and so on were distributed amongst the whole Company and the game of follow-my-leader began. The ground the men stumbled over was pitted with shell holes and slashed by trenches. Things went fairly well for a while, until a fellow carrying a heavy bag of sugar dropped his load to rest his aching shoulders, tired of waiting for a 'blow' that never came. Those behind him did the same, then he went on; but the others lingered, thus the continuity of the file was broken. The leading people (who carried no burdens) proceeded without a halt. Fitful messages passed up and down the ragged file of food carriers: "Pass it down, 'lost connection'."

"Lost touch in the rear".

"Steady in front".

"Why the 'ell don't you go steady in front?"

Crash, a clatter, a blast of blasting by someone who has slipped over. He picks himself up and carries on.

"Mind the hole!"

"Too late, I've found it" – from one who has stepped on nothing and collapses.

"Why don't they pack the bloody war up; they know they can't win!"

The safety valves were working well.

The guide in front had lost his way. That bag of sugar never reached its destination, for, after a series of minor adventures, it fell into a narrow trench, became wedged, and was discarded by its disgusted custodian.

The men were silly through want of sleep. They had had scarcely any for forty-eight hours and had been on the tramp for about ten, hastening to relieve the 5th Division.

Many wounded were borne along; in some cases carried by German prisoners.

At last the marching men saw, through the faint light of dawn, the men in the front ranks of the Battalion sink to rest at a hillside; and so, with one accord they too dropped down. It was as though a big invisible ball had suddenly sped down that long column of living ninepins and bowled them into unconsciousness. No one knew how long he slept; it seemed but a few moments when the R.S.M. walked along calling them to resume their journey. At this point, the Company gladly handed over the loads.

Notes

1. Major C.H. Dudley Ward, *The Fifty-Sixth Division, 1st London Territorial Division 1914–1918* (Naval & Military Press, repr. edn, 1921), p. 49.
2. The burial of the dead after a major action was critical both to maintain morale and for reasons of hygiene. The task was universally disliked but using men of the same unit to recover their fellow soldiers was an appeal to comradeship. Burial of enemy dead often proved a surprise as troops discovered that their opponents also had families and home lives not so different from their own.
3. 'Strafe' – a term used by British soldiers to describe a bombardment by shells. The origin is the German song 'Gott strafe England', which was also known as the 'Hymn of Hate'.
4. Shrapnel shells exploded in the air, projecting 'shrapnel balls' forward as they did so. 'Minnies' were German heavy mortars called 'minenwerfer'.
5. The 'forty' here refers to a virtually full platoon of men.
6. A reference to the work of the famous British cartoonist Bruce Bairnsfather. In one of his works two soldiers are pictured in shell hole with the caption 'If you knows of a better 'ole, go to it'.
7. The division was in fact the 17th (Northern) Division, which had a large element of soldiers from Yorkshire in its ranks. One of these was 41956 Private John Andrew Robertshaw, who served in the 12 Manchester.
8. These questions related to the nature of the position, strength and hostility of the enemy, positioning of stores, etc.
9. This is an example of a major factual inaccuracy in *The Platoon*. Italy declared war in 1915 and Austria had been at war from the start of the conflict in August 1914.
10. This is a description of the first tanks. They were first used in action on 15 September 1916 on the Somme.
11. The BWD records this as taking place on 22 August 1916 and records that the battalion was located at Millencourt from 23 August 1916 to 3 September 1916. On 25 August Lieutenant T.C. Tate took command of D Company. The bayonet training referred to may correspond with the arrival in the battalion of Major H. Campbell on 27 August 1916 but may also refer to Lieutenant Colonel R. Campbell, referred to in chapter 1.
12. Lucifer was a common nickname for matches, and this also might be an allusion to the song 'Pack Up Your Troubles in Your Old Kit Bag':

    Pack up your troubles in your old kit-bag,
    And smile, smile, smile,
    While you've a Lucifer to light your fag . . .
13. Throughout the war the 'Cockney chappie' was a constant humorous stereotype. One result was a book entitled *The Best 500 Cockney War Stories* (London Evening News, 1921). Also see A. Robertshaw, 'Irrepressible chirpy cockney chappies. Humour as an aid to survival' (*Journal of European Studies*, 2001), vol. 31, parts 3 and 4, no. 123, pp. 277–87.
14. 'Fred Carno' was the stage name of Frederick John Westcott, who was a theatre impresario of the British Music music hall fame. Among the comedians who worked for him were Charlie Chaplin and Stan Laurel. They were part of what was known as 'Fred Carno's Army'.
15. The BWD confirms this as 3–4 September 1916, when the battalion arrived at a tented camp area known as the Citadel (Trench map sheet 62dNE2 Meaulte) located on the road between Bray and Fricourt, on the Somme.
16. Field postcards, known as Whizz-Bangs because of their speed of delivery, were a

pre-printed message system on which the sender deleted or underlined the appropriate phrases. If anything was added other than the address the card was destroyed by the military censors.

17. 'Poilu', literally, 'hairy one' – the common nickname used for a French infantryman. The French hated the title almost as much as British soldiers disliked being called 'Tommy'.

18. The reference to 66lbs is interesting. The author was not in a position to weigh his uniform and equipment, although he could estimate the load. The figure of 66lbs is, however, given in the volume of the *Official History of the Great War* that covers the Battle of the Somme. This was published in 1932 and would have been available to the author through a public library, or perhaps he bought a copy. The date of the publication fits very well with when the editors believe that this account was written. Brigadier General Sir James E. Edmonds, *Military Operations France and Belgium, 1916, Volume I: Sir Douglas Haig's Command to the 1st July 1916, Battle of the Somme* (London, HMSO, 1932).

19. As all webbing equipment looked the same, it was important to identify your own set if you ever expected to recover it and its contents. Indelible pencils were issued to all Non Commissioned Officers (NCOs).

Chapter Four

Leuze Wood

It was full daylight when the men climbed the hill to cross the plain at its summit – a plain of death. The 7th Royal Irish Fusiliers had attacked on the previous day and the ground was strewn with the bodies of those who had been shot down from the waves of attacking men.[1] One, with a horrible hole in his head, still clung to a bucket of Lewis gun ammunition.[2] Another appeared to be in a dreamless slumber, so calm and peaceful he looked. The captured position was in a sorry state, blown to devastation by British artillery and by the Germans after their troops had been driven out. Everywhere dead Huns lay about, with stubbly beards, blanched faces and glazed eyes; wearing their brutal-looking jackboots. One lay half charred at the entrance of a smouldering dugout, as though he had crawled out and died.[3] At dusk a company attempted to cross the stretch of open ground leading to Leuze Wood. The platoon went with it, advancing from shell hole to shell hole. They were doing well until a low-flying German airman spotted them and dropped coloured lights.[4] Thus signalled, enemy artillery opened fire. The farther the men advanced the more intense the shelling became; piling up the dead and wounded. The strategists then decided that the job was not all that urgent, so the survivors were ordered to retire to their starting place. Heavy shelling continued all night.

Next morning another attempt was made. The company reached the wood, which they found unoccupied. On the way there, Godfrey had seen a cunning sniper's post at the extreme north-east corner of the wood overlooking the plain. A little platform had been built high up in the boughs of a big tree from which was hanging a ladder, now broken and limp, obscured by the trunk. What murderous work had that Boche perpetrated from his point of vantage ere his light had been put out! This blackened wood of skeleton tree trunks was surrounded by hidden snipers who found it easy to pick off men as they endeavoured to dig themselves in with their entrenching tools by connecting shell holes together; feverishly working under intense shell fire. Tubby Steel was wounded in the shoulder, and poor Slocombe killed, as well as several July the First men, before the order to retire was given again.

The Company was relieved that night and went back a mile or two to a trench in an artillery camp. There the men rested and slept notwithstanding the shocks and noise of the guns.

The first thing Calder did next morning was to parade at the aid post and obtain tablets from the M.O. When he returned to the trench he learned that Taylor had been slightly wounded in the head. The following morning the whole battalion paraded and went forward to a big dump where each man, or pairs of men, quickly received a load (a bundle of spades and picks, or boxes of bombs or a case of ammunition) and went on in Indian file[5] towards Leuze Wood (Lousy Wood to the troops).

This was in preparation for another attack on the morrow.[6] The way led across open ground straight to the wood: before long the Boche rumbled something, for he subjected the whole train to an intensive gruelling. The operation was a costly bit of work, costly in human lives and limbs. Swift searching shells rained down and made the way ghastly with the sight of writhing men and those stricken dead. A shell dropped just behind Knight and his mate who were carrying between them a box of s.a.a.[7] It wounded a couple of men close by and lifted the sergeant-major unhurt into the air.

As the two continued slowly along they met Lawley, who was returning, having just deposited his load; but seeing the weak state of Knight's partner he insisted on taking over his end of the box and going forward again, notwithstanding the intensity of the shelling.

The platoon got to their own trench in the early hours of the morning. The battalion was in support to the brigade, awaiting orders to move forward. Men not put on guard immediately lay down on the bottom of the trench, pulled their groundsheets over their heads and fell fast asleep.

There was one spot, however, where a niche had been cut in the side of the parados into which a man might curl up. Gawkey Rudd had found it, and although the morning was well advanced he was so much under the influence of Hypnos[8] that he did not recognize the voice of his Company Commander when that gentleman endeavoured to rouse him to ascertain the whereabouts of Mr Summers. Shaking the sleeper the O.C. said:

"Wake up, this man!"

Grunt.

"Wake up; what's your name?"

Two grunts.

"Do you know who I am?"

"Buzz off!"

"Wake up, will you!"

"See yerself off, bugger you!"

"Where is Lieutenant Summers?"

"'ow the 'ell do I know?"

"Damn the man! You'll be for company office when we get out!"

But Gawkey was snoring again.

Short rations appeared from somewhere and were issued to the closely packed men, waiting for zero hour. It was now four o'clock: the warm sun was shining down.

Suddenly the British artillery let loose its tornado of thunder and death. Young Smart, who was standing with Barnet, kept up an excited "'old that one, Fritz!"

Then the men climbed the parapet and went forward. The noise was so deafening that they could not hear the enemy shells coming towards them. The platoon went on in extended order, as rehearsed. Mr. Summers led the way a few paces ahead. He carried a swagger stick in his hand, as was his wont on parade.[9]

Suddenly a fierce flash struck him; his face went purple and he went down on one knee, as a knight at his accolade – the sword of death had touched him. His men pressed on through the barrage and jumped into a German trench. There amongst the dead and demoralized they fought. One big fellow pointed his bayonet at Godfrey and lunged. Godfrey parried, brought his right foot forward, swung his rifle up and round and smashed the butt into his opponent's face. The German dropped his weapon and crashed to the ground. Gawkey Rudd tripped over a corpse and fell down. A Boche rose from a shell hole to throw a bomb, but it fell short, exploded and blew him to pieces. A flying segment landed on one of the Lewis gunners, wounding him. Barnet, maddened at the death of Mr. Summers, laid about him like a demon. There were desperate bloody struggles farther along, the two sides bombing each other across a rough barricade.

As night fell, the platoon was in danger of being out-flanked, so a message "they are working round us" was passed along. The fight waxed hot, and many a feverish request for bombs went through.

Then a mob of Huns tried a frontal attack on the survivors of the platoon. The Lewis gunner turned his weapon upon them; the riflemen gave rapid fire, jostling each other to repel the invaders. At times, they were firing across a rampart of corpses. All night long the heavy shelling continued as the wounded passed to the dressing station; slowly limping along, impeded by the living and the dead, their only support the slippery sides of the trench, and agonising at every step. At intervals a very bad case was borne along on a stretcher, preceded by the call 'make way, there' but rarely, as the bearers were few. The Division had fought forward in the pitch darkness of night against a stubborn determined enemy, resolved to defend Combles and the area in the vicinity of Leuze Wood at all costs. At one time it was surrounded on three sides. The dawn did not help, as it brought with it a thick mist, blanking out the possibility of air reports.

This 56th London Division formed the right flank of the British army and joined hands with the French. The disputed ground lay between Ginchy and Combles. The relief came at two or three o'clock in the morning. The platoon went back with the rest of the Company into some support trenches and immediately commenced carrying work; more and more bombs, to the front line: those deadly iron eggs invented by the ingenious Mister Mills.

The strain of the week's efforts and the scarcity of food had drained the men of vitality. On each journey, Parks carried two large boxes of bombs; but his fingers had lost their strength to retain their grip on the rope handles, so that the boxes kept slipping to the ground. He tried carrying them upon his shoulders with little improvement, but he managed to stick it.

And still the wounded dragged past; a never-ending procession of pain, British and Boche alike. One of the latter, a middle-aged man nursing an ugly wound, went his melancholy way alone, without escort, without molestation.

The tramp farther back to a camp near Maricourt took two hours. They arrived at an arid plain wide enough to bivouac[10] the whole Brigade. Each man received some tea, a small piece of fried bacon, but no bread – the first issue for two days – then slept for an hour in a small hole in the ground. But the rations came a few hours later. Afterwards there was time to scrounge for water to wash and remove seven-day beards. Blake assisted Sergeant How to make some sort of cover with their groundsheets. The Company-sergeant-major had been killed, so How, being the senior sergeant, had been promoted to take his place. He appeared to be in a great hurry to let the men know what he had become, for he took off his tunic and commenced to remove his stripes. Having done so, he began to draw with a copying-ink pencil the rough outline of a C.S.M.'s[11] crown on the lower part of each sleeve. Blake, who was scraping some of the mud from his puttees with his jack knife, said nothing, but he thought: "Master How has not grown up".

The constant arrival of big batches of prisoners provided some diversion with a general rush towards each party as it came into sight and moved with ragged step to a large barbed-wire cage. One man, enveloped in a large groundsheet, paced the ground like the Moody Dane.[12] Another sought the aid of a sentry to bandage a sore arm. It was a motley crowd; most of whom had done their best to kill only a few hours before.[13] A small party of British officers rode up to watch. One, a fair-haired young man, was the Prince of Wales.[14] Lawley told Thomas: "The last time I saw him he was in civvies; about three years ago, one summer night. My girl and I had been up West and decided to walk to Victoria Station via the park. As we were passing the Queen Victoria Memorial, he came along with a friend towards the Palace".

"Now you'll have something to talk about when you write to your girl", said Thomas.

"Unless its censored", was the reply. "That reminds me of a woman I know who wrote a letter to her husband out here and got it returned by the censor marked: 'You talk too much'".

That morning the crippled Brigade had held a church parade.[15]

The platoon's losses were severe; nearly half had been killed or wounded. Sec. Lt. Summers, the C.S.M., Corporal Green, Whitty, Lance corporal Thorn, Steel, Slocombe, as well as many others. The threatened confrontation of cheeky Gawkey Rudd with his Company Commander on the disciplinary charge was off; both had been wounded.[16] Mason, who was always good for a laugh when being seen dozing on the fire-step off duty, mouth wide agape, had died of his wound whilst being conveyed across the channel.

Calder, cheerful and generous; he, too, had 'gone west',[17] leaving a sad gap. Back in the village he had shown Knight a photo of his pretty fiancée dressed in a nurse's uniform.

Blake had made enquiries during the day concerning the fate of the merry band that had come with him from England, and had been divided amongst the battalion. In the ten weeks here twenty per cent had become casualties (killed and wounded).[18]

As evening advanced the new sergeant distributed extra battle stores amongst his platoon. He pushed a big pair of wire-cutters into Barnet's unwilling hands with the quip: "Souvenir of the Great War".[19] Then the battalion set out through the mud, interminable mud: at every step a man's boot lifted pounds of it. They passed a light cart being pulled by twelve mules to keep it running.

It was past midnight when the men halted at an old trench system. The guns were all around them ceaselessly pounding the enemy.

Early next morning the Company went farther forward, to the rear of Leuze Wood, and dug itself in, being in reserve. An attack on a ten-mile front was about to begin.

Lawley and Thomas were talking and laughing. The subject of their hilarious conversation was about the antics of their new Company Commander on the way up some days ago. It had been raining miserably all that day, so in consequence he had had recourse to the insidious solace of Roger Rum; too much of which had induced in him a mania for speed, notwithstanding the treacherous nature of the ground.

A lad in front of Lawley had slipped into a shell-hole.

"Never mind the hole" shouted the officer. The words had hardly left his mouth when he fell against Lawley, spluttered "I beg pardon, my boy", and fell flat on his face in the mud!

"What happened after that?" asked Thomas.

"Well, we carried on; but soon afterwards a message was passed along: Mr. ——— (I didn't catch his name) is now O.C. Company". Roger Rum had been carried off on a stretcher – ill!

A counter-attack was expected, so a sentry was posted in each fire bay. Because of the shortage, each man stood there nearly all night. The dawn found a lamentably thin line of watchers, the majority weak with dysentery, nervous strain, and lousy to boot. It was fortunate for them that no Germans came.

The weather changed to glorious sunshine; the tortured earth looked up to an exquisite azure sky.

When in due course the relief came, Sergeant-major How gathered the Company together and led them on as fast as he could go. His speed was attributable to two causes, good health and wind-up.[20] Some of the men were hard put to it to keep pace with him, so straggled behind.

Joseph Johns Steward and Emily on their wedding day,
14 October 1922. (*Family collection*)

This family group was photographed at some point in the early 1930s. It is possible that
the young boy is Joseph and Emily's son Eric. Joseph is standing on the extreme right.
(*Family collection*)

The front cover of the Attestation paper signed by the author on his enlistment. Similar records that survived German bombing in 1940 can now be viewed at *www.ancestry.co.uk.*

The author's AFB103 (Casualty Form Active Service), which provides a series of chronological entries relating to his movements, both with his unit and as an individual. (*www.ancestry.co.uk*)

Army Form B. 103.

Casualty Form—Active Service.

DURATION OF WAR

The author's map of
France and Belgium
found with the
manuscript. He appears to
have removed the map
from a copy of the 56th
Divisional History and
then underlined places of
significance in red.

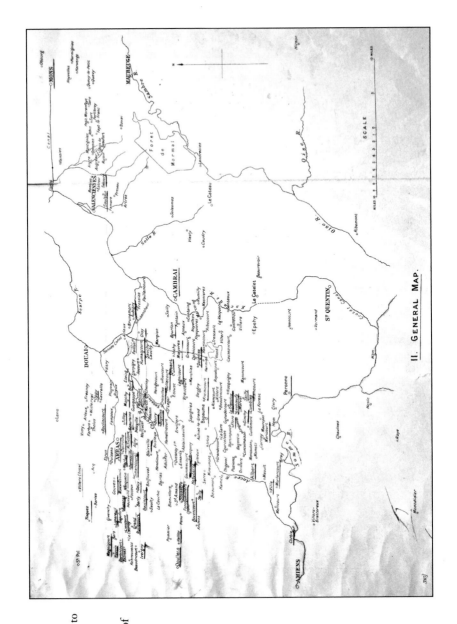

II. GENERAL MAP.

'Arf a mo, Kaiser' – a period postcard depicting a popular image of the archetypal 'Tommy' of the Great War. The image typifies the attitude that the 'Tommy' could endure and overcome any hardship provided he had '*a lucifer to light his fag*'. (*Editors' collection*)

(*Below*) A typical view of a British battalion resting while on the march, ten minutes' rest in every hour being the usual practice. Marching was the usual form of transport for the infantry and certainly features as part of the author's experiences. The officers are separated from the other ranks and are standing to the right. The lack of helmets and the wearing of early gas mask pouches suggest that this image was taken somewhere in France or Belgium in late 1915 or early 1916. (*Editors' collection*)

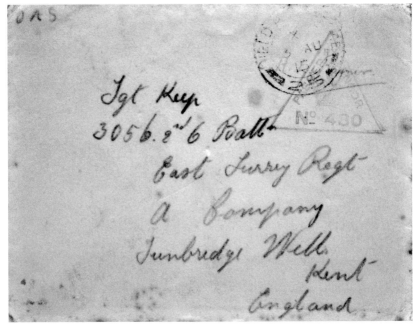

The importance of mail to the troops resulted in the Royal Engineers operating an extensive postal service, with Army Post Offices being established wherever troops were serving. This envelope serves to illustrate the basic details necessary for a letter to reach the correct serviceman: regimental number, rank, name and unit. (*Editors' collection*)

A postcard 'silk' sent from the Western Front to a member of the editor's family. Locally produced, thousands of these were sent back by the troops instead of plain or normal pictorial postcards. As decorative pieces, silk postcards are now highly collectible, especially those which illustrate the various regimental and corps badges. (*Editors' collection*)

Leuze Wood, the scene of the 13 Kensington advance in September 1916. This was Joseph's first important action, and Major Dickens was killed in the attack. It was over this ground that the 7 Royal Irish Fusiliers had attacked, and Joseph and his colleagues passed the bodies of their fallen. (*Editors' collection*)

The importance of hot food for the troops is frequently referred to by Joseph; meals were provided by regimental cooks using field kitchens such as this one. (*IWM*)

Troops were not always content with their rations: sometimes a simple change in flavours would suffice. (*Editors' collection*)

THE ETERNAL QUESTION
" When the 'ell is it goin' to be strawberry ? "

Sketches
of Tommy's life   A regular carouse of coffee and fried eggs is one of the things we always
Out on rest - Nº 5   have when we get to one of these villages.

When out of the line troops could be billeted with locals, as illustrated in this postcard. (*Editors' collection*)

In Arras in 1917 Joseph was billeted in Schramm Barracks, a French Army barracks located within the city. (*Editors' collection*)

Arras was not a safe billet and until mid-1917 was always within range of the German guns. (*Editors' collection*)

Life was not always as comfortable and was at times, as this trench scene clearly shows, basic. (*IWM*)

Poor conditions applied equally to supporting troops, as in this Royal Army Medical Corps relay post. (*IWM*)

Area of the 13 Kensington advance (towards camera) at Neuville Vitasse on 9 April 1917. (*Editors' collection*)

An officer inspects the rifles of men just out of the line. Such inspections were regular events for the author. The level of 'bull' required for each was dependent on the rank of the inspecting officer or, as demonstrated in the manuscript, the whim of an individual officer. (*IWM*)

It is clear from the narrative that the author was a member of the platoon's Lewis Gun section. This late war image illustrates the Lewis Gun team on the left of the unit. (*IWM*)

A Lewis Gun section on its way out of the line at Arras in April 1917. The unit is not identifiable but the man standing in the middle row with his hands crossed bears a striking resemblance to Joseph Steward. (*IWM*)

In Chapter 12 Joseph describes passing the grave of a Victoria Cross winner at Lagnicourt. Captain P.H.C. Cherry VC, 26 Australian Infantry Battalion, was killed in action on 27 March 1917 leading an attack on the village. This image shows the grave as described by Joseph. (*AWM collection*)

A modern view of 'Bank Copse' looking towards the railway embankment attacked and captured by the author's platoon on 22 August 1918. (*Editors' collection*)

The last patrol: the bridge over the Canal du Nord, as described by the author. The German machine-gun positions examined by Knight were located on the left of the bridge. (*Editors' collection*)

Name.			Corps.		Rank.		Regtl. No.
STEWARD Joseph. J.			13 Lond R		Pte		7515 493489

Medal.	Roll.	Page.		Remarks.
VICTORY	R13/101 B3	316		
BRITISH	do	do		
STAR				

| Theatre of War first served in | | |
| Date of entry therein | · | · |

K. 1380

The author's Medal Index Card showing his entitlement to the British War Medal and Victory Medal. (*www.ancestry.co.uk*)

The British War Medal and Victory Medal issued to the author. (*Editors' collection*)

Joseph Steward (right) in Home Guard uniform. The man wearing ARP uniform on the left is Stanley Herbert Hawkins, and in the centre, wearing an Air Cadet uniform, is Joseph's nephew Laurence Hawkins. (*Family collection*)

Joe and Emily on the left of a family gathering in the late 1960s. (*Family collection*)

Godfrey, weak with dysentery and worried by thoughts of his wife's continuing ill health, went on alone.

The night grew dark; the way strange. He tried to make his way towards the artillery. A swift stream of gas-shells passed over his head and fell thudding a few paces beyond. Feeling that he might crawl around all night and then be no nearer the Company, he decided to try for a ready-made 'funk hole'[21] and there sleep until daybreak. He stumbled over some full sandbags, felt them, and found that they surrounded and half-covered a hole cut in the ground. Holding by his hands he lowered his legs and felt the space below with one foot: it collided with somebody's head. A startled "Hi!" and an apologetic withdrawal put a quick finish to that venture.

He was luckier at the next attempt; he found a cavity in a bank, so crawled in and immediately went to sleep. It was daybreak when he opened his eyes. Stretching his cramped limbs, he took his rifle and again set out to find his Company. He had gone not more than a couple of hundred yards when he was sickened by the sight of several dead horses, ripped and mutilated by shell-fire. There had been a heavy fall of gas-shells during the night: Godfrey had lain oblivious of it all, for the kindly wind had blown the poison past his bivvy.[22] By alternate shuffles, rests and enquiries he at last came upon his Battalion in an old trench system a few miles behind the firing line. By this time it was midday.

As for the Company, it had arrived there only half an hour before. The Sergeant-Major had completely lost his bearings and led the men wandering in the wilderness all night.

When Godfrey went to draw his rations he was immediately told to attend sick parade. The medical officer, after examining him to make sure he was not a scarecrow, wrote 'hospital' against his name on the sick list. He was ordered to hand his bombs[23] to the C.S.M., then report in half an hour, to repair to hospital. An N.C.O. was put in charge of the party, given instructions and told to get going. Their sole conveyance was shanks's pony,[24] so they shuffled along the road, a woe-begone squad.

Godfrey rated himself for being so contemptibly feeble, but he could not shake off the debility. After tramping about five miles the party was seen by an army lorry-driver who stopped and gave them a lift to a casualty clearing station.[25] There they piled into a wooden shed and were served with bread and butter across a counter. As they sat waiting, a cheerful padre gave them cigarettes. Then someone came and marked their hands with indelible[26] pencil to indicate their destination. They talked very little; their ego was spent; but it was heaven to sit there in that quiet hut far away from hell-fire.

After dark a lorry fitted with seats drew up. The party travelled farther and farther back into a country where trees flourished and the undisturbed earth grew green. It was a journey of pain for one poor lad with a wounded foot, groaning every time the lorry jolted over a hole. At length the lorry pulled up at a large plot of ground covered with big white tents. It was the rest-camp at Corbie,[27] near the road to Amiens. By way of greeting, the men were given steaming meat extract.

Although it was past midnight, a medical officer examined and questioned each man; after which those who had rifles and equipment handed them in, in exchange for numbered tickets, and were shown to their sleeping quarters in a big tent. Here, rolled between two thick blankets upon the floor, Godfrey enjoyed the first real sleep for a long time.

The camp was without soap or towels. Godfrey had none; his were at the battalion dump together with his shaving kit. But an obliging neighbour came to his rescue. The friendly act enabled him to remove his mask of grime and an unloved beard. That alone lowered his temperature several degrees. He joined a long queue outside a hut waiting breakfast, so spent the fifty minutes studying the cap badges, shoulder titles and physiognomies of the men around him, who had come from many units.

Every morning the M.O. went around the 'wards' taking temperatures and so on. Some of the inmates were very bad, dysentery being the chief malady. There was a middle-aged man squatting opposite Godfrey, who tried to convince the doctor that his eyesight was failing.

"I don't believe you!" rapped the doctor decisively.

Godfrey smiled at the M.O.'s perspicuity, for, earlier that morning, the lead-swinger had watched him lacing his boots and had called across: "Got one to spare, chum?"

Later, he became more acquainted with this ticket-worker. One day the man was turning out his haversack when Godfrey spotted a used green-coloured combined leave and railway pass.

"What's the use of keeping it; its out of date, so you can't use it again," he said. The answer he got was a crafty grin.

On the morning of the third day, Godfrey joined a small party who were lined up to be discharged from the hospital. The M.O. came to him, gave him a hard look and asked whether he felt all right. The lad replied "I think so, Sir" – he wanted to get back to his friends.

So, no longer an invalid, he was pounced upon, in true army fashion, for a fatigue. After tea, he collected his rifle and equipment, drew dry rations for the journey and walked with the others out of the camp on to the highway, to get back to his battalion – somehow.

By tramping and lorry-thumbing Godfrey got to Fricourt at dusk. He fell in with two lads who, like himself, were seeking their battalion, which happened to be in his division. All their enquiries were fruitless. It was now dark, so Godfrey decided to go no further that night, and invited his companions to kip with him; but, timid souls, apparently fearful of being 'shot at dawn' if they delayed, they continued their journey, and probably wandered in a circle all the livelong night. He selected a grassy deserted spot sheltered by some bushes, against which he stood his rifle. He took off his equipment, made a pillow with it, and covered himself with his groundsheet.

He lay there thinking of home, of his young wife's ill health, and wishing he could get to England to see her. What happy times they had spent together in the past: excursions to Brighton, ending up with drinks in The Falcon at Clapham Junction.[28] He remembered a customer there named Miller who used to amuse them with his mimicry. On this happy thought he fell asleep and dreamt:-

He was standing at the roadside thumbing a lift, which would take him on the first stage to Blighty. A lorry driver slowed down for him to climb into the back, where he was pulled in by two soldiers. The van was full of laughing joking men, happy because they were going home on leave. Godfrey, too, was going: had he not got his 'pass', bought from that old lead-swinger at Corbie on payment of ten francs? So he joined in the singing. He made one with the men when they got on the boat at Calais.

During the crossing he wondered whether his luck would hold when he got to London; suppose a 'red cap' should ask him to show his pass? At any rate, he had carefully rubbed out the pencilled dates with the assistance of a small cylinder of rubber shock-absorber extracted from the lining of his steel helmet, and made the alteration.[29] He parted with his new chums at Victoria station and caught a train to Clapham Junction. From there, he walked along to The Falcon for a drink. The pub was full of men and women war-workers and the unfit. Whilst he was drinking, he looked round the partition that separated the public and saloon bars. There, amidst all the chatter, sat his wife, laughing and joking with the man Miller.

Godfrey's first impulse was to tear round and create hell. Instead, he bethought himself and walked the three streets that led to his home. Fuming, he waited in the dark, ready to smash in Miller's head. The two came along, all unaware, then saw him. His wife fell in a faint. The other, scared at the murderous expressions on Godfrey's face, turned in terror, his avenger rampaging after him. Godfrey in his fury was catching up on him when his heavy boots slid along the smooth pavement, sent him down on his back and gave him a sharp crack on the head.

When he pulled himself up, his eyes lighted upon green grass and the friendly bush that had sheltered him in the night. His rifle, that had struck his head when it fell, lay across his body.

A soft early-morning breeze fanned his cheeks as he sat up, trying to disentangle his thoughts. The dream had been so graphic – the rowdy fellows in the lorry, the passers-by in London, the people in the pub, his wife with that man Miller.

After a while he shifted his rifle and took from his haversack the feast that the War Dept. had doled out to him on leaving the rest camp: bread, margarine and jam, washed down with a few mouthfuls of Adam's ale from his water bottle. Then he girded his loins and pressed toward the mark, namely, his battalion's transport lines. Through diligent enquiries and much peregrination, he found them at Morlancourt. This village was still inhabited by French folk who, with characteristic shrewdness, had opened estaminets and small shops.

Godfrey learned that his battalion was in the firing line but was expected to be relieved that day. So he (together with others who had returned, and a draft of newcomers from England) was not sent up.

The boys tramped in just before midnight – that is to say all except Godfrey's platoon. His friends had clicked a fatigue, the most distasteful of all: burying the dead. He watched them come in on the following day. Some were mere youths, 'Derby Men'[30] who had joined while he was away; and the expression of mute suffering on their faces brought a lump to his throat. He hastily divided amongst them a cake that had arrived for him in his absence.

The roll-call was taken by the Regimental-sergeant-major, who stood on a farm wagon and called out the names to the crowd below; the troops answering: "Here, Sir", or, for absent ones: "Wounded, Sir" – "Killed, Sir" – "Missing, Sir". And so on. The platoon was brought up to something like strength by the addition of men from the draft. They were, as usual, of diverse temperaments.

Fenn was a quiet stick of a dry humour; who found a welcome chum in Barnet the happy-go-lucky. Heriot was a reticent man, stolid and reliable. Burril, a cheerful chatterer, had left his milk round to another.

The sleeping quarters were tents. By reason of the close attention of enemy airmen, lights were forbidden. Blake was sitting smoking in the gloaming one night listening to Godfrey relate his recent doings. When told about the dream in the meadow at Fricourt, he laughed it off, saying: "I have those sort of mixed-up dreams myself sometimes. They are ridiculous and not worth a second thought".

"How did you get on in the line?" asked Godfrey, changing the subject.

"After a few hours 'easy', we went up and over the top again. Helped to capture part of Bouleux Wood, took a lot of prisoners and some machine-guns. The division on our left took Morval and Lesboeufs".

The platoon stayed in this place, called the Citadel,[31] three days; and although one was the Sabbath there was no abatement of the 'training programme', which included that pet of the parade ground, sloping arms by numbers.

Those who wished to attend communion, which was held in the outskirts of the camp, were allowed to do so. It was a memorable scene. On a gentle slope carpeted with grass, the padre had set up a small altar and a tiny shrine of wood delicately carved. The khaki-clad men knelt in semi-circles facing the altar whilst the priest ministered to them; the black and white of his vestments contrasting vividly against the green field, the blue sky and the golden sunshine. A caressing breeze ruffled the hair of the kneeling men, the warm sun poured his benediction upon their heads: but ever and anon the deep boom of the distant guns sent the imagination forward to the battle zone with its

> Sweat, writhings, anguish, laboring of the lungs
> In that close mist, and cryings for the light;
> Moans of the dyings and voices of the dead.

Once, while the Company was at drill, the Colonel strolled up and made a short speech. He said the Battalion had done well in the last 'stunt', having saved a critical flank. He read a letter from the commanding officer of another battalion expressing thanks; then went on to tell them that they would have to go up again (audible 'blimies'); but when their allotted task was done they would be transferred to a quiet sector where they would remain for some time.[32] After that, it rained for hours; increasing the volume of mud in readiness for the next sojourn in the trenches.

Notes

1. This advance took place in the early hours of 6 September 1916. The 7th Battalion Royal Irish Fusiliers [7 RIF] had attacked on 5 September 1916 and been caught in the open by barbed wire entanglements and machine guns. They suffered 273 casualties. According to the BWD at 5.30pm on 6 September 1916 D Company was ordered to move forward and occupy Combles Trench (Trench map sheet 57cSW3 Longueval) to the east of Leuze Wood. This had been reported by contact aircraft as being clear of the enemy. As the company advanced, the men were caught in the open by heavy shellfire and forced to withdraw. Heavy fighting took place throughout the day with heavy enemy artillery fire and counter-attacks down through the wood. The battalion was relieved on the night of 7 September 1916 and withdrew to Casement Trench (Trench map sheet 62cNW1 Maricourt).
2. The author's interest in the fate of the man carrying ammunition for a Lewis gun indicates that he is, quite possibly, a member of a Lewis Gun section himself.
3. The reference to a smouldering dug-out is an indication of the use of incendiary bombs. On 1 July 1916 German soldiers had emerged behind the attacking waves from dugouts that had not been damaged by one or two grenades thrown down the steps. To prevent a recurrence of this, troops adopted a variety of weapons to destroy dugouts, one of which was Thermite bombs, which used up the oxygen and caused the timbering to collapse, killing or entombing the occupants.
4. Although soldiers on the ground had a limited perspective on the battle, they were always aware of aircraft. Quite clearly this German observer was using flares to call for an emergency artillery shoot on the advancing British.
5. 'Indian file' – the name given to a formation in which one man follows another. This is quite different from what many people imagine as being the standard formation for British troops. By 1917 'worms', 'blobs' and 'arrow head' formations were far more common than advancing in line, as seen in films and television recreations.
6. The BWD records that this attack took place on the morning of 9 September 1916 with the battalion in support to the 12 and 4 London. When called forward on the evening of 9 September 1916 the battalion crossed from trenches near Leuze Wood to the Guillemont road and advanced north along the western edge of Beauleux Wood. They reinforced the leading units in the second objective and remained there during the night.
7. 'SAA' – small arms ammunition for rifle or machine gun.
8. 'Hypnos' – the Greek god of sleep. Soldiers in action can get very tired and this exchange is probably not fictional.
9. 'Swagger stick' – a small metal-tipped cane usually only carried on parade.
10. According to the BWD the battalion had been withdrawn on the morning of 11 September 1916 and moved to a rest area at Billon Farm on the Fricourt–Bray road.
11. 'CSM' – Company Sergeant Major.
12. 'Moody Dane' – Prince Hamlet from Shakespeare's play.
13. Enemy prisoners fascinate soldiers and film taken during the war shows British

soldiers gathering round to look at them. In some excerpts British soldiers are seen handing over cigarettes or rations to men who had been trying to kill them only hours before.

14. The Prince of Wales, later Edward VII, served in the Grenadier Guards, but was not allowed into action. He tried to visit the trenches whenever possible and it is not impossible that the author saw him behind the lines at some point.

15. The BWD records that a church parade took place on 12 September 1916 and in the evening men visited the 'Bow Belles' divisional concert party.

16. According to the BWD between 6 and 10 September 1916 the battalion suffered four officers and thirty-three other ranks killed, ten officers and 207 other ranks wounded and one officer and four other ranks missing. SDGW records that on 9 and 10 September 1916 the following officers were killed: Major C.C. Dickens (Charles Dickens' grandson), Second Lieutenant R. Dawes and Second Lieutenant W.A.T. Sanders. One of the two subalterns mentioned is represented by Lieutenant Summers but it is not possible to confirm which. All of the officers killed are recorded on the regimental panel on the Thiepval Memorial to the Missing. In the case of Major Dickens, the area of his original burial was marked after the war by his family, who placed a cross at the site. The original cross was replaced in the 1990s and the current private memorial is still located at the site. One of the other ranks killed in this action was Private Percy Mundy, a member of the 15 London draft with Steward. An obituary for Mundy appeared in the October edition of the Boscombe Congregational Magazine. Mundy is also commemorated on the Thiepval Memorial to the Missing.

17. To 'go west' was an expression from before the Great War. It may be derived from the fact that condemned prisoners on their way to Tyburn 'went west' out of London to their place of execution.

18. SDGW shows that only nine of the hundred men who constituted the 15 London draft had been killed by 12 September 1916, indicating that the author's figure of 20 per cent is incorrect. All of these men died during the action at Leuze Wood on 9 September 1916.

19. The term Great War had been previously applied to the conflict with Revolutionary and Napoleonic France that ended in 1815 at Waterloo. It was being applied to the war that started in August 1914 by the beginning of 1915.

20. 'Wind up' is a reference to being 'windy', or having the 'wind up', meaning to be scared. This term appears to have been first used in the war. An officer's uniform on which the insignia had been moved from the cuff to the shoulder, making the wearer less conspicuous to enemy snipers, was called a 'wind-up tunic'.

21. The term 'funk hole' had its origins in the Boer War and described a simple dugout or shelter in the trenches.

22. 'Bivvy' – a shortened form of the word bivouac.

23. He would have been issued with two Mills bombs that were usually carried in the tunic pockets. The RAMC were very keen to ensure that dangerous items such as these were not carried by the sick or wounded.

24. 'Shanks's pony' – a popular expression which means to walk, rather than ride. The least severe category for evacuation comprised 'walking wounded', who were expected to make their own way to the rear, although under some form of medical supervision.

25. Although the author describes Godfrey's arrival at a CCS, it is more likely that he would first have arrived at a Corps Main Dressing Station [MDS]. The MDS for

XIV Corps was located at Dive Copse on the Bray–Corbie road. He would then have continued on to the Corps CCS, located at Corbie.

26. Both iodine and pencil marks were used by the RAMC to indicate either destination, as here, or the nature of the treatment which had been received.

27. The arrival of Private Godfrey at Corbie relates to his arrival at a CCS. According to the XIV Corps War Diary, 5, 21 and 34 CCSs were all located at Corbie in September 1916. The location allowed for the onward transportation of the wounded to the coast by both road and canal. WO 95/914, TNA.

28. This pub, close to the railway station, still exists, having survived both the Blitz and more recent 'development'. The railway line from Clapham Junction goes to Brighton.

29. The author must have had a close look at the helmet he was issued with to work out that it was possible to remove the small pieces of chopped up rubber tube that formed the 'buffer' between the helmet shell and the wearer's skull.

30. 'Derby Men' refers to those who had 'volunteered' rather than face conscription under Lord Derby's scheme. See the section 'The Platoon in the Great War', p. XXXX.

31. This corresponds with the BWD for 28 September 1916, when the battalion came out of the line having been engaged in the Leuze Wood area, in the capture of Bouleaux Wood and in the advances around Morval and Lesboeufs. The battalion moved to a tented camp at the Citadel (Trench map sheet 62dNE2 Meaulte) on 30 September 1916. The CO at the time was Acting Lieutenant Colonel W.W. Young, who commanded the battalion from 28 June 1916 to 27 October 1916.

Chapter Five

The Battle of Attrition

The battalion set out at noon: the main roads were thick with traffic of all kinds. The platoon arrived with its company at 2 a.m.: the journey had taken fourteen hours. They had come via Trones Wood, and were in the support line between Flers and Lesboeufs. The night was given over to digging a new trench in No Man's Land: two companies joined in the task. The Boche did not allow them to have it all their own way; he sent his devil's fireworks over thick and heavy.[1]

"And people in Blighty are saying the Germans are running short of shells", said Thomas, wiping the beads of sweat from his forehead with the back of his hand. The men had no drinking water. A party had been sent out for some the previous day, but had not returned. Just before his company went forward to take over the front line, Knight determined to find a stick of some sort to assist him from slipping and sliding into shell holes in the darkness. By a strange fluke, he came across a plain, stout wooden crutch; it was a mystery how it got there. As he handled it, it crossed his mind that he might have to part with it before long, to a 'walking wounded'.

Going up at dead of night, the company came under violent shellfire, which continued into daylight. Splinters were whizzing everywhere, dropping with vicious hisses in the sides and bottom of the trench. Sometimes a fellow stopped one: if it went into a 'safe' part of his anatomy he smiled – he had got a cushy one[2] which meant a respite from the rack. Heriot was one such. A small jagged piece embedded itself into the fleshy part of his backside. Lawley, who was near, tore the trousers and examined the wound – a red round mark about the size of a florin[3] – and placed a field dressing upon it. Heriot's face blanched with pain, but showed a quiet content. Leaning against the side of the trench, he imperturbably sorted out the contents of his haversack, placing shaving materials and other articles in his packet. The remainder he distributed amongst the section. He shed his equipment; and as it was made of webbing and Park's was leather, the latter effected the exchange.[4] Then the wounded man said he would make an effort to hobble out through the trenches. The rough crutch was standing by. "It's hail and farewell" said Knight, as he handed it over.

They were so close to Jerry that sounds and movements had to be minimised. When the night of their relief came, a group argued regardless during a temporary pause: something German and deadly exploded amongst them and made a sad mess. A stretcher was found for a badly wounded man. Fenn and three other new men were detailed to carry him on their way out.

The hot sun during the day had partially dried the surface of the earth; but a few minutes after the start a sharp shower made the ground like slippery glass, and the sky blackened. The bearers could see only a few paces ahead. They were hampered all the way by shell holes and many trenches over which they stumbled, jolting the heavy man, who was groaning with pain. For direction they had nothing to guide them, so carried on through the black night. The young bearers had almost lost heart; but the steadiness and forceful character of the corporal in charge spurred them on. At length, as dawn drew near, they came to the spot where the rest of the platoon was lodged. Here, a dressing station had been set up and the RAMC took over.[5] Meanwhile the wounded left in the front line were suffering agonies as men of the relief passed and repassed over them. Helpless under the shellfire, their wounds growing septic, tortured by thirst, they languished. One poor fellow, suffering from a stomach wound, took a discarded bully beef tin, and out of it drank his own urine.[6] The battalion stretcher-bearers worked like gods night and day; but what were they among so many? At this time, it was attack, attack, attack. It was called a war of attrition. So the battalion went up again. The rations were carried by all the men to the kicking-off trench. The attack took place in the afternoon. When the leading company reached the German line the only defenders the troops met were crazy with shell shock, gibbering amongst their dead. The place was being pulverised with dreadful exactitude by the concentrated fury of enemy guns endeavouring to blow out the attackers.

Godfrey and another stood in a fire bay[7] when a shell burst on the parapet above their heads. When the black smoke had cleared away they heard an explosion in the next fire bay where they thought Smart and his chum were crouching. They ran round, and then heard cries coming from the top. Godfrey crawled out and found Smart badly wounded with the other lad dead beside him. He lifted the boy and carried him down to the trench, where he laid him on the fire step. Smart's puttees and trousers had been ripped off by the explosion. Somehow, he raised a leg against the side, but it was broken in two with one part dangling away from the other, joined only by a fleshy thread.

"Rub me leg, rub me leg; I've got the cramp!" cried the poor boy.

"It's not cramp, mate", said Godfrey, sickened at the sight. Luckily, a stretcher-bearer was found, so Smart was carried away there and then. The Huns made those trenches a veritable inferno; they were levelled with the top in many places. The company commander, wounded several times, went out of the line after much persuasion, for he was an obstinate fellow. C.S.M. How was badly shaken up and useless. The platoon sergeant and many of his men were knocked out. Parks was killed. Finally, not an officer was left in the company; one sergeant took command, with a lance corporal. The platoon had been made up to strength with men fresh from England. Some had gone west[8] before their names had been learnt by the others. One lay dying a long time in a firebay, and the survivors took turns at visiting him, helplessly seeing the forlorn expression in his glazed eyes as he looked up at them. A few paces off, the trunk of a corpse projected from a 'funk-hole' in one side of the trench. The falling earth had half buried its victim, pinioned his arms and left a ghastly thing. Here and there were mounds where living souls had been swiftly and completely engorged.

The stench was loathsome at the foul condition of the trench, sodden with slime and reeking with German excrement. Wild-eyed, apprehensive, numb, the London men withstood for hours the raging holocaust. They were ignorant of the state of the battle and out of touch with troops on their right and left. They wondered whether the Boche was preparing for a counter-attack. They knew that in their weak state the fight they would put up would be, though desperate, a poor one. But at long last, the shelling decreased, and they were left alone. Late that night an officer arrived from somewhere and collected together the survivors of the company. In the small hours, they reconnoitred a shallow trench about a hundred yards in front of their demolished one. It was unoccupied, apparently ignored by the enemy.

A party that had volunteered to take rations along could be seen making their way along the battered trench in the rear. Each time these men came to view in the gaps the snipers fired; when they scampered across the open space to deliver the goods they met with a sharp volley. Unhappily, some of the bullets found their billet; so that the food was brought to the hungry men at the dear cost of their comrades' blood. Although there was enough food for all, there were only two mouthfuls of water for each man. All that day and during the night whispered words passed along: "Make sure of fire-steps",[9] "Keep a sharp look-out", "Counter-attack expected", and so on. But no Huns came. Perhaps they too were exhausted.

A few nights later men of the Fourth Division effected a relief. It was an awkward changeover because the narrow trenches were choked with churned-up earth. Moreover, the Irish troops wore full packs on their backs.[10] So the departing men climbed out on top. The whole place was flooded with moonlight: the enemy snipers were in their glory. It meant a succession of short sharp sprints and flops down – the outstretched hand sometimes dropping on the cold face of a dead man staring up through the silver moonlight into eternity.

After a while, the platoon dropped into a communication trench, where they joined the rest of the company. Here a sergeant, acting as O.C.,[11] was doing his best to find the way out. Jerry rumbled them and strafed with whiz-bangs and other forms of explosive spite.

At last a runner from battalion headquarters appeared and showed them the way: first along a trench, then out on top, past a black forbid-ding skeleton wood, away, back tout de suite,[12] hurrying from that place of torment and marvelling that they were alive. There was a halt where BHQ had left a dump of empty water tins and rum bottles. The men clustered round and held inverted vessels to their mouths in the hope that perchance a tiny drop would touch their parched lips – but other hands had been there before them; one or two of the new draft men took their mess-tins and scooped up dirty water from shell holes and drank it. Godfrey thought they were asking for dysentery; although his own craving intensified as they marched along. As they passed along the Trones Wood road Barnet's eyes searched for one thing only, a petrol tin that might still contain a drain of water. He saw a French soldier dump a tin on the roadside, so fell out, seized it, tilted it to his lips and took a big mouthful – of petrol! He spat it out, dropped the can on his foot and swabbed his mouth with a rag once known as a khaki handkerchief.

They met a water cart on its way to the line. One of the fellows offered the driver a ten shilling note[13] in exchange for a drink; but was refused: "I can't do that, mate; you'll have a drink of tea soon".

But it was a long dreary drag. Frane was limping distressedly along-side Thomas who was swearing garrulously: he cursed, among other things, wars, makers of wars, the French roads, his own fate, and the weight of his rifle, which he kept shifting from one shoulder to the other. They passed a wayside Calvary, the sight of which seemed to quiet him down somewhat. Frane staggered and almost fell. "Give me your bondook,[14] chum", said Thomas, marching beside him.

The company halted with the battalion long after midnight and bivouacked in a field off the main road. Here rest and drink came at last – and a nightcap of rum from the quartermaster for those interested. For the next two days the platoon was hard at it cleaning arms, equipment and clothes. Much of the time was spent in digging the layers of dried mud from their puttees and overcoats. Knight managed to bathe his sore feet in a shell hole. On the third day the Battalion rose at two in the morning and moved off in the dark at four to the strains of its drum and fife band. Many troops were met, British, Colonial and foreign; and although these men were marching into the furnace, they exchanged hearty greetings and sang as they swung along: "We beat 'em on the Marne, We beat 'em on the Aisne, We gave 'em 'ell at Neuve Chapelle: And here we are again".[15] At one o'clock the battalion halted at a field outside Vaux-s-Somme. A little later a joyful surprise came in the form of a column of French busses driven by coloured chauffeurs muffled in fur coats. The footsloggers were swiftly borne far back to a pretty little French village nestling among the hills, named Vaux-en-Amienois.[16]

The platoon had a new Company Commander, the third in three months.[17] He had the men out for two hours before breakfast and, not content with physical jerks, got them running. This was too much for empty stomachs and debilitated bodies, causing some to fall out, others to faint; leaving those who were made of cast-iron bodies to finish the course. There was much dysentery in the village; some chronic cases had to be sent to England. It was said that an enquiry was held among the chiefs of the Division to ascertain the cause of the outbreak. A special parade for inspection of water bottles and mess-tins by O.C. Companies was ordered. The rank and file had their own ideas. A few suggested that Jerry had, of foul purpose, left the bacteria behind him.[18] The verdict of the majority as ever was: 'too much plum and apple jam'.[19] Sunday intercepted the eight days 'training' at this village as there was a compulsory church parade. Sardonic Thomas said there would have been no need for compulsion had a bath parade been substituted. "Another instance of hypocrisy" he said. "Buttons and brass-work polished; bodies dirty and lousy". One day the whole Battalion paraded for inspection by one of the generals. All the men were dressed in full marching order and polished up in excelsis – outwardly. Their Commanding Officer kept the men standing still with full packs on backs for an hour and a half, waiting for the arrival of the great man. Eventually a dispatch rider dashed up on his motorbike to deliver a message: the general could not come.[20]

Things took a better turn in the evening; a pay parade changed the boredom of the billets into the conviviality of the estaminet.[21] Blake could not keep his eyes off an attractive girl serving drinks. Knight, who was with him, smiled and said:

"The first female face we've seen since we left that railway refreshment room at Rouen on June the thirtieth".

"And now it's mid October," said Blake, still following mademoiselle with his eyes.

The good cheer of the place was somewhat damped by the arrival of an NCO who whispered a rumour that reveille would be at an unearthly hour next morning, for an early move. Sure enough, everyone was up at 4.30 a.m. Two hours later, the battalion left the wee village behind. The weather was warm and sunny, the marching men in good spirits. The battalion halted for dinner at a place called Crouy. The appearance of the field-cookers was greeted with cheers as the hungry men lined up for their stew. Afterwards they relaxed; glad to be leaving 'the bloody Somme'. The blowing of whistles brought the mid-day meal to an end and the men to their feet.

The battalion reached its objective (Sorel, on the road that crossed the river Somme to Abbeville) at five o'clock. The platoon was billeted in barns where, for the next three days, the men were actually left in peace except for rifle inspection. It puzzled them that the new O.C. had not turned them out for squad drill and that farcical running – until they learned, to their glee, that he had gone away.

The last stage of the exodus began at five o'clock on the morning of the fourth day, when the battalion marched to Longpre and entrained. As usual, the men were not told where they going, and could only hazard a guess; but as time went by they realised that they were northward bound.

Notes

1. According to the BWD the battalion at this time was engaged in actions around Le Transloy and Les Boeufs. During the period D Company was under the orders of 12 London.
2. 'Cushy' – soft or comfortable; in this case a wound that would take you to safety. From the Hindustani.

3. A florin was a two-shilling coin of similar size to a modern ten-pence coin.
4. The mention of the exchange of equipment is a very specific indicator of attitudes common to soldiers in the Great War, but which would mean nothing today without interpretation. The basic equipment of Regular and Territorial soldiers was the 1908 Mills Web equipment. Made of woven cotton, it was comfortable, well balanced and coloured khaki to conform with the soldier's uniform. On the outbreak of war the Mills Company had insufficient looms to make all the equipment that was needed and an alternative 1914 Pattern made of sewn and riveted leather was manufactured. Regular soldiers regarded this as very second-rate; worse still, as it was issued to the New Armies it was the badge of the wartime volunteer and amateur. In consequence, experienced soldiers, or those who wanted to be seen as 'old hands', would exchange the leather equipment for webbing whenever possible.
5. This must be a reference to the battalion RAP that would have been located at an easily identified point so that the battalion stretcher-bearers [SBs] could easily find the post.
6. Treatment for the wounded included, wherever possible, a hot cup of sweet tea, but this was denied to those with stomach wounds.
7. Trenches were divided into fire bays and traverses. The fire bay, which could accommodate three or more men, was constructed with a fire step on which a man could stand to shoot over the parapet that faced the enemy. To prevent a shell which burst in a trench causing too much damage, each fire bay was divided from the next by an angled traverse which provided a narrow passage way but was not used for fighting. The parapet, the front of the trench, faced the enemy and the parados faced to the rear.
8. Recently arrived reinforcements sometime comment on the unfriendly reception they received from more experienced soldiers. This can be explained, at times, by the natural fear that there was little point in making friends with someone who might not last long once the unit went into battle.
9. Fire steps were provided in fire bays so that a man could fire his rifle with his elbows resting on the parapet.
10. It was unusual for troops to wear their large packs into the line but in cold or wet weather the ability to provide the men with a great coat and blanket would dictate that this might occur despite the congestion that would result.
11. 'OC' – Officer Commanding, normally attributed to the officer in charge of a company.
12. 'Tout de suite' is grammatically correct, but when spoken the phrase sounds like 'tout suite'; it means 'right away'. Soldiers' French was often a triumph of hope over linguistic knowledge and reduced the term to 'toot sweet'.
13. Almost two weeks' pay for a private soldier.
14. 'Bondook' was a term used for a rifle – sometimes spelled Bandook from the Arabic for a firearm – and arrived in the lexicon of the British soldier from the Hindustani version of the word. Given the army's long-standing commitment to 'Policing the Empire' and in particular India, it is hardly surprising that many terms in use during and after the Great War have their origins among the 'old sweats' who had seen service on the Indian subcontinent.
15. The battles mentioned in the songs are those in which the BEF fought in 1914 and 1915 at a time when the 'Colonials' had not yet arrived on the Western Front. This could be seen as friendly rivalry or a deliberate provocation.
16. The BWD states that the battalion was relieved on the night of 9 October 1916 and

moved back to Trones Wood. On 10 October 1916 it arrived at Mansell Camp near the Albert–Peronne road and then by 12 October 1916 to Vaux-sur-Somme.

17. The BWD confirms that Lieutenant T.C. Tate, who had commanded D Company since 25 August, was wounded between 4 and 6 October 1916. The BWD details casualty returns for 8–9 October as twenty-five other ranks wounded and one missing. This, however, excludes figures for D Company, which had been detached from the battalion. Figures given for 9–10 October include D Company's and show eight other ranks killed, two officers and fifty-seven other ranks wounded and seven other ranks missing. This may reflect the narrative account of the extensive shelling experienced by the platoon.

18. It has been suggested that the serious outbreak of dysentery resulted from the arrival on the Somme of troops who had previously served at Gallipoli. These soldiers had picked up persistent forms of the disease and this now spread to others when they took over their trenches or billets.

19. Plum and apple was the most common of the jams issued.

20. The BWD records this event on 19 October 1916 while the battalion was billeted at Vaux-en-Amienois and engaged in training and rest. The battalion remained here from 12 to 20 October 1916, when it moved to Wanel.

21. There is no British equivalent for the estaminet as it combines the qualities of a pub, café and restaurant. They were never large and were usually found in villages or small towns. They provided beer, coffee, food – egg and chips was always a popular choice – and sometimes wine. Even today poor wine is called 'plonk' because the request for white wine by British soldiers was rendered as 'Van Blonk'. Estaminets also meant female company.

Chapter Six

In Rest

The battalion detrained at Merville in the afternoon. The Division had reached the Neuve Chapelle area, preparatory to relieving the 61st Division in the Richbourg l'Avoue–Laventie line. The platoon marched with the company to Estaires, a two hours journey.[1] Six days were spent in the town, where the men were given a real rest. They had a few parades; and as for food, they were given good roast meat. The platoon was billeted in a small storeroom in a brewery; and their luck was in. The men had clean straw to lie on, water in plenty, and hot water from the boiler for their morning shave. Every dinner time a bucket of beer was brought, gratis, by a workman. And they could buy eggs and chips and coffee in the town provided they had the wherewithal.

Most welcome of all was the bath (after a lapse of twelve weeks) in a large tank of creosoted water, finishing in another containing clear water. They were not required to go back to their lousy underclothes. The fresh garments came in all sizes and shapes – but who cared?

As Jack Lawley said: "I feel like the man out of whom the devils were departed, clothed and in his right mind".

When the platoon got back from the ablution shed, they saw some new faces. Also, returned to their unit, were Savage and Marvell, wounded at Hebuterne in the summer, and Gawkey Rudd, who had been wounded at Beauleaux on September the ninth. And there came back an old sweat[2] by the name of Steenie, nicknamed The Bruiser, an ex-boxer. Of the new men, Kettle was a London ex-bus conductor. He sported a small moustache and – one could see – had an unflappable disposition; very useful when in a fix. Private Strong, a big-boned countryman, but gentle withal. The boys were going to take to him. Harry Russel seemed a mere boy. Bobby Thomas, looking at the youthful face, thought "he has no business to be out here in this bloody shambles".

Wills, too, was young, bright, excited in his new environment. Sergeant Jonah had been posted as the platoon sergeant. Then there was Corporal Blown. He had been transferred from another company. It did not take long to know why: Private Barnet, with cockney acumen, summed him up: "'E lets yer know wot 'e is; frowing 'is weight about". Second Lt. Wren became the new platoon officer.

One morning Cpl. Blown, Lawley, Blake and another were detailed to mount guard over five privates who were in the clink[3] awaiting court martial.[4] For the time being the prisoners were kept in a room off an ex-cinema hall. One of the men was a tall pugnacious individual who was under arrest for striking an N.C.O. He kept up a tirade against the military police for pinching (according to his version) some of his rations whilst he was under their charge. He strutted the floor at intervals dramatising parts of Shakespeare. He said he had been an actor. He was continually making tea with the aid of a mess-tin under which he lighted a tiny stove consisting of a tin lid and a piece of candle wrapped in a portion of flannel.[5] It was a mystery how he managed to procure all the dry tea and candle; but the flannel he cut from the tail of his shirt, which by that time was in ribbons and halfway up his back. On one occasion, having made his tea, he spread some plum jam on a piece of bread and got some on his fingers. With a dramatic gesture he stood staring at the red mess, then, in a simulated voice of anguish, cried out: "Will all great Neptune's ocean wash this blood clean from my hand? No; this my hand will rather the multitudinous seas incarnadine, making the green ONE RED!"

Then suddenly his mood changed to dismay; he dropped the lot and made for the exit. One of the guards put his foot out to intercept him, but he jumped over it, opened the door, closed it behind him and knocked three times. The guard rushed after him shouting, "What's the game!"

"That play", panted 'Macbeth', "I shouldn't have said it; its unlucky".

"Come and stop ―― about" said his captor.

It transpired that only by the ceremony of the knocks can an actor exorcise the ill luck that smites him if he quotes 'Macbeth' off stage.

"You're so fond of quotations, Mac; I'll give you one," said Lawley.

"What, from the Immortal Bard?"

"No, from the immortal St. Paul".

"What's that got to do with the spot I'm in? Well, what is it?"

"It is hard for thee to kick against the pricks" quoted Lawley.

"Bah! I can't stand these lance-jacks,[6] dressed in a little brief authority".

"Watch it!" snapped Corporal Blown.

In a corner of the guardroom lay another prisoner, rolled in a blanket. He spent most of his time feigning illness and sloth, his face turned against the wall. The regimental police[7] said it was an act put on by a crafty malingerer.

The actor once raised a laugh when he paused in his strutting, looked down at the fellow with mock solemnity, and said: "Rest, rest, perturbed spirit". Lawley was enjoying himself; he had taken this 'card' to his heart!

When Corporal Blown led his small squad down the village street away from the guardroom, he caught sight of the Brigadier approaching.

"Do I give 'eyes left' or 'eyes right'?" he asked over his shoulder. This was Blake's chance to give him the wrong answer, but he desisted. Knight paid a visit to Estaires church; there to see a fine wooden pulpit, carven with large figures of St. George and the dragon, confessionals of carven wood, and a supposed fragment of Christ's cross. On leaving the building he saw a captured German spy dressed as a workman.[8] The easy conditions put everyone in a good humour. At night the platoon had sham fights in its billet. But the combatants gingerly kept clear of Godfrey when he commenced his Indian club exercises by swinging two rifles simultaneously; for none relished a crack on the head from one of those heavy flying butts.

The battalion left Estaires at 8.30 next morning and marched about four miles to Laventie, a town nearer the front line. The platoon was marched to its billet,[9] a house by the roadside, where the rooms were so filthy that they cried out for decontamination.

On the afternoon of the third day, Mr. Wren got his platoon sitting in the billet and explained to them the positions to be occupied in the line and the overall programme. A new kind of gas respirator was issued and tested in a cellar of the broken church. It was an immense improvement.[10] In the evening a letter, sent by the Fourth Army Commander, General Rawlinson, was read out, thanking the Division for its work on the Somme. Laventie had suffered severely from shellfire in the past. Now, however, the enemy refrained from strafing it, the reason being (said the know alls) that there was an unwritten understanding that the British, in their turn, would not shell Aubers, a similar small and useful town just behind the German lines. Laventie civilians had, therefore, seized the opportunity to minister to Tommy's wants with hot coffee, eggs and chips, and vin blanc avec citron; also souvenirs in the form of cheap aluminium finger rings and silk handkerchiefs worked with garish colours for the wives and sweethearts at home.[11] A march of more than half an hour took the battalion to the front line. This was a succession of sandbagged posts or barricades spread along a flat waterlogged land; their sides crumbling away. The barbed wire barriers out in front, too, were weak and shattered.

The Fifty-sixth Division was a dabster at putting its house in order. So, on the second night, Sgt. Jonah got his platoon to assist in strengthening those defences. All the men worked quietly and quickly, unhampered by the desultory rifle fire, then packed up just before five a.m. The new platoon commander, Mr. Wren, was a small sub.[12] with a big smile; whose antics helped to beguile the monotony. When in the line his favourite pastime during the day was to shoot at the tiny whirling arrows of the weathercocks with his revolver in competition with Sergeant Jonah. At night, the prowling rats claimed his attention when he was not on a special duty. If out with a wiring party he would walk up and down the line of work and, being short-sighted, oft times trip over wires and fall headlong into shell holes full of cold clammy water, cussing and blinding like an ordinary private! This Little Titch of No Man's Land got wounded, was sent to hospital, and did not return, much to the regret of the platoon and the relief of his company commander. The conditions here were execrable; the trenches filled with water, at one point reaching up to a man's puttees. No Man's Land was flooded, making patrolling very difficult. It was found that the Germans had retired from their own slimy trenches at some spots.

Back at billets, the Company was inspected by another O.C., a fat comfortable-looking major fresh from England. One could see at a glance that he was fed up. Fed up, he watched the troops training; fed up, he paid them. He went to the platoon's billet one evening to inspect their gas respirators. A goodly portion of the aforesaid pay had been transferred to the pockets of estaminet proprietors in exchange for the elixir of mirth; so it was a full-throated merry group that stood singing songs, swaying in unison with Bobby Thomas's baton and stamping its feet. Sgt. Jonah was challenging Bruiser Steenie to fistic combat; Barnet and young Wills were holding shoulders, swaying and dancing. Some chaps were playing pontoon; others mouth organs, or the fool. Into this medley the fed-up major fell, accompanied by the C.S.M. who yelled "Party, 'shun!" But the order was drowned in the medley of noise. Finally, order was restored and the gasbags inspected. Shortly after that episode, the Major disappeared. It was rumoured that he had managed to get back to England — no doubt glad to get away from those uncouth fellows of the First Battalion.[13]

Christmas was at hand; but there was no let-up in the training programme. But the troops were not required to salute the happy morn with fixed bayonets. Even attendance at the church service was voluntary. The cooks had worked hard preparing the special dinner: pork, beef, vegetables and pudding. It was ready at 4.30 – and so were the men, as the last meal, breakfast, had been at 7.30 in the morning.[14] The men lined up in a queue in a long barn and were served by sergeants (mess-orderlies as an act of Christmas grace),[15] then squatted on the floor to eat. Knight was unlucky over the pork, which he had been hankering after; the last slice having been served just before his turn came. When the diners were half-way through the course Sergeant Jonah called out "Roll up for your pudding". Countryman Strong rushed up with his mess-tin half full of meat and mashed vegetables and got the server to deposit his portion of duff and custard amongst the lot. There was a free distribution of beer to those who wanted it. During the meal the Commanding Officer looked in and drank the men's health. The R.S.M., who accompanied him, said, by way of good cheer, "I wish you all good luck next time you go over the top". A chorus of mock groans greeted this clanger.

With the disappearance of the feast, the dixies and the sergeants, the big barn was cold and draughty again. Someone started up 'Take me back to dear old Blighty', and most of the men joined in. After a while they switched from the swinging to the yearning:

"There's a long, long trail a-winding to the land of my dreams …"

At this, Godfrey jumped to his feet and said "I'm off to the estaminet". The others followed, except one or two quiet ones who had managed to hold on to a book despite all the upheavals. Blake was absorbed in 'Twenty Years After'. He had got to chapter thirty-six where Dumas described the locality of an ancient battle – La Bassee, Estaire, Vieille Chapelle, La Venthie.[16]

The cheerless billet could not damp the spirits of the troops when they returned and proceeded to lay out their simple beds. One or two had to have them made for them.

Sergeant Jonah had collided with the big heap of muck that lay festering outside in the darkness. One side of his uniform was saturated with black mud and garbage. Nonetheless, his face wore a seraphic smile of dreamy content while his fellows scraped him. "Come on Omar Khayaam", said Blake, pulling off the sodden socks, "let's get you to kip". Young Wills surveyed the sorry garments; "'e wont 'arf 'ave a shock in the morning".

"Don't you worry; he's well in with the quarter bloke",[17] said Burril.

One by one the candles were extinguished against draughts and prowling rats. Thus ended the platoon's Christmas Day. They had fared better than their comrades in the trenches.

On Boxing Day the Commanding Officer, evidently thinking some-thing was needed to purge the ill-effects of his battalion's Yuletide orgy, took his men all round the country on a route march, equipped in full marching order. The remainder of the day was spent in poshing up for the Brigadier's inspection on the morrow; scrubbing, spitting and polishing. The inspection was a tedious affair. The men were on parade three hours, wearing their full packs; and told to stand still most of the time. Two days later it was the turn of the Corps Commander; but the great man could not come, so the inspection was cancelled, to everyone's relief – at least <u>almost</u> everyone![18] But there was a treat in the evening: motor lorries took the troops to La Gorgue, nearer Estaires, to enjoy a performance by the Divisional Concert Party, Bow Belles.[19] The men packed into a large hall. Just before the show started high ranking offi-cers were conducted to the front seats. One or two vulgar fellows way back greeted their entry with a dirty epithet; but as this was rather timidly spoken, it was lost in the hubbub. The last day of 1916 was a Sunday; so the platoon physical-jerked and squad-drilled. Result, men disgusted, N.C.O.s browned off,[20] officers uninterested.

Notes
1. According to the BWD, the battalion arrived in Estaires on 23 October 1916 and remained until 29 October 1916. During this time it took part in company and battalion training and inspections. On 27 October 1916 Lieutenant Colonel J.C.R. King assumed command. Until the end of October the battalion provided working parties to the Divisional Commander Royal Engineers [RE].
2. 'Old sweat' – a soldier with considerable experience.
3. 'Clink' – the Guard Room.
4. TNA figures provide details of five men from the battalion who were sentenced to death by Field General Courts Martial [FGCM] between 1916 and 1918. Two of these men, Privates S. Course and W. Gardiner, were tried on 14 October 1916 for cowardice. Course's sentence was not confirmed and Gardiner received five years' hard labour. No members of the battalion were executed during the Great War, all of the sentences being commuted to periods of penal servitude.
5. The method used here in which sand bag could be substituted for shirt was in

common use in the Great War. It produces a smokeless fire, which was important in trenches where cooking fires would attract enemy fire.

6. 'Lance Jack' – a lance corporal with one stripe. The lowest rank of NCO.

7. Regimental Police – members of a unit who were appointed to guard prisoners and keep order within the battalion. They are often described as Military Police but this is not the case. The Military Police were (and still are) an independent branch of the army responsible for the maintenance of discipline and the investigation of crimes behind the lines. They were also responsible for traffic control and the establishment of stragglers' posts.

8. All too often German spies 'dressed as workmen' were workmen. Suspicion was intense on both sides of no man's land and civilians risked being executed if they could not explain their actions or motives.

9. 'Billet' – a house, barn or stable used for accommodation.

10. This refers to the introduction of the small box respirator, which was a great improvement over previous models of gas protection. It was equipped with two glass lenses for vision and the gas was removed by means of a box filter carried in a satchel on the wearer's chest. Initially issued from September 1916, it was in service until the end of the war and in a slightly improved version remained in use well into the Second World War.

11. Although many families have this sort of souvenir in their collections of military memorabilia, the idea of soldiers shopping is alien to many people's concept of service on the Western Front.

12. 'Sub' – a sub-lieutenant or second lieutenant. The lowest commissioned rank.

13. According to the BWD the new company OC referred to is likely to be Major E.L. Parnell, who joined the battalion on 7 December 1916 and departed on 12 December 1916, not as claimed returning to England but to take command of the divisional training battalion.

14. The BWD entry for Christmas Day records a football match between the battalion and 12 London; the battalion won 5–0. At 4.30pm Christmas dinner was served to the other ranks by officers and senior NCOs and they were visited by the CO.

15. The tradition of senior ranks serving the men continues today.

16. Alexander Dumas's novel *Twenty Years After* is the sequel to *The Three Musketeers*. Much of the action, set in the mid-seventeenth century, occurs in the region later to be the Western Front. R.H. Mottram later used the phrase in the title of his book, *Journey to the Western Front, Twenty Years After* (London, G. Bell & Son Ltd, 1936).

17. The quartermaster [QM] responsible for providing supplies and clothing.

18. The BWD supports this, citing route marches on 26 December 1916 and an inspection by the Brigade Commander Temporary Brigadier General G.G. Loch on 27 December 1916; the Corps Commander's inspection on 29 December 1916 was cancelled.

19. The BWD reported that the divisional concert party, 'the Bow Belles', performed in the evening and 420 men of the battalion attended.

20. 'Browned off' – fed up.

Chapter Seven

Neuve Chapelle and Winter 1917

Early in January, the Company moved to the front line in the Neuve Chapelle area. The trenches were so waterlogged that duckboards floated uselessly. Each firebay was just a trench cut out of the earth, in which a pair of sentries would stand after dark to keep watch over No Man's Land.

Barnet and Fenn took up their positions there one dark night while the rain poured a monotonous tune on their tin hats. It was bitterly cold. They stood together stamping their feet, and from time to time shaking their itching bodies tormented by lice. They gazed out upon a dreary stretch and heard the incessant cries of a night bird perched on a blasted bush. An enemy rifle flashed and cracked, a machine-gun rattled noisily, and at intervals, a heavy long-distance shell lazily passed over their heads with a drone that reminded them of a tramcar passing in Blighty. Now and again, a verey-light shot up, illumined for a few seconds the misty gloom then fell and fizzled out. Some of the troops used to say there was but one German soldier, an aged man, occupying the opposite trench, whose duty was to move along to various posts and fire star shells to delude Tommy into believing that Jerry's line was full of troops![1]

The rule for sentries was: one hour on and two off, during the night; another pair relieving. The only 'relief' they got when they stood down was freedom to stamp along the few yards to try to get some warmth into their frozen feet. Shelter there was none. The platoon spent six days and nights of this.[2] Without doubt the most looked-for event of front-line life in winter was the rum issue during morning stand-to. After a foul night, the men used to hail with pleasure the appearance of the brown jar under an officer's arm. The amber magic drove the chill from the stomach, enlivened the heart's action and revived the spirits. It was good to see the rose of dawn displace the purple on a comrade's nose and see the light of hope rekindled in his eyes. Certain peculiar people in Blighty, who would have withheld this medicinal dram, might have modified their views had they spent but one of those bleak nights out there.

Going back to their billets at Riez Bailleul when relieved, the troops resembled little old men, weak-kneed, swollen-eyed, backs and shoulders in excruciating pain through being unable to recline their bodies and rest their heads, under the constant weight of their equipment and steel helmets, and the grip of the gas respirators on their chests. And lousy withal.[3] Little Wills was so weak that he hobbled along alone. When they reached the billet Frane dropped on the floor in the dark without shedding his equipment and lay thus in a sort of stupor. The field kitchens stood in the yard. The two cooks had made tea for the platoons. Corporal Blown called out: "Thomas and Lawley, fetch the tea". Blown had conceived an antipathy against these two, he seemed to resent their background and friendship. Also, he was under the impression that Thomas had applied for a commission.[4] Each time the platoon was out of the line he had to adhere to a proper rota for the mess orderlies. But he knew that a turn in the trenches would break the rota. What better opportunity for annoyance than to pounce on Thomas and Lawley immediately they came out.

So "Thomas and Lawley, fetch the tea". Thomas told Jack Lawley that they should gib against this, but his chum said that was just what Blown was waiting for, so that he could make a charge of refusal to obey an order. So they carried on, with impassive faces and inward chuckles, knowing they had the laugh of him. As they were drinking their char,[5] Jack smiled at Bobby and said "Hoist with his own petard". The score was evened up one evening, in the estaminet, when Blown bounced in, went up to a serving girl and ordered "Un beer Mabel".[6] The girl looked him up and down, then said in indignant English "I am not your belle!" Thomas, who was standing by, put his arm playfully around mademoiselle's waist, grinned at Blown and said, "She is not your belle!" Blown glared hatred at Thomas, gulped down his beer, and shot out.

The middle of January found the platoon again assisting in the defence of the front line.

At 3 a.m. one morning a raiding party came up whilst the men were standing-to-arms in their firing positions.[7] The raiders passed through and quietly climbed over the top. For camouflage, they wore white overalls and weird pointed cowls on their heads. Lawley remarked that they looked more like the ghosts of dead inquisitors than twentieth century warriors.

As he spoke, a torrent of screeching shells skimmed his scalp and smashed down upon the Boche front line. Then the barrage lifted; but before the raiders could rush their objective, the Germans were standing-to shooting. The raid was a failure; not one Jerry was captured. With crimson spots upon their white suits, the adventurers limped or were carried back to their own lines. Two stretcher-bearers bore a dead man, his snow-suit befouled with dirt and blood. The last bomber was following his party out of the line when the enraged enemy let loose the fury of his fiery anger.[8] The raiders could retire; but the unlucky men whose duty it was to hold the front line caught the full force of Fritz's retaliation. Burril and the other gunners were in one shattered fire bay when two more men came in. "It's not safe to bunch up together like this," he told them. A few seconds later came a violent explosion, a blinding flash, a cry, a splash of something falling into the water of the trench, and vile smoke wreathing around. When the gunners pulled themselves together, they found that one of the two men had received the deadly thing all to himself, for his severed trunk and limbs were floating in the water at their feet. The dead man had recently re-joined the battalion after having a spell in hospital recovering from a wound got on the Somme. It was a night of horror; hideous death jumping all about the trench, maiming, killing, deranging. Those poor mortal remains were taken from the bloody water and put into sandbags.[9] With the coming of daylight the enemy shelling slackened and the men stood down. Fenn went round the traverse on his left and there saw Barnet squatting dejectedly.

"Cheer up mate; you're lucky to be alive!"

"It aint that; I aint 'erd from 'ome for a long time," replied Barnet.

"Well, you might get a letter when rations come up". Fenn walked back, watching the sun break through. Out there the ground between the two armies was covered white, the belt of barbed wire was festooned with glistening pearls of ice. Here and there the sunshine touched rubies of blood scattered in the snow. The rations arrived and were distributed by Corporal Blown. While Fenn was eating his scrap of bacon and bread he heard Barnet singing cheerfully.

"Ah! he's got a letter at last", he thought. A few minutes later shrapnel crashed overhead; and the singing stopped. Fenn waited for a resumption of the song; but there was silence. He went round the traverse, and found Barnet slumped against the side of the trench. A shard of shrapnel had cut through his steel helmet and pierced his brain. He was holding the letter from home.[10]

Two days later, the battalion was relieved and went back to Riez Bailleul.

With the object of nurturing the troops' morale, the Brigadier had told the N.C.O.s: "Do not make the men fed up". This directive did not penetrate Corporal Blown's dark humour: the two friends were still the butt of his rancour over the tea fatigues. He did get a jolt once, when Frane spoke up:

"Corporal Blown, why do you always pick on those two; why don't you stick to a proper rota?"

"You shut up, and don't try to teach me my job".

"You're not doing your job fairly. And another thing; it would be more to your credit if you treated us like human beings".

This hit Blown on the raw; he shouted "Right! You'll be on a charge for insolence".

"Oh —— you and your charges" snapped Frane.

"Now you will be for it!" retorted Blown. So inoffensive little Frane was put in the guard room to await court martial.

That night most of the platoon stayed in their billet as they had no money. The talk centered round the abortive bombing raid.

"Wot's the use of going on; we're not getting nowhere; we might as well throw in the towel", said Steenie.

"I'm surprised at you, Steenie, after what you've gone through", said Godfrey.

"That's jest it; wot 'ave we got to show for it all?"

"You don't propose to let Jerry walk in, do you?" said Blake. Thomas joined in: "He walked in this place once, raping and mutilating women".[11]

"A lot of that's propaganda", replied Steenie.

"Well, I can take you to people in Laventie who found their daughter dead in her bedroom with a bayonet stab through her body. That's a fact, not fiction; I've spoken to them myself", said Thomas, "and the same thing happened at Estaires and Armentieres, until the barbarous beasts were driven out".

"Is that why the Germans are called 'Huns'?" asked Snipe.

"That's right," said Blake, "because the Kaiser once told his troops, 'You must be like the Huns under Attila'."

"Attila's army invaded French and Italian towns, burning, looting, ravishing, murdering: as far back as the fifth century".

Fenn sat alone and downcast at the loss of his effervescent chum. He had asked permission to have Barnet's aluminium ring, and now wore it on his finger as a keepsake. He remembered the walk back from the estaminet on Christmas night, singing arm in arm with this lad of the shiny cheeks, rubicund nose and honest grey eyes – who need not have gone back to face the enemy, because the M.O. had told him that, being ruptured,[12] he would be certified as unfit for the trenches. Fenn thought of Barnet's mother and how she had written to say that she did send letters, which never reached him. How good it was that the last one reached him in time!

During one of the six-day 'rests' the battalion was inspected by the Commander-in-Chief, Sir Douglas Haig.[13] In preparation, and with feverish haste, tin hats were painted a nasty sickly brown colour and the Division's dagger sign stencilled in red on the side of each. On the eventful day, the men paraded at 8.15 for preliminary inspection by their officers, which lasted a trifle more than three hours. In the afternoon, the battalion, led by its drum and fife band, marched to the Lestrem road and formed up in line. The road was closed to traffic, with umpteen military police and brass hats all agog. The troops remained unperturbed. After a long wait, when packs grew heavy and patience thin, of a sudden the band struck up the general salute, the long line of bayonets flashed, and the awakened troops stood stiffly at the present. If there were any avid militants in the battalion thirsting for the thrill of a close inspection, they were quickly disappointed. The Field Marshal had been detained (so it was stated). Standing at the head of a group of generals and staff-officers on a little eminence at the road side, he took the salute as the battalion marched past. That was all. On the way back to billets, the oracles' talk of 'something coming off' met with shouts of 'windy'. Later that evening Kettle remarked: "'aig gave 'em the bird over our tin 'ats; 'e said the show was very good, but we looked too posh for fighting troops". So off came the unpopular paint and the bold red London dagger, by the simple process of rubbing the helmet in the earth.

During the battalion's next tenure of the trenches, south of Neuve Chapelle, a successful bombing raid was carried out by using the 'element of surprise'. The night before the raid three men went out and blew a gap with ammonal[14] in the belt of German barbed wire, luckily without arousing suspicion. At dawn, the stand-to and stand-down took place as usual, and sentries posted. A slight artillery bombardment (merely the usual morning strafe) caused the Germans to keep low, with never a suspicion of a raid. The bombers reached Jerry's trench without casualty and discovered him sans equipment, frying his breakfast.[15] Without more ado, the flabbergasted sausage-eaters[16] were bundled over their parapet and rushed across No Man's Land. As the raiders returned, Lewis gunners gave them covering fire by raking the flanks of the enemy trench and so keeping down any who felt a natural desire to shoot. The action was so successful that it set the pattern for all future raids by the Londoners.

A rumour was current that the United States had entered the arena.[17] And there was another surprise for Jerry: one morning as he stood-to and watched the light increase he discerned a large placard standing in front of the British barbed wire which read (in German) "If you want any food, come over here".[18] The platoon did not think that funny: breakfast ration that morning could have been easily consumed by one of the men; and a complaint had to be sent to the officer. They let off steam by shooting from a trench mortar a great winged projectile nicknamed a flying pig which was so devastating that it made even the relentless Prussians sit up; for they protested against "the inhuman thing".[19] The news from other fronts was heartening. The enemy was retreating in many places. War correspondent Philip Gibbs wrote on February 28th:

'Last night the German troops abandoned Gommecourt and Pusieux and our men followed the first patrols who had felt forward and took possession of the salient which keeps to the line of the part surrounding the famous old chateau. This entry into Gommecourt without a fight was most sensational.[20] It was here on July the first, 1916 that waves of London men of the 56th Division assaulted an almost impregnable position, and by the highest valour and sacrifice broke and held its lines until forced back by massed gunfire which threatened them with annihilation. Many of our dead lay there, and the place will be haunted for ever by the memory of their loss and great endurance. At last the gates were open. The enemy's troops had stolen away in the dusk ....'[21]

Notes
1. This kind of rumour was common in quiet sectors of the line. As enemy soldiers were so rarely seen, it was easy to imagine that there was no one there. A tragic result of relaxation could be an enemy raid or a sniper's bullet.
2. By 1917 long stretches in the trenches were increasingly infrequent. The toll on the soldier's health was too great. Four days became the usual time a unit spent in the front line before relief.

3. Despite the use of killing powders and steam laundries, lice remained a common problem for soldiers in the Great War, even in winter.
4. Some antagonism was shown to men in the ranks who applied to be officers, and NCOs sometimes resented the possibility that one of the 'men' could be giving them orders in a few months.
5. 'Char' – tea, from the Hindustani.
6. This is not the most mangled phrase used by British soldiers, and misunderstandings, sometimes comic but others more serious, were common.
7. According to the BWD the raid outlined took place on the night of 19 January 1917 and involved one platoon of A Company commanded by Second Lieutenant Young and a party of bombers, with a platoon commanded by Second Lieutenant Wash providing a covering party in no man's land. The raiding party was held up by barbed wire and failed to reach the enemy lines.
8. The BWD recalls twenty-one other ranks killed, wounded or missing, including three sergeants killed.
9. According to SDGW, there were eight fatalities, including Sergeants Innes and Oborn and Lance Sergeant Prior. It is not possible to confirm if these men were killed as part of the raiding party or by the enemy retaliatory fire. CWGC records show that Sergeant Innes is buried at La Gorgue Communal Cemetery (Plot III, C, 2) and Sergeant Oborn and Lance Sergeant Prior in Pont du Hem Military Cemetery, La Gorgue (Plots II, D, 20 and 21 respectively).
10. The BWD makes no mention of this but SDGW identifies the only casualty on 20 January 1917 as 7913 Private Albert Barrett. The battalion was relieved on the evening of 21 January 1917 and returned to billets in Riez Bailleul. The CWGC records that Private Barrett is buried in Pont du Hem Military Cemetery, La Gorgue (Plot II, E, 4). The similarity between Barnet in the account and the real Private Barrett indicates the author's full knowledge of the event.
11. Stories of German atrocities circulated widely in 1914 and although some were real, others reached mythical status, such as the Canadian sergeant crucified with bayonets. In consequence, many soldiers became sceptical about the truth behind such stories.
12. The weight carried by soldiers has historically caused a large number of injuries and a soldier would have been exempt from service until treated.
13. The BWD places the warning for the inspection as being received on 12 February 1917 while the battalion was in reserve at La Fosse. The battalion paraded on 13 February 1917 and marched past the Commander in Chief on the Lestrem–Bethune Road; they had previously been inspected by the General Officer Commanding 56th Division, Major General C.P.A. Hull.
14. Ammonal is an explosive used in civil mining and military operations.
15. The raid referred to took place at 7.15am on 17 February 1917 under cover of a short barrage and all participants had returned by 7.26am. The raid took five prisoners and killed approximately forty of the enemy at a cost of one officer and thirty-three other ranks wounded and four other ranks killed. SDGW supports this, detailing four other ranks killed, including Sergeant A. King, who, according to the CWGC, is buried in St Vaast Post Military Cemetery (Plot IV, D, 7).
16. 'Sausage eaters' – a common nickname for Germans, especially at breakfast!
17. The United States of America entered the war on 6 April 1917.
18. From early in the war German agriculture was crippled by the manpower shortage, which resulted from the mobilisation of the army. This situation was made worse by the Allied naval blockade.

19. The 'flying pig' was the nickname given to the 9.45in (240mm) trench mortar. Its projectile could be easily seen in daylight and did resemble a porcine projectile.
20. The Germans abandoned Gommecourt as part of their planned withdrawal to the Hindenburg line. This well constructed system of defences had been prepared well behind German lines during the winter of 1916 and allowed the German Army to withdraw in the early part of 1917. This effectively shortened their overall lines by thirty miles (fifty kilometres). The fact that the 56th Division, which had suffered such devastating losses on 1 July 1916, was the unit that captured the village was significant both to the men of the division and those at home.
21. Philip Gibbs was a correspondent who wrote for the *Daily Telegraph* and *Daily Chronicle*. It might also indicate that the author's family collected newspaper references to the 56th (London) Division and these cuttings were available to him when he wrote this account.

Chapter Eight

The Battle of Arras

Early in March, the Division was withdrawn from the Neuve Chapelle area, to commence rehearsals for the spring offensive, afterwards known as the Battle of Arras. The 49th Division took over, the 56th being transferred to General Snow's VII Corps in the Third Army.[1]

The battalion went back to Merville and entrained for Doullens in the south.[2] As they pulled out, Burril remarked to Lawley who was sitting by him: "Glad to get away from this place; it gave me the willies". But Lawley didn't answer; he was laughing at his thoughts.

"What's the joke?" asked Burril.

"D'you remember I told you about a curious chap among the prisoners I helped to guard at Estaires?"

"That actor bloke you called Macbeth?"

"No, not him, the chap who rolled himself up in a blanket and made a pretence of being barmy. I've just been told about him. It appears he had his court martial and was acquitted. But when he went back to the guard room to collect his kit he jumped to it like a two year old. Back in his Company he started to do the daft and dirty dodge all over again until everyone got sick of him, so he was sent to a labour battalion.[3] If you ask me, I think he was the actor!"

The journey to Doullens took six hours, after which a four hour march brought the men to the village of Ivergny, which was to be the battalion's training centre for the next two weeks. The platoon's billet was a barn. Blake dropped his rifle and equipment on one of the wire beds and went out to assuage his thirst. When he got back to the billet, Snipe, who was sitting on one of the beds nursing his swollen feet, asked:

"Been on the scrounge?"[4]

"No; I went to get a drink, but had an encounter with la belle dans sans merci".[5]

"Who?"

"The estaminets were closed, there wasn't a pump to be seen, so I knocked at a door; I could see she had some inside. But she said 'napoo

104

water'[6] and shut the door. I didn't think a daughter of France could be so cruel. I found a butt of rainwater farther on, so helped myself to that".

Now intensive training for the coming offensive began, even before breakfast. In a wood a mile or two from the village two companies fought each other in mimic attacks.

Private Frane was not with his platoon. He stood in a nearby field with his back against an artillery wagon. His arms had been spread out and his wrists tied to a wheel. A group of French children stared at him. He was serving part of his 21 days field punishment number one sentence for insulting an N.C.O.[7] The strenuous training culminated in a dress rehearsal minus shots, shell and Huns[8] at Gouy-en-Artois; a ten-mile march nearer the firing line, over atrocious roads.

Sleet fell during these operations. On their way back to camp, everyone was drenched. The Colonel wanted the men to march themselves dry; but the Medical Officer prevailed upon him to order them to retire to their huts and get between blankets just as they were.[9] For once, the M.O. got his way; his plan succeeded for the blankets absorbed the moisture, which heated bodies drove from wet clothes.

This confinement to bed tickled the platoon, as they lay there side by side on the floor of the barn all afternoon, indulging in the luxury of a compulsory lie-in.

They passed the time in banter, argument and song. Rolled in their blankets, they resembled rows of resuscitated corpses.

Godfrey, who had been listening to the wrangling of two gladiators about the morning's manoeuvres, had had enough, so he challenged across to Fenn:

"What about a song, Chirgwin?"

The argument stopped, and Fenn, who was a fan of the White-eyed kaffir, took the stage.

"Ladies an' Gent'men: 'Lily of Laguna'.[10] 'I know she loves me, I know she loves me, 'cos she tol' me 'cos she says so; She's the lily of Laguna, She is ma lily an' ma rose".

Then someone remembered Harry Weldon in his football sketch; fooling about as a goalie on the stage; and the song he sang about his wife:

"She wakes me up in the middle of the night, Just as I'm in clover, Blows a little whistle in m' ear and ses, ''Arf time, change over'."

"Those were the days", sighed Lawley, then added, "It's about time some of us got some leave".

"Talking about music halls", said Burril, "I went to the Old Surrey once, in Lambeth Road, to see a silly melodrama. I stood in the middle of a crowd waiting to go in. When the doors were opened there was a rush and I was literally lifted off my feet and carried in (I was a youngster at the time)".

"What was the play called?" Wills enquired.

"The Death or Glory Boys". Burril grinned at the recollection. "It was about two officers: one was pointing a revolver at the other demanding: 'Say you will marry my sister!' over and over again".

"What 'ad 'is sister got to do with it?" Wills went on.

"I can give you a pretty good guess", said Blake.

Burril continued: "All I remember was the other bloke saying: 'You may take my life, but you cannot take my Victoria Cross!' I thought it was barmy; but the audience just lapped it up".

Steenie lay stretched, contentedly smoking a pet clay pipe. When asked about his last leave, he said, between puffs, "What with the dawdling train to the coast and 'anging about for the boat, it was dark before I got to Blighty, and all the pubs were closed, so I 'ad to go straight 'ome. When we got to bed I said to the missus 'You'll have to 'elp yerself tonight, mate; I'm fagged out'."

Blake was lying on his back; his hand cupped behind his head, dreaming of his sweetheart:

"Pillow'd upon my fair love's ripening breast; To feel for ever it's soft fall and swell; Awake for ever in a sweet content".

The battalion's next move was to Achicourt. Some of the troops were placed in ruined houses; but the platoon's new officer, Mr. Thorn, had to lead his men through to a wide bare trench in front of the village. It snowed that night and all the next day.

After dark, the platoon stood in the road while Mr. Thorn explained to them the job that had to be done. They were going up to help dig the assembly trench, or, as he put it, 'the kicking off place for the show'.[11] The men went forward in small sections to minimise casualties, and after a tramp of a couple of miles turned into a trench where they found themselves wading through a stream of liquid mud that almost reached their knees. They took this as part of the job; but when they reached their destination, they discovered that they could have got there by keeping to the dry road. They dug steadily and quietly for several hours during a heavy snowstorm; not unduly hampered by the enemy and got back before dawn without a casualty. The cooks got busy and made tea for them.

During a rest on the following day Lawley told Blake how last night's quietitude in No Man's Land reminded him of those nights on the Somme just before July the first when General Hull[12] made his audacious decision to shorten the distance between his Division and the enemy. It meant busy preparations in the daytime, and extraordinary doings in the darkness of No Man's Land, with the Engineers taking part. After three nights of intensive work, the new assembly trench was finished, 250 yards nearer the enemy. Then the wiring parties went out to fix the entanglements. Hundreds of men carried all kind of stores, etc, – !there were about three thousand men in No Man's Land, and Jerry didn't know it".

"Incredible", said Blake, "but there must have been many casualties".

"No; under a hundred".[13]

A few days later, another Company relieved, and the platoon went to the billets in the village. These were tottering houses, with roofs that let in the rain and snow, but vastly better than the trench.

The days were spent in resting and the nights in busy preparations for the coming attack. One night the rifle section under Sergeant Jonah went out and cut some gaps in their own barbed wire so that the troops would be able to pass through easily on the eventful day. The Boche rattled his machine-guns at them, but they got the job done without a casualty and arrived back twenty minutes earlier than the men who had been working in front of them.

A huge joke among the ranks was how they were being made a fuss of in a quiet way: the stews were rich and thick, in contrast with the dixies of 'camouflaged water' and floating lumps of yellow fat that too often confronted them. And – wonder of wonders – the men were actually awakened one morning by a cook who waited upon the whole platoon with a dixie of tea. Mr. Thorn, too, treated them to new-laid eggs which he obtained from one of the few inhabitants pluckily remaining in the village.

Easter was approaching. On Good Friday the Chaplain held morning prayers and communion in the protestant church, attended by all sorts and conditions of men. He did not ask those who stayed for communion whether they had been confirmed or whether they were non-conformists, or Roman Catholics, or agnostics. To him at that moment they were children of God about to hazard their lives for a cause; and he felt that they felt they wanted something to hang on to. So, of the platoon, went Burril the rip, Bruiser Steenie, Kettle the casual cockney, little virginal Wills, saucy young Snipe, Chirgwin Fenn, and Lawley among others.

In the afternoon, the men got busy with pencils and pads composing their letters for home. They were written with a simulated cheerfulness not felt, and a guarded description of the state of affairs.

Then they all began to reminisce about pre-war Good Fridays. Kettle, the London bus conductor, stroked his moustache and remarked: "Good Friday never made no difference to me".

"What did you do Bruiser?" asked somebody.

Steenie, who was on his feet curvetting in an imaginary ring, responded with a display of the fistic art against an invisible sparring partner.

Burril, with his skittish little chuckle, said that he had to do his round with the milk.

Marvell then told them that he once picked up a tart in the Waterloo Road.

Frane, the victim of Corporal Blown's spleen, did not take part in the conversation. He looked pale and ill. He had just re-joined the platoon from the guardroom.

Lawley remembered that on one Good Friday he had enjoyed a performance of Stainer's 'Crucifixion'.[14]

Knight told him that Sir John Stainer had made it a practice to go to his own school each year when the boys sang a long piece accompanied by a student orchestra. Asked how that came about, he said Sir John and his singing master were old college friends. "To us boys he wasn't a bit like a man who could compose sacred music; he was bald and short; but we liked him – especially did the solo boy who always got half a crown".[15] Lawley then began to hum 'Fling wide the gates'.

"Jesus Christ was a great teacher, but I think he was only a man like us", said Thomas.

"I dunno", replied young Wills, "my dad and me know a lot about 'orses, so I think it wasn't no ordinary man to get on a colt what 'ad never been broke in and to ride it through all that shouting".

"And they were the very people that yelled 'crucify him!' a few days later" said Thomas.

"No Bob, you've got it all wrong" interposed Lawley. "The Palm Sunday enthusiasts were his friends, the Galileans who had come with him to Jerusalem. It was the Judaeans, the political faction, that insisted 'crucify him'."

Corporal Blown burst in with an "On parade!"

The platoon moved to a village that had just been evacuated by the enemy. It lay waste. The buildings were rubble-heaps. The graves were gaping open; the gravestones smashed and hurled into the street. The dead had been disturbed by the fiery tempest. A village of ghosts and vampires.

Each man took a long scaling-ladder from a dump, put it on his shoulder and went forward up the road that led to the assembly trench, a rough stony road.

Frane, who was in the file, set his jaw and soldiered on until at last the sore pressure of the wood on his back forced him to his knees and to the ground.

Sergeant Jonah, who was walking nearby, lifted the heavy ladder and called to Strong to carry it. Then he said to Frane "You could have reported sick this morning, you know". But Frane said "I want to go with it".

When the men reached the deep assembly trench they stood the ladders at intervals, then returned to their billet before dawn.[16] Battle stores of all kind were issued during the day.

As night fell, the battalion left the village and marched half-way to the line.

As dawn was breaking Knight, who was Number-one-on-the gun, drew his revolver from its holster and began to wipe it with an oily rag. The other gunners were busy filling the circular magazines with cartridges, forty-seven to each.[17] Lance Corporal Love, who was in charge of the team, came round the traverse to see them.

"A very good Easter morning, chaps".

"Wot 'opes!" said Burril, half in jest.

It was sunny in the afternoon. Blake lay on the parapet of the trench and watched a practice barrage sweep that stretch of No Man's Land, which the battalion would cross on the morrow. The village beyond was belching flames, smoke and debris.

At dusk the battalion, bristling with the accoutrements of battle, made its way to the assembly trench; which it deepened still more against intense enemy shellfire. The night was very cold.

Gawkey Rudd, always one to snatch sleep whenever possible, several times sat on the bottom of the trench, but was forced to get up and work an imaginary treadmill to get a little warmth. There was no room for the men to move about, as the trench was packed full.

A small party under Sergeant Jonah stole out to the German barbed wire and cut gaps through. They returned without a casualty.[18] The rations arrived; ham and bread and water, and were distributed in the dark hours of the morning. Then Mr. Thorn and the sergeant went along with the rum issues – just a tot, and very soon forgotten.[19] An order was passed down that greatcoats had to be left in the trench. By this time everyone was busy. Leather jerkins were put on over tunics and under equipment; groundsheets were rolled and strapped on. Spades were stuck down backs. Bombs were placed in handy pockets. Lewis gunners gave their weapons a final overhaul. Finally, rifles were checked and bayonets fixed. The sky darkened, rain and sleet fell. As they stood waiting, Knight smiled at Steenie, who responded with a laconic "under starter's orders".

Blake glanced at Fenn, who looked depressed. "Cheer up, Chirgwin!" he heartened.

But Fenn said "I don't think much of my chance this morning".

"You stand as good a chance as any of us".

But Fenn shook his head.

Godfrey, Russel and Edgley had been included in the reserve personnel, so had gone back.[20] The guns were thundering on a fifteen-mile front from Croisilles to Vimy Ridge, including the Hindenburg Line.

Mr. Thorn looked at his wristwatch. It was 7.30 a.m.

"Get ready!"

"Over!"

Up the scaling ladders, out of the earth, "over the top, and the best of luck!" No longer were they moles, forced to burrow and slink in the ground, but dogs of war.

The din was deafening. The men spread out and went forward in waves, as they had done at the dress rehearsal – but this time there was the Boche barrage to face.

It tore up the ground all about them; snipers hidden in bits of buildings added to the casualties. These men were picking off officers and N.C.O.s.

Lance-corporal Love took over Knight's gun to give him a break (as they had about four hundred yards to cover), when he was shot in the face and went down. Marvell dropped the panniers of Lewis gun ammo he was carrying and knelt down to give Love some aid, but Sergeant Jonah, coming up, ordered him to keep going. Gawkey Rudd got his feet twisted, sprawled over and was nearly run down by a tank.

The German barrage slackened, but the snipers intensified their deadly skill. Fenn was shot in the head, Lane fell mortally wounded, and loveable Jack Lawley passed through 'the gates'.[21] Skinner was slightly wounded, together with Corporal Blown. The sergeant-major was killed.

As the attackers neared their objective, several Germans left their trenches and came forward to surrender. One such, a pale-faced youth with dark red hair, wearing no equipment or headgear, put up his trembling hands to Private Kettle, who cocked his thumb over his shoulder towards the British trenches and told him to "fuck off dahn there".

More rain and sleet fell – an Easter Monday excursion!

The strain was telling on Marvell; the rough ground, the bobbing up and down with his heavy buckets of ammo, and endeavours to keep up with his lighter-burdened brethren took most of the wind out of him. He was sorely tempted to dump some of the stuff; but his better self urged him to hang on to it: it was as well, for he and Knight were the only gunners to reach the objective. In making his way through the broken-down barbed wire, he caught his foot in a strand and went sprawling on his face. His rifle and bayonet clattered off his shoulder, the magazines fell with a crash, and in shooting out his hand to break his fall it fell with full force on a long sharp barb that stabbed its poisonous spike into his flesh. He picked himself and his appendages off the ground, and without further mishap jumped into the enemy trench.

The stubborn Germans fought bravely; but most of their mates had incontinently retreated. One big chap, however, went for Wills with a trench dagger, but the little fellow dodged between his legs, and Steenie floored him with his fist.

In the trench, there were deep dugouts, where bombs had to be pitched down to rout out and capture startled prisoners. Snipers had to be dislodged from their perches in the ruined buildings. This conquered village was called Neuville Vitasse.

Mr. Thorn appeared, pleased as punch: it was the first time he had been over the top. The strain having relaxed, he talked to the survivors like a big brother. But he grew sad as he thought of the next-of-kin, to whom it would be his duty to write his letters of sympathy on their bereavement.

"What happened to Frane?" he enquired.

"He's finished; I saw him hanging on the wire" Rudd replied.[22]

Three hours later, another battalion of the brigade passed through, and wrested more ground from the harassed Boche.[23]

The day was going well. On the left Telegraph Hill had been captured; the gallant Canadians were nearing their conquest of Vimy Ridge, north of Arras.

Thomas took a look around the wrecked village. Amidst the mass of fallen bricks and timber the remains of a house still stood, exposing a room where a large painted crucifix hung on the wall by a bed. Dead Germans were lying in the street together with British lads.

At night, a party of men went back to the assembly trench and brought the overcoats to the company. They were welcome, for the weather had turned into black winter again, although April had advanced nine days. To unfreeze their feet the men got out on top and jumped about, describing a big dark circle in the snow.

Two days later, Blake was sent to the rear with a bag of surplus bombs. On his way, he came upon an open grave, wide, clean-cut and square, made large enough to hold the bodies of his dead comrades. They were not stretched out, but lay just as they had fallen; therefore, they appeared to be asleep.

Fenn was there; his chum's cheap aluminium ring on his finger. Blake was deeply moved by the serene expression on his friend's face. The hole in the cheek made by the sniper's bullet was so small that it was as though Lily of Laguna had found the lad sleeping and left the red trace of her kiss upon it. How he would be missed, that bright and gentle lad whose voice, when conditions were vile, had heartened them with songs that exorcised the demon of despondence.

A few paces from the grave, a gun was being prepared to exact a penalty from the enemy.

Returning to the village, Blake saw where a new grave had been dug. Someone had brought the large coloured crucifix from the shattered house and placed it above the body of poor Frane, taken down from the barbed wire.[24]

On the sixth morning the battalion moved forward, scotching up for the troops that had passed through them. It had no sooner reached one line of trenches and stood-to than it was off again to another more advanced. This it did three times.[25]

Disorder was everywhere: arms, equipment, bandoliers of ammunition lay scattered about, mute evidence of the enemy's hard-pressed retreat.

During an interlude, young Snipe clapped a Hun helmet on his head and one of their gas masks on his face, and then picked up a deserted rifle and did a little arms drill. "Your mum ought to see you now," laughed Bobby Thomas.

After a bitterly cold night, the men of the platoon stood shivering in the grey dawn. Mr. Thorn went round with his runner, carrying the rations. He had fetched them himself, to give someone a rest. He was a real friend to them. He lived – or rather existed – in the same slimy gulley, endured the same shell fire and was tormented by the same species of lice. Before dusk had quite robbed the Boche of visibility he would climb out and go to company headquarters with his daily report; followed not infrequently by the reports of the said snipers' rifles.

This little man had been engaged in the prosaic routine of a Civil Service office before the ruthless claws of war caught up and deposited his inoffensive body into the shambles.

Shortly after stand-down the sentries, peering into their periscopes, shouted that a crowd of Germans was advancing to attack. Tom, Dick and Harry jostled one another to the fire steps and set-to with umpteen rounds rapid and streams of lead from the Lewis guns. The result was devastating; the Jerrys turned and bolted, leaving their wounded and dead behind.

After dark, the whole company worked to improve its position: N.C.O.s digging with the men. A covering party had gone out to No Man's Land to protect them; Knight and Burril with their gun, together with two riflemen, Marvell and Frager.

They found a shell hole, where they arranged to work in pairs; two on the lookout and two to rest their eyes; an hour at a time.

With gun poised, the watchers peered over the dark ground; while the frost stung their ears and the callous wind cut across their eyes. It was quiet enough for them to hear the faint sounds of the men digging in the trench behind them.

Laggard time dragged wearily on.

At last, Knight whispered to Burril, who was watching with him, "nudge them to take over". So Marvell came up and crouched behind the gun, with Frager. The latter's hands were shaking violently, and he began to moan:

"We're in a terrible state; what will happen to us?" The sharp rattle of a machine-gun broke the quiet.

"The place is collapsing; it's falling down!"

"Wake up and shut up!" whispered Marvell at his side.

"It's no good: we're finished. What will they do to me?"

"Why don't you shut your bloody trap!" hissed up Burril through his teeth.

The lad's body was trembling. Knight was scared; "It's a more than wind-up," he thought. Then to Frager: "The relief won't be long, chum".

Something shrieked through the air towards them, tore into the ground in front, covered them with chunks of mud and scattered shrapnel over the litter of No Man's Land.

Seconds later another explosion above them forced their heads down upon their shoulders. After that, there was a lull. Knight called up to Marvell, "What's the gun like, Harry?".

Marvell spread his hand over the magazine pan and catch, then felt along the radiator casing and put his finger into the barrel-mouthpiece.[26]

"Are you all right?" asked Knight.

"Yes, I was just feeling the gun. She seems O.K., except for two dents in the outer casing. And two in my tin hat" he added as an afterthought.

Although it was quiet again, Frager was whimpering: "Mother, mother, what shall I <u>do</u>, what shall I <u>do</u>!"

"He's gone dotty", thought Burril.

Suddenly the lad began to clamber out of the shell hole, and Marvell had to pull him back. Knight was desperately anxious. He worried lest a stealthy Boche patrol might try to scupper them in the blackness and confusion. He said he would take over the gun; the others to keep Frager under control. The shells began dropping again nearer and nearer. Frager was struggling:

"They're smashing the door down; they're smashing the door down!"

"We'd better knock him out" said Burrill.

Knight wondered whether he himself was going crazy. The lad's cries kept beating against his brain; and he could do nothing. He looked up, hoping to see a chink of dawn, when the order to withdraw would come.

But at last, a shadowy figure emerged from the trench, crossed the stretch to the shell-hole, and told the men they could go back.

Collecting together the precious gun, the ammo, and their stiffened limbs, they crawled away from that damnable spot.

Under the daylight and his changed environment, Frager had become quiet; but his fellows watched him narrowly.

Food had been scarce: water there was none. Private Woolton lay wounded. Young Wills was crying with the pains of trench-feet. Now, adding to the enemy fire, their own shells fell short; and Frager raved again. Sergeant Jonah called for the stretcher-bearers to take him away.

Only towards evening did the bombardment slacken, for the men to take stock of themselves. Two stooped over a dead lad who lay half-immersed in a puddle of water and took some of the liquid in their mess tins. They had a little dry tea, but where to find the fuel? There were no bits of wood lying about; 'Tommy's cookers'[27] were but a memory. Burril said he would go for a scrounge. Twenty minutes later he returned with his find – a little rifle oil. Bits of rag were torn from shirts, dipped in the oil, placed on a cigarette-tin lid under a mess tin, and ignited. After an hour or so of patient watching and guarding the precious little stove in the parados, the water boiled.

That evening, as the light was failing, Mr. Thorn gave the glad news of a relief: "Tonight, boys, for sure". Whereupon Snipe tossed his tin hat into the air as the watchful sniper's bullet hissed past. A little later a runner, lingering a second too long on the top, received one in his ankle.

So, they collected their small belongings, put the guns and other warlike equipment together ready for quick removal, and waited. Under cover of the dark, two or three took spades and tenderly placed their dead in the warm bosom of mother earth.

The men of the relieving Division, at full strength, were hard put to it to squeeze themselves in, so the others had to get out on top; then, having handed over, did not wait to watch them settle down!

Mr. Thorn led his platoon to a distant village. Great heaps of rubble confronted them at every turn. Half way through, the officer stopped and examined his map and wondered whether they were running into enemy ground. A few minutes later a solitary British soldier appeared from somewhere and was able to direct them to the right road. He told them that the village had been stormed and captured a few days previously by another brigade of the division.

It was a painful tramp for cramped limbs and debilitated bodies. One man, carrying a Lewis gun on his shoulder, slipped on the lip of a deep shell hole and slipped from top to bottom, swearing "This is a bon bloody war!"[28] He was pulled out by the nearest in the file amid cheers and laughter; so happy were they all to be leaving that place of torment.

It took a long time to get back from Heninel to Neuville Vitasse (the village the battalion had helped to capture on Easter Monday morning).

Some distance back, near Beaurains, the field kitchens were reached, where a halt was made for an issue of tea.

Then the battalion moved off again. As they marched, the R.S.M. went alongside the men, and told them they were going right out to a village far from the firing line, for a 'rest'.

Half an hour later the troops entered Achicourt. The gaping graves had been filled in, the roads repaired; the town made into an important dump, alive with men, bristling with guns and shells, and warm with a large array of wooden huts.

The rumour that they were bound for Arras went down the rank. It was six in the morning when the battalion straggled into the outskirts of the martyred city.

A war correspondent stood by the side of a spic-and-span French military policeman on duty, and was making notes. A few days later his account appeared in a London newspaper.

'A bedraggled remnant slowly limped in. Not a mother's son would have been recognised, with their bent backs, haggard looks and bearded faces surmounted by dank points of tangled hair protruding from beneath steel helmets that had slipped to ludicrous angles. Their puttees were loose, slimy and torn; and in many cases lousy shirts were visible through rents in trousers ripped on enemy barbed wires. One fellow had got his equipment into a terrible tangle, had given up in despair, and carried the lot slung over one shoulder, as he silently trudged along'.[29]

Notes

1. Divisions were frequently transferred between both corps and armies, depending upon the military circumstances. Often a soldier may have known his divisional commander by sight, but rarely the commander of higher formations. This is not because such officers were remote from the men, but rather was a question of numbers. A corps consisted of two or more divisions, around 30,000 men and an army not less than two corps. In consequence, even the most active commander at this level could not hope to see, let alone meet, all the men under his command.
2. The BWD dates the move from Neuve Chapelle to Ivergny as taking place on 10 March 1917 with the men travelling via Doullens. The battalion spent approximately two weeks in the area training in mock attacks, digging trenches, route marches and sports.
3. Labour units were formed from the Army Service Corps [ASC] early in the war for a variety of labouring and construction tasks. The Labour Corps was formed in

January 1917 and grew to 389,900 men (more than 10 per cent of the total size of the army).
4. 'Scrounge' – this did not mean to steal personal items, rather it implied taking food, firewood, or kit from the military or civilians.
5. 'la belle dans sans merci' – literally 'The beautiful, in without mercy'.
6. This is a corruption by British soldiers of the French 'Il n'y en a plus' – 'there is no more'.
7. One of the sentences a court-martialled soldier could receive was Field Punishment Number One, which took the form of periods of time shackled to a fixed object, usually a wagon or limber wheel, in an area away from the line but where his comrades could see him. This punishment was regarded as mild by the Regular army of 1914 but would have been shocking to the author and his comrades. See C. Corns and J. Hughes-Wilson, '*Blindfold and Alone*'. *British Military Executions in the Great War* (Cassell & Co., 2001).
8. The author makes clear in this chapter the increasing emphasis placed on training soldiers at platoon level and, as here, in larger formations. The spring of 1917 had seen the introduction of a new training pamphlet, '*S.S. 143 Training the Platoon for Offensive Action*'. This changed the way in which units were handled and placed great emphasis on the importance of mutual support and flexibility of tactics at platoon level. This had to be rehearsed in the most realistic of circumstances as frequently as possible.
9. In the BWD the weather for 29 March 1917 is described as very wet and may account for the discussion between the CO, Lieutenant Colonel King, and the RMO.
10. 'Lily of Laguna' was a popular music hall ballad of the period. Written in 1898, the lyrics are racist by modern standards and would usually have been sung by a white performer who had 'blacked up'. Hence the reference to the 'white-eyed Kaffir'.
11. Although this meant, literally, a theatrical entertainment, the term 'show' was applied to a forthcoming attack, as here.
12. 'General Hull' – Major General C.P.A. Hull, 56th Divisional Commander on 1 July 1916.
13. Although this may appear impossible to the reader, it is again evidence of the author's memory and use of detail. The event referred to by Lawley occurred during the 56th Division's build-up for the attack on Gommecourt on 1 July 1916. Following a decision to shorten the distance between the opposing trench lines, a new British front line 400 yards nearer the German line was required. Using almost 3,000 men of 167 Infantry Brigade, this feat was achieved during the nights of 25–28 May 1916. According to the Divisional History, *The Fifty Sixth Division 1914–1918*, p. 23, an estimated 2,900 yards of front line and 1,500 yards of communication trench were dug during this period. The BWD records that 13 London were not engaged in digging the trenches but provided covering parties, protecting the men working. These events are also well described by A. MacDonald in *Pro Patria Mori. The 56th (London) Division at Gommecourt, 1st July 1916* (Diggory Press, 2006), pp. 88–100.
14. Sir John Stainer was born in Southwark, South London, in June 1840 and died in 1901. Based on the evidence given here it is quite possible that the author met the composer or knew something about his work to encourage singing among boys from his old school.
15. Half a crown was a coin worth two shillings and six pence. In 1917 it was five days' pay for a private soldier.
16. According to the BWD the battalion moved to the Achicourt area and took over a

section of the line on 1 April 1917. On the night of 2 April 1917 the entire battalion was engaged in digging assembly trenches.

17. The weapon discussed here is the Lewis gun, which was termed an 'automatic rifle' although it might be better described as a light machine gun. The circular magazine held forty-seven rounds. The number one on this weapon was the firer and was issued with a pistol. The other members of the Lewis Gun Section carried rifles and additional ammunition for the Lewis gun. The reference is further evidence that the author was a member of a Lewis Gun Section. By spring 1917 this section was one of four within the platoon. The others were made up of bombers, who were specialist grenadiers (rifle bombers who could fire grenades from their adapted rifles), and the sniper, scouts and moppers-up who were trained on marksmanship and bayonet work.

18. The BWD during this period records trench routines and the pre-assault bombardment. There is a report on the night of 8 April 1917 of twelve men of D Company led by Second Lieutenant W.K. Mortlock going out to cut gaps in the enemy wire while under heavy machine-gun fire.

19. The rum issued before an attack and on occasions in cold wet weather was very alcoholic but the amount provided for each man was so limited that even an abstainer would not be able to get 'fighting drunk', as some people have suggested.

20. Before a major attack roughly 10 per cent of the battalion's officers, NCOs and other ranks were classified as 'left out of battle'. The idea was that in the event of a disaster they would form the nucleus of a new battalion.

21. The 'pearly gates' of Heaven.

22. 'Hanging on the wire' – a common expression used to indicate that a soldier had been killed in or on the barbed wire.

23. The BWD entries for 9 April 1917 record the battalion's advance into Neuville Vitasse and the attack on Moss Trench (Trench map sheet 51bSW1 Neuville Vitasse). Both this trench and Telegraph Hill on the battalion's left were successfully taken.

24. The casualty figures for the day record that D Company suffered two officers and twenty-eight other ranks killed and wounded. In total the battalion lost almost one-third of its strength, mainly through shellfire. SDGW suggests two casualties who may correspond with narrative characters. Lance Corporal Love may represent 493086 Private H. Lovell, while Company Sergeant Major Howe is almost certainly 490123 Company Sergeant Major Howes. In addition to these two, SDGW records a further twenty-nine other ranks killed. According to the CWGC Private Lovell is buried in Wancourt British Cemetery (Plot IV, F, 1) and Company Sergeant Major Howes, originally buried in Beaurains Road Cemetery, is now commemorated on a memorial wall in London Cemetery, Neuville Vitasse.

25. The BWD between 10 and 19 April 1917 places the battalion in the area of Wancourt. The enemy counter-attack referred to occurred at 9pm on 16 April 1917 and was successfully repulsed.

26. The Lewis gun was vulnerable to damage, and dirt in the mechanism or even a hard knock could make the weapon impossible to fire.

27. 'Tommy cooker' – a small, solid fuel cooker in a tin which could be purchased from home or in a YMCA store.

28. 'Bon' – good, from the French.

29. This may be a further reference to the work of Philip Gibbs, the official newspaper reporter referred to earlier.

Chapter Nine

Out of the Line

The battalion quartermaster – a fine old friend – watched the troops tramp in. The Adjutant, bareheaded, went up the street to smile them in and chaff them about the sore chins they would have tomorrow. Then he stood at the door of the big billet to recognise some old faces he knew, escaped from the fires again.[1] A large building that once had hummed with busy workpeople afforded shelter for the whole battalion, one floor to each company. The room, which the platoon shared, was largely composed of curious cubicles of a size that barely accommodated the length of a sleeping man. But each of these tiny compartments was furnished with two blankets and a small piece of candle, placed there by a thoughtful quartermaster-sergeant.[2] Hot beef extract, dixies of steaming tea and some Roger rum welcomed them. There was a big pile of letters, parcels, newspapers and periodicals that had been held back from the battle zone. The letters were eagerly read, notwithstanding tired eyes and the lure of the blankets.[3] Bruiser Steenie sat on the floor, unrolled his ragged puttees, tugged off his boots and relieved his feet from their fortnight's confinement. He chuckled as he read his missus's gossipy letter, then rubbed his big hands together in contentment, rolled himself in the warm dry blankets and slid into deep sleep. Not a few of the others thanked the God of battles for their deliverance as they laid themselves down. It was then 8 a.m. The men were allowed to sleep until one. At two o'clock they all had a hot meal.[4] After that the soldiers besieged the washrooms to remove from their cheeks and chins the beards that Nature and Mars had imposed upon them. That is to say, all but the Lewis gunners. They were ordered to fetch their guns from the limbers somewhere within the city and clean them.[5] Knight brought his to the billet. The weapon had been with him in execrable places; so he had to spend all the evening restoring it to its parade brightness. He did not mind; he thought this job could suit him for the duration. His thoughts went back to the previous night; the long cold vigil in that shell-hole trap of No Man's Land, the screeching shells; the struggles with the unbalanced lad; and his own mental strain. Now it was all over. He got his wash and shave just before the orderly-sergeant called out 'lights out'. He made his way back to the cubicle in the dark and, with a quiet feeling of exaltation that he had climbed out of Avernus[6] that dreadful night, went to sleep.

Everyone was astir the next morning; they had to be packed up and outside their billets by eight o'clock. The company paraded in the street and made for a piece of vacant ground outside the city. Thomas and Kettle were marching together and speaking in undertones. The subject of their talk was the return of the captain who, as O.C. Company, rode on horseback in front. He had ordered his men to march out with sloped arms.

"He's come back, now the scrapping's over; all regimental," said Thomas. "Look at the chaps; they're too weak to slope arms properly – talk about Fred Karno's army!"

"I'd like to knock the grinning bastard orf 'is 'orse," said Kettle.

When all the battalions had gathered together, the whole brigade left by motor vans and lorries and travelled south to the Somme district, arriving at Bayencourt in the evening. Next day (Sunday) a few of the survivors who had taken part in the attack at Gommecourt last July went across to the old battlefield. Gruesome relics still lay there, scattered about the barbed wire and trenches.[7] The Germans had retired a short while before, followed by the British, who had established a new line.

On the following Tuesday the battalion was suddenly ordered to march to Gouy; a five hours journey.[8] On arrival, the Colonel issued an edict that he would inspect billets. The Company Commander straightway got the wind up, himself inspected the men's kits and gave strict orders that the men be kept standing outside their huts until the C.O. paid his visit. Sardonic Blake remarked that it was absolutely necessary in order to save the Persian rugs being ruffled and the tapestries disarranged. It was a long cold wait for swearing, stamping men. Burril growled: "Why the hell can't they see about some baths instead of fussing about billets!"

"The spirit of the troops is excellent", wrote Sir Douglas Haig.

The platoon was strengthened by the arrival of a fresh draft. After which it marched with the battalion to Simencourt, then on to Arras. Heriot returned; his wounded posterior having been made sound again. An empty house afforded the platoon shelter. Squatting in their billet before lights-out, Godfrey made acquaintance with Singen (one of the new men). He wanted to find out what the mad world had been doing while he and his companions had been busy chasing the Germans out of the Hindenburg Line.

He learned that America, infuriated by Germany's unrestricted submarine warfare (the steamer Laconia had been torpedoed,[9] with the loss of American lives, at the end of February), had declared war on April the sixth – Good Friday.[10]

The Russian Empire was breaking up. The Guards Regiment had mutinied and stormed the Winter Palace. The ex-Tsar and his family were under arrest.

A small man named Lenin had arrived at the Finland station to meet the advance guard of "the international proletarian army" with their war cry "Long live the world-wide socialist revolution!"[11] Godfrey perceived that his quiet informant was a man of parts.

As they were getting their equipment ready for battle order, Blake talked to another newcomer, named Manley, who was putting a small bible into his haversack.

"It's all right; I'm not the religious sort", said Manley, "but I found it in the cattle truck on my way up, and got interested in The Book of Kings".

"I'm a bit of a bibliophile myself", said Blake.[12]

Godfrey looked across to Blake and told him that the captain had gone off again. "This time he got himself included in the reserve personnel".

A few hours later, the men moved off by platoons to a support trench near Monchy.[13]

Captain Barnett had taken over as Company Commander, and lost no time in describing the plan of the coming battle to his men. Brigade was being held in reserve to the other two brigades, which were now in line ready for a big attack in conjunction with the French.

The 'trench' shared by Knight, Thomas and three or four others was about twelve feet long. Taking their spades, they dug deeper; it was hard chalk. As daylight approached they stopped delving and stood to.

All the men had been strictly adjured to refrain from giving the Boche the least sign of their presence.

"Well, stone me!" ejaculated Snipe.

The others followed the direction of his eyes. There, in broad daylight, the Colonel and some officers were passing along the top.

After that exalted infringement, some of the men cast aside the warning and scrounged about above ground. Enemy observation balloons hung in the sky. Then the firing commenced; it rained vicious shells all day.

But during the night the firing slackened. The day dawned beautifully sunny: it was Sunday. One of the new men, named Baker, looked at his watch; it was eight o'clock. He said his parents would be at Holy Communion.

Suddenly a loud ominous sound broke the peace and – perchance at the very moment, those faithful lips touched the chalice – the horrid carrier of death descended.

With a deafening explosion, it burst among the men in the trench on Knight's right.

To think that that bright Sabbath of blue and gold could hold such an awful thing!

Knight and his companions (except Baker who had been killed by a shell splinter) seized spades to release the buried ones, then looked to the others. Four men were dead. For two it had been their first time in the firing line. Five were wounded. Thomas and Knight tore out field dressings and hastened to give first aid. Thomas was blaspheming all the time; railing against the Almighty, for suffering such a thing. "Don't blame God; get on with the bandaging", said Knight.[14]

That night the battalion relieved a Scottish regiment in the front line. Their dead lay all about. As the platoon was making its way along the narrow trench, the man in front of Savage stooped to awaken a Jock who was curled up on the side. Shaking him, he said: "Wake up, chum, your relief's here". But the sleeper stirred not – nor will he, "til Gabriel sounds the last rally". He had been relieved.

A section of the platoon was sent to man a shell hole out in front.[15] A heavy downpour was succeeded by several hours of sunshine. The Boche fired his shells over to the support line; so the section basked happily in the warmth when not on the watch. They were left alone, too, for none dared to come to them in the daylight.

Godfrey, one of the team, decided to have a sun-bath combined with a louse-out. He untied the strings of his box-respirator and dropped it to the ground, together with his webbing equipment. Off came his tunic and his shirt. He spread the latter across his knees and went straight to the armpits where with gory thumbnail he wreaked his vengeance. That done, he pulled off his puttees, removed his boots, stripped off his trousers and had a crack at the crutch in whose heat the crawling lice had laid their eggs.[16] As he bent over his task the sunlight played on his fair hair and caressed the comeliness of his naked body.[17] But for the business of the lice, he could have been the young Apollo relaxing at Troy.

The contagion of cleanliness spread to some of the others who took off their cootie shirts and joined in the slaughter.

Burril, who had not disrobed, said: "If the Brigadier saw you chaps now he'd have a fit. He used to explode if he saw anyone minus his respirator".

After stand-down that evening the outpost were ordered to retire to the front line whilst the artillery bombarded the enemy position. At the conclusion the men returned.

Afterwards, when the company was relieved, the platoon went back to the spot where a single shell had wrought such havoc amongst them on the previous Sunday.

The men were suffering through an acute scarcity of water. Blake, Steenie and Snipe were squatting in the trench. Steenie took his water bottle in his thick labourer's hands, and shook it. He held it suspended for several minutes then pulled out the cork. He put the bottle to his lips, took one mouthful, rolled the cool liquid round his tongue for several seconds before swallowing it, then resolutely rammed home the cork.

Blake grinned and began to mimic the words of the Medical Officer in the big open amphitheatre at Havre: "Although at times water would be scarce, you ought always to spare a little with which to wash your teeth, your arm-pits and the vulnerable parts of your bodies".

Steenie grimaced: "I s'pose some bleeding base-wallah said that", he remarked. Then to Snipe: "What you looking so miserable about?"

"He's drunk all his water" said Blake. Steenie caught the appealing look in the lad's eyes, then handed him his water bottle without a word.

That evening the two front battalions made a sudden assault upon a German trench, which they badly needed.[18] Startled rockets of green and red shot up into the twilight mists as the artillery pounded the enemy.

As the Londoners ran forward, they saw Germans scampering away to their second line. The captured trench was full of dead; some prisoners were sent back together with six machine-guns.

Shortly afterwards a Lewis gun team was ordered forward to occupy a crater. Burril, Knight, Blake and Thomas with two others hurried along. Their path led through a communication trench; and they quickly found that it was being subjected to a most murderous shelling. As they progressed, it intensified. The explosives fell like hail, along the rims of the trench, in the trench, in front of the men, behind them, but never on them. They tore along, every step taking them deeper into that howling hell; but determined to reach their goal. They reached it; the six unhurt.

They shot out from the end of the furnace into a great hole in the earth that had been made by a mine. A medley of men were sheltering there, waiting for the fierce barrage on the communication trench to weaken.

Helpless wounded on stretchers, with their bearers, walking wounded, German prisoners with and without guards, exhausted runners, and a poor youth, whose toes had been shot away, crying in his agony – all were there.

Eventually the little team passed out of that place, crossed the open, to the crater they had been ordered to guard and hold. The enemy contented themselves with slinging H.E.s[19] across; there was no counter-attack. All the objectives gained in the evening's fighting were held. That night and the following day passed without event.

At dusk, a fresh party came to the relief of the team, who returned to their platoon. The way back through the choked communication trench was comparatively quiet compared with the nightmare of the previous evening.

"I still can't think how we got through; I don't mind admitting I was praying all the way" said Blake to Burril.

"And you wasn't the only one – Thomas was doing the same thing" said Burril

"What, Thomas?"

"Yes, he kept saying 'O God, save us'. I thought he was an atheist".

"No, an agnostic" replied Blake. "There lives more faith in honest doubt, believe me, than in half the creeds" he quoted.

The sergeant told Godfrey that the battalion expected to be relieved that night. When the time came the platoon hurried out as fast as could go; glad to be away from that infernal brown strip.

The company carried on until the men were behind a ridge. Here they halted and lit up: that is to say, the provident few who happened to have saved a cigarette from their issue.

After a short rest, they continued on, through the night until they reached a wide plain. There, afar off, shone a single light. They made straight for it; an electric light on a high pole, placed there to give direction. One of the chaps remarked: "That's a sensible idea" and began to hum a tune:

'Clear before us through the darkness Gleams and burns the guiding light'.

The battalion tramped the roads until it came to an old trench system near Tilloy, and stayed there that night. It was 1 a.m. Piles of accumulated letters and parcels were waiting; and there was an issue of hot beef extract.

Next day the battalion moved to the big Schramm Barracks in Arras.[20] In less than a week the troops were off again; this time to the village of Berneville, south-west of Arras, a three hours march.[21]

Notes

1. The BWD records that the battalion was relieved on the night of 19 April 1917 and moved back into Arras. It was met by the quartermaster, Captain Ridly, and was billeted in a large building on the Boulevard Crespol.
2. It is interesting to see how much difference this kind of care made to the attitude of the troops and how greatly it could be appreciated.
3. Throughout the war mail was both sent from and received at the front. In addition to cigarettes, food and luxuries the contents of letters did much to maintain morale. In a period before public or mobile telephones a few lines scribbled by a soldier or his family members might be the only contact between them for a year or more. In these circumstances the failure of mail to arrive could be a disaster.
4. The pattern of activity for units that had come out of the front line.
5. The Lewis gun section used horse-drawn two-wheel limbers to transport the heavy weapons and ammunition on the march. These were left behind with the other transport when the unit went into action.
6. In classical mythology Avernus was the entrance to the Underworld. In Greek it means 'without birds', and was originally the name of a volcano in Italy, where the gas and fumes had killed the wildlife. This is another example of the author's knowledge and love of literature and mythology.
7. The 56th Division was not the only unit to mount a pilgrimage to the battlefield of 1 July 1916. Men from the 4th Division went to the site of their assault near Serre to look for fallen comrades.
8. The BWD notes that on 21 April 1917 the battalion was moved by bus to Bayencourt and then to Gouy on 25 April 1917. On 28 April 1917 the battalion returned to the Tilloy area of Arras.
9. The Cunard liner RMS *Laconia* was sunk by a U-boat on 25 February 1917 with the loss of twelve lives.
10. This is the correct date for Easter 1917.
11. One wonders how much of this information would, in reality, have been known by the men in the trenches. It is one of the few occasions when the author uses information that could only have been known in retrospect.
12. As Blake describes himself as a bibliophile, and we know that the author certainly was, is Blake a self-portrait? William Blake was a poet and artist and it is not difficult to see that the literary and artistic associations of the name might have tempted the author.
13. The battalion's CO at this time was Acting Lieutenant Colonel King and the war

diary dates this move as 3 May 1917. There is, however, no reference to shelling or casualties.

14. SDGW details one fatality on the day, 493433 Private S. Barclay. The CWGC records that he is buried at Saint Marie Cemetery, Le Havre (Plot Div. 62, I, B, 2), which would indicate that he died of wounds received earlier and not on the day in question. The battalion moved into the line on the night of 4/5 May 1917 with D Company in Bullet Trench (Trench map sheet 51bSW2 Vis en Artois).

15. By this stage in the war both sides were increasingly making use of shell holes as defensive positions rather than relying on formal and easily targeted trench systems.

16. The process described here was called 'Chatting' as the lice were known as Chatts; their removal was invariably accompanied by talking, from which is derived the familiar term to 'have a chat".

17. This reference to the male body might be surprising to a modern reader but the aesthetic appeal of the human form, of both sexes, formed part of the artistic appreciation of the period. Hence the reference to 'the young Apollo relaxing at Troy'. Misunderstandings relating to the assumed sexuality of war-time artists and authors can, in some cases, be traced to this cultural perspective.

18. This attack took place at 8.30pm on 11 May 1917 and the two battalions (14 London and 4 London) captured Tool Trench and Cavalry Farm (both Trench map sheet 51bSW2 Vis en Artois).

19. 'HEs' – high explosive shells which burst on the ground, as distinct from shrapnel shells which exploded in the air.

20. The BWD records that the battalion remained in support until 14 May 1917.

21. The BWD indicates that the battalion arrived at Schramm Barracks in Arras on 15 May 1917 and moved to Berneville on 19 May 1917.

Chapter Ten

Training for the Next Stunt

On the Sunday following, a church parade was held, attended by the Brigadier-General. Three days later, he inspected the brigade.[1] After he had gone the Adjutant promulgated a sentence of court martial, while the prisoner stood there under escort. Then the officer read out another, quashing a man's sentence because of his subsequent bravery in the field. Now there was work to be done, to dig trenches for practice 'stunts',[2] and to make a shooting range. So the platoon shouldered picks and shovels and marched forward to a field on the outskirts of Simencourt. The men finished in the afternoon, then went to their fresh billet, a large wooden hut originally built for French troops, fitted with tiers of wired bunks. It was Empire Day.[3] The stay at Simencourt lasted more than a fortnight.[4] The weather was glorious; the countryside gay with many coloured wild flowers and smiling cornfields. The troops enjoyed a kip every night, and once a week walked to the bottom of the street for a warm bath. Most afternoons and evenings were free for lazing, or for playing games or estaminet conviviality. And there were letters and field cards to be written.

Godfrey had received a letter from Sam Smart in England, enclosing a photograph of a group of men dressed in hospital blue.[5] Sam was sitting smiling in a chair in the centre, his knees covered by a rug. Both his legs had been amputated. Godfrey's thoughts flew back to that horrible day at Lesboeufs when he carried the lad into the trench from the top and was sickened at the sight of the poor boy's dangling shattered legs.

To boost morale, inter-companies competitions in shooting, drills and so forth were held.

One day the whole brigade had field sports, with races, tugs o'war, jumping, disc throwing, and a trotting race for the transport men and their mounts.[6] The platoon had been awakened at half past five that morning by the battalion bandsmen who marched down the centre of the wooden hut, rattling and blowing their instruments with crazy abandon.

The blare crashed into the deep slumber of Gawkey Rudd, causing him to jerk himself up on his wire bunk and wonder what damnable engine of Satan the Boche had newly invented. A moment later, he was joining in the general laughter.

One afternoon Harry Russel sat in Madame's kitchen, operating a small wooden coffee machine, grinding the brown beans into gold for that lady, who was making a mint of money out of the troops, who gladly exchanged their francs for coffee, deux oeufs[7] and chips. As he turned the handle he broke into a gay little song in a high falsetto voice. The woman abruptly stopped her ironing; the girl Marie ran in from the yard. Their surprise gave way to laughter when the youth minced up and down the small room signifying in atrocious patois that he was going to be a soubrette at the battalion concert. At this Madame excitedly gabbled something to Marie, who disappeared and presently returned with an armful of clean female attire, which she carefully spread out, on the table – a chemise, drawers, petticoat, stockings, a pair of shoes and a dress – for the lad's inspection and approval. He laughed and said the idea was tres bon.[8] Madame giggled and rubbed her fat palms together. So Private Harry Russel, with his smooth, pink, boyish face, tripped on to the concert stage that evening, amid a riot of wolf-whistles and boisterous cheers, wearing a blonde flapper's wig[9] and Marie's garments – except the dress, which he had exchanged for something more risqué to excite the lads.

The next Sunday, after church parade in a field at the back of the billets, the battalion left the village in the evening light and marched to Gouves. But the troops were called out at 3.30 next morning, had some tea and a scrap of bacon, then waited a long time outside in a downpour before setting out for Arras. It rained all the way. On reaching Schramm Barracks[10] Sergeant Jonah's platoon took off their drenched uniforms and remained semi-naked for the remainder of the day. Snipe sat grousing: "I don't know why we have to put up with all this heavy-handed treatment!"

"Discipline", said Godfrey, "that's why we've got to put up with it. Discipline in drill, on the march, on manoeuvres, and in a tight corner".

"Hark at the old soldier!" laughed Harry Russel.

"Joshua's troops knew the meaning of discipline" said Manley.

Blake, surprised, looked up: "What, have you still got that bible?"

Manley went on: "Joshua had his troops circumcised with sharp knives, and they submitted, although the enemy wasn't far away. What price that for discipline?"[11]

Kettle was all derision: "That was barmy," he said, "They'd all be massacred".

Manley, nonplussed, referred to his bible for answer: "They abode in their places in the camp, till they were whole".

Next morning the battalion left Arras to move nearer the firing line. But the platoon stayed behind for a few days, to work for the Town Major.[12] No one approached to give orders, so the men went out on the scrounge amongst the deserted ruins. They found a queer assortment of articles, much of which they carried to the room they occupied. The Colonel would have burst a blood vessel had he seen their billet. There were iron bedsteads, soft beds, tables, armchairs, mirrors, pictures, books, and a case containing several dozen boxes of sardines. Knight – although content with his usual couch on the floor – found and made use of a gilded chair upholstered in an artistic flowered material fit (had it been unsoiled) to give repose to the beautiful limbs of Marie Antoinette. Mr. Thorn, the platoon commander, sportingly allowed these amenities, and was only concerned to see that the billet and rifles were kept clean.

The Town Major's deputy got the men out in the afternoon to dig up a road and fill in a large shell hole made that morning in a street near the cathedral. Some civilians had been killed; the poor townspeople were still talking of the tragedy. How beautiful the streets of Arras had been; very wide, with avenues of stately trees, and restful green gardens stretching down the centre.

People were being killed every day by the relentless shells.[13] Nonetheless, some stubborn survivors still clung to their 'homes'. A few shopkeepers struggled on in an endeavour to get a bare living by selling souvenirs and cheap gifts to troops in temporary residence. One evening Burril strolled along and purchased a picture postcard worked in bright silk colours depicting the arms of Arras supported on either side by the tricolour and union flag, the stars and stripes and other allied flags. (To be sent to his grandfather.) A portrait in sombre silk of heroic Nurse Cavell (shot by the Boche brutes in 1915) would go to his cousin, who was a red-cross nurse.[14] He treated himself to a packet of photographs of nude smiling women displaying their full-blown breasts. Later on he showed them to Savage with the remark: "When I paid for them the girl behind the counter said to me: 'M'sieur – you no sleep tonight?'"

Their cushy job came to an end two days later, when the platoon packed up and rejoined the company. A two hours march took them to a spot near Beaurains.[15] There, in a wilderness of huts and tents, the battalion had halted.[16] Preparations were astir for a return to the trenches; so all arms were thoroughly overhauled. The Lewis gunners had a great surprise that evening; instead of being humped, the guns and ammunition were actually strapped to pack ponies, who went along with them towards the line. The searching enemy was sending over petrol shells.[17]

The final objective was reached after five hours progress; a reserve trench between Monchy and Wancourt.[18] To get to it the men had to go through a shallow tortuous communication trench, so narrow that their protruding equipment constantly jammed them. It was 1.30 a.m. At 3 o'clock they stood-to, it being midsummer. Some evenings later, Thomas sat on the fire step trying to shield with his groundsheet as much of his body as possible from a miserable downpour of rain, when word came along that the platoon had to go out wiring in No Man's Land. So after dark they went to the front line, shouldered wooden reels of barbed wire and iron pickets, climbed over the parapet and walked out.

Three men, Thomas, Long and Marvell, decided to work together, away from the others. Thomas and Long stuck an entrenching-tool handle through the centre of a big reel of barbed wire and held each end whilst Marvell started to pull the wire and fasten it to a picket. At that moment a German star shell suddenly sprang up, shots were fired, and Long dropped wounded. At the same time, Thomas felt a sharp stinging sensation in his left arm, so thought he had at last been hit. He got down quickly; the white light fell hissing beside him. Marvell could not be seen. Then a machine-gun opened upon them, sending a murderous hail of lead a foot beyond their heads. Thomas ground his face into the earth; Long lay groaning. A pause in the firing gave Thomas the opportunity to turn on his belly and peer across the dark. Another star shell shot up, and under the first faint ray of its ascension he saw a dark form moving; then, as the light increased, he realised his position – someone had fixed the line of pickets wrongly, so that the end one, which they had commenced to work upon, was close to the German trench.

Nearer still was Jerry's outpost, where two men operated together, one firing up the Verey lights to reveal the terrain, the other doing the sharpshooting. Thomas itched to have a crack at them, but he knew that would be senseless, with his gammy arm and the helpless lad beside him.

"Besides," he thought, "I didn't join up to be pushed about by dirty Jerries. Nor brow-beaten by their cocky officers".

With his good hand, he cautiously unbuckled the belt and peeled off Long's equipment, then made an effort to get him astride his back; but his wounded arm forced him to give up. A fine rain began to fall; and of a sudden, a furious tornado of shells pounded the front line. He lost count of time, and wondered what had happened to Marvell. Then, out of the gloom, he saw him crawling towards him. He got to his feet and whispered: "Long's wounded; get him on my back". The two Germans had sharp ears, and fired a burst from a machine-gun.

The trio made their slow way towards their trench, and had covered some ground when a sharp challenge stopped them:

"Halt – who are yer?"

Thomas recognised the voice; it was Rudd's. He was lying prone in a line of men with rifles cocked.

"That you, Gawkey: what are you doing down there?"

"We're covering the wirers behind us".

"Behind you! What a hell of a mix-up. What's Corporal Kemp think he's doing?"

"He's bin killed".[19]

Fifty yards back the three came upon the rest of the wiring party, who were packing up. It was two hours past midnight. As Marvell lowered Long to the fire step the glazed eyes of the corporal stared up at him. Then he went off to find stretcher-bearers. The battalion was relieved that night and went to Wancourt Village. Meanwhile, the two hapless dupes of No Man's Land made their painful way to the casualty station. From Wancourt the battalion moved back to Achicourt, now several miles behind the firing line. Then to the Arras road, where it met a convoy of motor lorries, which took the men westward to Liencourt, a village unsullied by the foul touch of war, smiling under leafy boughs, surrounded by rich pastures and made gay with many-coloured wild flowers.

The Division was now at rest.[20] The platoon had umpteen parades for intensive training, interspersed by baths at Berlencourt, a short distance away. An unusual movement was practised, a march-past for the King. He was expected, but did not come. Later, a bright boy on the staff had an inspiration. It happened one day on a brigade route march, when the band played in double quick time and everyone was expected to keep step with it. Officers and N.C.O.s were shouting, whilst the rank and file tried to emulate women dressed in hobble skirts.[21] The stony roads and full packs added to the difficulty – and the absurdity. Each time the band stopped playing a roar of derisory cheers went up. The whole exercise was a washout; it was not thrust upon the men again. More sensible were the inter-platoon and company competitions, when men tried their skill at bayonet fighting, shooting and cross-country running. There were some good boxing matches, too. A ring had been erected in a wide field. Bruiser Steenie took part in one. His opponent was a chap called Mutt from another company. Burril and most of the platoon were early at the ringside to support their big pal. At the end of the first round Mutt had won on points. As the second round progressed, he kept ahead, egged on by the jubilant shouts of his partisans; he swaggered about and pretended to toy with his opponent.

"Look at that!" exclaimed Kettle, "he's wiping his nose on Steenie's shoulder!"

But the Bruiser refused to be rattled, and boxed steadily on. In the next round, Mutt, furious at Steenie's composure, decided to knock him out. So, changing his tactics, he charged into him with vicious cuts to head and body, then dealt him a tremendous right to the jaw. The cockney boy's knees buckled. Then the gong sounded. With an exultant grin, Mutt walked back to his seconds. Steenie left his corner in the next round grimly determined to settle matters with this cocksure spoilsport. Swift as lightning he landed a left and right to the jaw so powerful that the fellow staggered and was driven back under a storm of blows.

"Go to it, chum!" yelled Snipe, jumping up and down in his excitement.

Mutt managed to get clear; but again was forced to the ropes under Steenie's remorseless pressure, until a terrific hook to the jaw followed by a fierce right sent him sprawling. There, amid the cheers and jeers of rival sides, the referee's rhythmic intonation counted the would-be champion out.

A new draft had arrived from England, all conscripts.[22] Eight were posted to the platoon. Three of the originals had returned. They took drinks together in one of the little estaminets. Two were Somme casualties; Tubby Steel, wounded at Leuze Wood; Drew had had a violent attack of dysentery; Skinner, wounded in the battle of Arras. This village possessed a town crier, aged eight. He would walk down the middle of the road ringing a hand-bell, halt, then when the old ladies popped their heads out of their windows, chant his notices with due solemnity. About this time the "honours and awards" for the Arras operations were announced. Captain Come-and-Go had been asked to name deserving cases in his Company, but said there were none to recommend! On the Sunday after the boxing match, the battalion left Liencourt and marched to Monts-en-Ternois, a three-hour journey. A short march next morning took the men to Petit Houvin railway station. The platoon, enveloped in full equipment, squeezed into a cattle truck. The 56th Division was bound north for St. Omer and the Fifth Army.

It was a tedious journey; it took four hours to cover the thirty-odd miles to St. Omer. Stiff and hungry, the men tumbled out of the trucks; the column lined up, then marched through the city; the band playing lively tunes; smiles from the belles[23] and hearty 'bon jours' from the older folk. A young man in civilian clothes was a rarity.[24] The troops passed out into the highway under a scorching sky. The use of water bottles was (sensibly) tabooed. But vendors of oranges accompanied them and did good business.[25] A two hours' march brought them in the evening to a fair-sized village named Moulle.[26] The platoon took over the upper floor of a big barn, approached by a wooden stairway, and slept comfortably under their greatcoats.

The battalion stayed in this place a fortnight.[27] The troops rehearsed warlike practices of all kinds and listened to lectures by the officers.[28] They did their training with light hearts: but the sort of thing that made them 'browned off' with the army was the following: One Sunday morning after church parade the men were told that the Brigadier intended to inspect their billets. Accordingly, they were ordered to form up in the yard and stand at ease until the great little man arrived. Sergeants and markers were posted at intervals to keep a look-out and pass the word when he approached, so that the men would be 'standing stiffly to attention' as he entered the yard. They were kept thus an hour and three quarters, their dinnertime came and went, and still the general came not. At length they were dismissed, hungry and disgusted. In the same village, on weekdays only, German prisoners were working undisturbed, being conveyed to and from their labours by motor lorries.

The rest period terminated with the usual field day. After the show, the men ate their dinner from their mess tins as they sat at the roadside. Ford (one of the new draft) then began to hum the double-quick tune the band had played on that brigade route march which had ended in such a fiasco. At this Peter Knight laughed, saying the affair reminded him of that time in England when some crank persuaded the war office to order all troops to wear a moustache.[29] Ford looked at Knight with incredulous eyes: "You're pulling my leg", he said.

"It's a fact. It was early in 1916, when I was in camp at Hazeley Down. Everybody swore about it. Some of the youngsters couldn't for the life of them manage a moustache – only a little bit of down".

"Did you do it?"

"Well, we had to try. But it didn't last long; the order was never enforced. It dawned on the Army how dam' silly it was".

The battalion moved off in the afternoon, led by the band. It rained nearly all the way back; indeed the days had been full of rain. Several manoeuvres had been washed out and lectures indoors substituted. The move to Belgium took place on August Bank Holiday Monday. The troops were roused at 3.30 a.m., and were regaled with a breakfast consisting of a tiny piece of bacon apiece, to which they added what portion of bread they had saved from the previous day. Mess orderlies were saved the trouble of fetching tea – there was none.

They marched six kilometres to Watten railway station and entrained in ordinary carriages. The train carried them through miles of luxuriant hop gardens to Steenvoorde, much nearer the fighting line. Then another march to some scattered farmsteads in the countryside. Here the battalion divided itself, the companies taking up their quarters in such shelters as were available. The colonel had left, and an acting C.O. assumed command.[30] The battalion was ordered to parade for his inspection. During this scrutiny there permeated slowly through the rank and file a conviction that a ...... martinet had turned up. 'Slowly' is the word: he was so long on the job that the troops were left standing on the road in full equipment avec heavy packs for nearly three hours. It was sickening to see him quibbling over trivial details. When at last he came to the platoon, he halted in front of Private Kettle and began to criticise one of the brass buttons. Mr. Thorn suggested that the button was a new one so could not compete with the others that had been burnished many times. But the C.O. would have none of it. So, the futile farce went on.[31] (In eight days time the men would be struggling in filthy bogs up to their waists, under high explosives and machine-gun fire in the attack on Glencorse Wood.)

The battalion made the next move in motor busses to a spot near Poperinghe, then marched to the vicinity of Dickebusch, about four miles from Ypres.[32] The following morning the companies prepared for inspection parades, when all the brass had to be aglitter – which, of course, made a deep impression on the enemy airmen hovering above! Three of the platoon: Burril, Blake and Knight, were placed on the reserve personnel list. Knight had been included at the last moment because his chums protested that, although he had been in every "stunt" since the Somme, he again was being passed over. Sergeant Jonah went back with them. An army order was read out emphasising the great importance of the present and future hostilities in this Ypres sector, which was to capture the ports then being used by the enemy as submarine bases. The Germans were putting up a stubborn and frightfully bloody fight to retain possession. The troops were warned against the new gas, virulent stuff that burned the body and ate into the eyes.[33] The lecturer said he had recently visited a brother officer in St. Omer military hospital. Several hundred artillerymen were lying there suffering from the effects of this gas. The keen gunners were prone to lower the eyepieces of their gas masks to get a clearer vision when firing.

Notes

1. See the last note in Chapter 9. There was a brigade church parade on 20 May 1917 and a brigade commander's inspection on 23 May 1917.
2. 'Stunt' in this context refers to an attack rather than a display of skill.
3. Wednesday, 23 May 1917.
4. According to the BWD the battalion moved to Simencourt on 24 May 1917. It remained there until 9 June 1917, moving again on 10 June 1917 to Gouves and on 11 June 1917 back to Schramm Barracks.
5. Wounded soldiers while in hospital were issued with a blue uniform, which was worn with a white shirt and red tie.
6. This kind of competition was felt to be important to maintain morale and encourage friendly rivalry between units. It also helped to build up fitness. It may, however, be surprising to many readers that while some members of the BEF were in the trenches, others in the same army were competing in field sports and demonstrating equestrian skills.
7. 'Deux oeufs' – two eggs.
8. 'Tres bon' – very good.
9. 'A flapper' – a fashionable young woman. It is not clear whether this performance was a part of the permanent entertainment troupe 'the Bow Belles', but it does indicate the popularity of female impersonators in wartime shows.
10. Schramm Barracks was a French Army barracks located in the town of Arras and occupied by units of the British Army operating in the vicinity of the town.
11. The level of religious knowledge is a good indication of how much bible study there was in the curriculum of the day and how many of the men were church-goers.
12. Towns under military control were run by an officer known as the Town Major, who acted very much as a non-elected mayor. Working with a workforce of troops under his command, he was responsible for sanitation, discipline, billets and transport through 'his' town.

13. Shelling from the autumn of 1914 extensively damaged Arras and contemporary photographs show the damage to both public buildings and private housing.
14. These embroidered postcards, known as 'silks', were a common souvenir and hundreds of thousands of them are still to be found in the collections kept by families of men who saw service in the Great War.
15. Beaurains, south of Arras. The Commonwealth War Graves Commission's headquarters for northern France is now located at Rue Angele Richard, 62217 Beaurains, France.
16. The BWD details the battalion strength at this time as twenty-four officers and 741 other ranks.
17. Incendiary shells designed both to cause casualties and to illuminate potential targets.
18. The battalion left Schramm Barracks on 20 June 1917, moving to trenches in the Guemappe sector, where it remained until 26 June 1917.
19. The BWD for this period records that Second Lieutenant Posnett and six other ranks were killed and Second Lieutenant Stredwick and twenty-four other ranks wounded. There is no evidence for a Corporal Kemp being killed but SDGW records Private F. Kimpton being killed on 26 June 1917. The CWGC records that Second Lieutenant Posnett is listed on the Arras Memorial to the Missing and Private Kimpton is buried at Wancourt British Cemetery (Plot VIII, H, 8).
20. The battalion was relieved during the night of 26 June 1917 and moved into reserve at Harliere, where it continued to provide working parties. The battalion moved back to Achicourt on 2/3 July 1917.
21. Hobble skirts, fashionable before the war, greatly restricted the wearers' ability to take normal steps.
22. On 2 August 1917 the BWD records that Major V.A. Flower and a draft of eighteen men arrived from England. On 4 August 1917 Major Flower assumed command of the battalion as acting lieutenant colonel, and Major Higgins reverted to second in command. Major Flower had previously commanded 22 Battalion (Queens) London Regiment [22 London] and had been invalided back to the United Kingdom suffering from a hernia.
23. 'belles' – indicates the good-looking young women in the town.
24. Unlike Britain, France had universal military service and on the outbreak of war all men of military age had been called up.
25. There is a story that apples were popular in the trenches because they could be eaten with one hand. Oranges, however, need to be peeled and in the conditions of the trenches the men kept one hand for eating and the other for holding what passed for toilet paper. With the chance to 'clean up', oranges would be much more welcome.
26. According to the BWD the battalion moved on 22 July 1917 to Monts en Ternois and on 23 July 1917 to the St Omer area, where it was billeted at Moulle.
27. Between 23 July 1917 and 4 August 1917 the battalion remained there and was engaged in training.
28. The BWD confirms much of the detail given here, with the battalion taking part in battalion, company and platoon training. The brigade bayonet fighting competition was won by A Platoon, D Company. There were also boxing and football competitions.
29. For some time it was a regulation that all soldiers that could do so should grow a moustache to make them look more military. A number of men refused and at the point when court martial appeared likely the High Command realised the absurdity of the situation and the order was rescinded.

30. According to the BWD on 14 July 1917 Acting Lieutenant Colonel King was replaced as CO by Major J.E.L. Higgins MC. On 1 August 1917 Captain R.E.F. Shaw was replaced as Adjutant by Captain R.D. Barnett. It is highly likely that this is the same Captain Barnett named as the D Company OC at the beginning of May 1917.
31. This kind of obsession with small detail is frequently referred to by other authors with experience of military service. Although it may appear petty, the logic of this kind of thinking is that if a soldier cannot keep himself and his buttons clean, then he may also neglect his weapon. If this fails, he is placing himself and his comrades in danger. It is worth saying that older buttons are indeed easier to clean than brand-new ones.
32. The battalion arrived at Steenvorde on 7 August 1917 and Captain Lewing was appointed OC D Company.
33. This is a reference to Mustard Gas, which had just been introduced into the arsenal of weapons used by both sides.

Chapter Eleven

The Ypres Salient

Meanwhile, the battalion had reached Zillebeke, about three miles west of Ypres.[1] Then the Division moved into that part of the line: Westhoek, facing Glencorse Wood.[2] Weighed down with their heavy equipment and battle extras, the platoon picked its way to the support line, along narrow slippery duckboards raised on piles above the mud and flanked on either side by bogs, decaying death, ordure and stale gas. They had covered half the length when an exploding shell shook the footway; Gawkey Rudd stumbled, lost his balance and fell on to the foul mess. Kettle stretched out his rifle to Rudd, who gripped it, got one leg on the duckboard, was helped on, and straightway vomited. Then another shell fell close, wounded Kettle and flung him right into the obscenity. Steenie spread-eagled his body half on the duckboard, half outside in an attempt to rescue the helpless man with his hands – only to watch him slowly sink and go under. Swearing and protesting, the big fellow was laboriously pulled back by his mates, and the file went forward.[3]

It was black night when the platoon, after delays and uncertainties, reached its position. It had been mercilessly shelled all the way. There were no trenches as such; only a line of shallow ditches and shell holes half full of muddy water, among which the men distributed themselves. It was hopeless to try to dig deeper than two feet; underneath that lay a sheet of water. The Division had taken over with immense disadvantages. It had come to an unfamiliar part of the line, with little or no time for reconnaissance, to relieve a division equally ignorant – having been there only twenty-four hours – under constant shell-fire churning up their miserable holes. Outlines of the scheme for projected operations were hurriedly sent out by Corps Headquarters. More and more orders followed in quick succession. In consequence, worried regimental officers were hard put to it to pass the necessary instructions to the men.

At a quarter to five next morning (August 16) the Division commenced its attack on Polygon Wood.[4] It encountered for the first time big white reinforced-concrete forts so strong that they withstood

138

the barrage. Protected by these 'pill boxes',[5] the German machine-gunners let loose their fury, inflicting grievous losses on the advancing men. The remnant, forcing forward, encountered troops, which till then had been held back in accordance with the enemy's new system of 'defence in depth'.[6] The struggle went on all through the morning, until Glencorse Wood was gained.

The assault on Polygon Wood to the north-east was met by intense fire from the flanks as well as the front, followed by a counter-attack. The exhausted Londoners fought back desperately over that foul ground but were forced to give way. Another counter-attack later, even fiercer than the first, would have overwhelmed them had not their supporting battalions come to their rescue.[7] The line was held until the following night, when the Division was relieved by the Fourteenth.

The survivors of the platoon limped into a tent away back at Ouderdom early next morning. They sank into exhausted sleep until the afternoon, when mess-orderlies were detailed to get the dinner. There was more food than was needed, for many would not eat with them again. With Kettle killed and others wounded, including Drew, Skinner, Davey, Neal and Hurley. Ford was shell-shocked. Mr. Thorn, the platoon's commander and friend had been mortally wounded, and the company commander killed.[8] The acting-colonel had gone west.[9]

The battalion stayed at this camp at Ouderdom six days. The companies were reorganised, each forming two platoons from the remnants of its four.[10] Every day a programme of physical training, bayonet fighting and so forth was gone through; under the eyes of German prisoners, who took every opportunity to stare. Blake said he would give a lot to read their minds. Although the men were liable to be returned to the line at any moment, all the brass, clothing and equipment had to be kept shining bright. A newly-arrived company commander, Capt. Bull, who had been taking his ease (and whiskey) with the reserve personnel, away from the mire, blood and bitterness of the battle, lost no time in engendering hate among the long-suffering men of the company.[11] He inspected their tents and kits one morning; and although everything was orderly, it was not good enough for him. He confined the whole company to billets that evening. So Steenie, Rudd and company had to forego the pleasure of being served mild beer by the buxom Belgium lass, with her saucy quip 'That's the stuff to give 'em'.

The battalion did not go up to the salient again, but moved farther back.[12] The men rose long before the sun one morning, marched to

Poperinghe and boarded cattle trucks, which began to move two hours later. They detrained at Watten and marched to Moulle, the village they had occupied so short a while before with those who now, alas, were on the trail stretching beyond the grave. Sergeant Jonah, Blake, Burril and Knight rejoined the platoon. Bobby Thomas, now healed of the wound he got during the night-wiring fiasco, came with them.

The platoon had cause to remember the one Sunday spent at this place. After the church parade the men were kept standing outside while Capt. Bull again inspected the billets. Evidently, the only fault he could find was with Private Savage who had put a novel into a bomb bag. For this heinous crime, the culprit was sentenced to three days C.B. and pack drill.[13] After dinner the whole company had to scrub all equipment and polish brass work. Even this did not satisfy master Bull,[14] for, seeing an equipment that some finical fool had plastered with wet clay (as a substitute for the unobtainable khaki blanco),[15] he ordered everyone else to do likewise. The Lewis gunners were told to strip their weapons and clean them. Thus relieved from a tiresome parade, they spread ground-sheets on the floor and whistled while they handled the parts. While they worked, they looked out of the window and saw Private Savage with a pack on his back marching up and down, back and forth, with sloped rifle, and a regimental policeman barking out orders.

"It's a degrading sort of punishment, anyway: it's a good thing his wife can't see him", said Burril.

"Punishment be damned!" snapped Knight, flinging down the piston rod[16] he'd been wiping. "Bloody fuss over a book in a bomb bag".

"What was the book called?" enquired someone.

"The Laughing Cavalier".

Burril sat there, testing the trigger of the gun. He said: "This Captain Bull's going the right way to be accidentally shot for the purpose next time he's in the line".

"He's more likely to wangle himself away somewhere; I know his sort", replied Knight.

The battalion assembled on the parade ground at midnight and marched in the moonlight through sleeping St. Omer, then slogged on for four hours until the troops reached Arques railway station.[17] The platoon climbed into one of the cattle trucks, then sent two mess-orderlies to fetch dry rations for the day and hot tea from a field cooker in the station yard. The train left an hour later. As usual, military hush-hush kept the troops in ignorance of their destination. After swallowing the tea, the men settled down to smoke, chat or snooze. Alas for the clayey glory of their equipment! Very soon it was besmirched by the grime of the truck. Blake sat reading a newspaper sent to him from Blighty.

"Hear, hear!" he ejaculated.

"What's that all about?" someone asked.

"Listen to this" said Blake:-

"Why in the name of all that is sane should the men on service in France be compelled to have all the bright parts of the equipment and uniform burnished till they are capable of use as a shaving-glass? The twinkling and blazing of the brass fitments discloses to the enemy the column and even the individual soldier, and is an inestimable help to the German flying man and sniper. For Heaven's sake, let us have finished with such puerilities!"

Knight sat hunched up in the truck. Again and again the revolting manner of Kettle's death obtruded upon his mind. He sought to obliterate the scene by recalling the friendly lad's suave cockney humour that nothing could smother – not even the C.O.'s preposterous criticism of his little brass button. He wondered what poor Kettle would say to the man should he encounter him on the way to Elysium? Would he tell him what he told the frightened Jerry in that other No Man's Land, to 'fuck orf dahn there'?

The train trundled along, going farther and farther south, away from the horrors of the dreaded salient. Oftimes it crawled, sometimes pulled up, when men of all races passed by: Americans, Portuguese, French, Belgians, Chinese, Anamites, and German prisoners.[18] Blake continued to read his newspaper. There was an article by Philip Gibbs,[19] the war correspondent, about the battle of Langemarck on August 16th:-

LONDON COURAGE

As yet I know very few details of the Irish side of things. I know more about the Londoners, for I have been to see them today, and they have told me the facts of yesterday. They are tragic facts, because for English troops it is always a tragedy to withdraw from any yard of soil they have taken by hard fighting, and many good London lads will never come back from that morass ... But there is nothing the matter with London courage, and to me there is something more thrilling in the way these boys fought to the death, some of them in the bitterness of retreat, than in the rapid and easy progress of men in successful attack. Lying all night in the wet mud under heavy fire, they attacked at day up by Glencorse Wood, in the direction of Polygon Wood. On the right they and their neighbours at once came under heavy blasts of fire from five machine-guns in a strong point, and under a hostile barrage fire that was frightful in its intensity. They could not make much headway. No mortal man could have advanced under such fire, and so their comrades on the left were terribly exposed to the scythe of bullets which swept them also.

A DREADFUL NIGHT

Men of London regiments fought forward with a wonderful spirit which is a white shining light in all this darkness – through Glencorse Wood and round to the north of Nuns' Wood, avoiding the most deeply flooded ground here, where was one big boggy lake.

Notes

1. The Ypres Salient had an unenviable reputation for its appalling conditions and danger. Fought over since October 1914, it was the area in which the Germans had first used both flamethrowers and gas. The waterlogged geology meant that conditions in the trenches were consistently worse than elsewhere on the British front. This was the first time that the division had been in the region and it arrived during the Third Battle of Ypres, otherwise known as the Battle of Passchendaele. The battle began in hot weather on 31 July 1917 and dragged on until November, when the village of Passchendaele on the ridge overlooking the city of Ypres was finally captured by Canadian troops.
2. An account in the BWD details the battalion advances on 16 August 1917.
3. There are numerous accounts of men lost in the quagmire of the Ypres Salient and the author may well have observed a man lost in the mud of the battlefield.
4. In the wake of a creeping barrage eight divisions attacked in atrocious conditions at 4.45am on Thursday, 16 August 1917 on a frontage of roughly 12,000 yards. The 56th Division was on the extreme right of the attack. The destruction of the 56th Division within the confusion of blighted woods on the Gheluvelt Plateau epitomised the desperate ordeals endured by the assaulting troops.
5. Pillboxes were a German innovation and were built in large numbers around the Ypres Salient. Each could protect a detachment of soldiers and was usually provided with positions from which machine guns could be fired. German practice was to shelter inside during a bombardment and then to emerge and fight from behind or on top of the structure when the infantry attacked. Pillboxes were rarely built singularly and each box could be used to protect another if it came under attack. The Tyne Cot cemetery contains the remains of five pillboxes and the Cross of Sacrifice is built on the central box.
6. This reference to 'defence in depth' helps to date when this account was produced. The move to the new tactic began in the spring of 1917 and the German Army was

able to use the technique very effectively by the summer. However, the under-standing of the tactic was limited to a few senior officers, even though many units had experienced its effect. It was only after the war that the nature of this kind of defensive tactic became known to the general public. The connection may be the *Daily Telegraph* newspaper. Sir Philip Gibbs wrote for the paper during the war and we know that the author kept his cuttings, suggesting that he was a reader of the paper. Between 1925 and 1935, when the editors believe that this account was written, the military correspondent of the *Daily Telegraph* was Basil Liddell Hart, an ex-Army officer who had served on the Somme and wrote extensively about tactics for his newspaper.

7. By mid-morning all progress in the centre and south halted; subsequent well organ-ised German counter-attacks forced British withdrawals. By early evening exhausted remnants of units were back or near their start lines. The end of the day saw no breakthrough; an advance of around 1,500 yards was made in the north, but virtu-ally no progress was made elsewhere. British casualties were estimated at 15,000. The official history, *Military Operations France and Belgium, 1917 (vol. II)*, compiled by Brigadier-General Sir James E. Edmonds in 1948, describes the day's activities as follows: 'The battle reports of the two London brigades of the 56th Division in Polygon Wood and east of Nonne Bosschen emphasise that the lack of preparation and the need for fresh troops close at hand to consolidate ground gained became evident soon after the objective was reached. The protective barrage, too, was weak; much of the shrapnel had the burst-on-graze fuse, effective enough on hard ground, but useless on the muddy patches and water-filled craters ahead of the troops.'

8. According to the BWD Second Lieutenant Ranson was the only subaltern killed during the day, which may identify him as the platoon commander referred to in the narrative. The BWD also identifies Lieutenant Swift as the OC D Company wounded on the day. Both of these subalterns were hit at about 7.55pm.

9. SDGW corroborates this, naming Acting Lieutenant Colonel Flower and Second Lieutenant Ranson as the two officers killed. It further records eighteen other ranks killed, seventeen of them on 16 August 1917. Following the death of Acting Lieutenant Colonel Flower, Captain R.E.F. Shaw returned to the battalion and assumed command; he was to remain in command until killed in August 1918. The CWGC records that Acting Lieutenant Colonel Flower is buried in Perth (China Wall) Cemetery (Plot I, E, 20) and Second Lieutenant Ranson is listed on the Menin Gate Memorial to the Missing.

10. The BWD records that between 9 and 16 August 1917 the battalion suffered two officers and eighteen other ranks killed and three officers and eighty-two other ranks wounded. The author of the history of the 56th Division offers an example of controlled restraint in his final verdict regarding this tragic attack: 'Maybe the confusion was inevitable, but it makes a sorry story in which the great gallantry of the London Territorials stands forth like something clean and honest in the midst of slime and mud.' (Major C.H. Dudley Ward, *The Fifty-Sixth Division, 1st London Territorial Division 1914–1918* (Naval & Military Press, repr. edn, 1921), p. 160.)

11. At this point the BWD gives no indication as to a suggested identification for Captain Bull. It may be only a coincidence but Joseph Steward's Attestation Papers were countersigned by a Captain Bull and this may have provided the inspiration for the name.

12. According to the BWD the battalion was relieved in the line during the morning of 17 August 1917 and withdrew to Cornwall Camp. The battalion remained at

Cornwall Camp until 24 August 1917, when it moved to the railhead at Reninghelst Sidings.

13. 'C.B.' – Confined to Barracks. Pack drill involves running or marching wearing a heavy pack. This was another sentence that could result from a court martial.

14. 'Bull' – bullshit.

15. Blanco manufactured the blocks of coloured paint used to make webbing equipment a uniform colour and provide some degree of waterproofing.

16. Another specific reference to one of the critical working parts in the Lewis gun: General Staff, *SS 448 Method of Instruction in the Lewis Gun* (HMSO, May 1917).

17. The BWD describes the battalion's movements to Watten by train and then by marching to Houlle, arriving by mid-afternoon on 24 August 1917. The battalion remained at Houlle and underwent battalion training until it moved on 31 August 1917 to billets in Beaulencourt. On 3 September 1917 the battalion moved into hutted camps at Fremicourt and remained there until 9 September 1917, when it moved forward into the line in the Lagnicourt sector.

18. By the summer of 1917 the Allied forces on the Western Front were truly international. America had entered the war, joining France, Britain and Belgium. Men from all over the British Empire were also serving on the Western Front but the demand for manual labour had continued to grow. As a result, both Britain and France decided to recruit around 200,000 additional labourers from mainland China and, in the case of France, from what is now Vietnam, then a French colony. These men were used to release troops from the vast network of docks, railheads and supply depots throughout France.

19. A third reference to this war correspondent.

Chapter Twelve

The Battle of Cambrai

The tardy train crawled into Bapaume, through the now restored Arras line, having covered the fifty-odd miles in ten hours. The Division had come down to that place of poignant memories, the Somme. The men marched through Bapaume, now in a sorry state of ruin and desolation, a stark host of skeleton buildings. Passing out, they continued until they reached a cantonment[1] of huts near Le Transloy.[2] A brigade church parade took place in the open on the Sunday, with the combined bands; attended by the Divisional and Brigadier-Generals. The division left for the firing line the following day. After three hours marching, a block of tents, pitched in a dark wilderness, was reached. In that solitary place, Captain Bull made his company march in with sloped arms, as if (to quote Harry Russel) they were passing the King at Buckingham Palace! Next day the captain left and went to 'hospital'.

The battalion moved on towards Lagnicourt. It passed a grave bearing the simple inscription: 'Capt. Cherry, V.C., M.C., A.I.F. Killed in action at Lagnicourt'.[3]

And now fresh drafts arrived to fill the hungry gaps. The Division's losses had been grievous. Its share in the battle of Langemarck from August the 13th to the 17th had cost it in casualties 111 officers and 2791 other ranks.[4] The villages hereabouts were in utter ruin. No civilian was ever seen during the division's three months in this sector.[5] Women and children were but images in the imagination. To relieve the monotony, the Corps Commander arranged trips to Amiens. Of course, only a small number could go. Burril was one. He sought solace in the arms of Circe of the Red Lamp.[6] But when he returned to camp he told Corporal Champion that he 'was unlucky', as 'she was old and dry'.

Baths had been fixed up amid the shattered ruins of Haplincourt, eight kilos[7] from the camp. One evening the orderly-sergeant made his way to the platoon's billet with good news for Godfrey and Marvell: their Blighty leave had come at last. The afternoon saw them marching with the company to the baths and marching back again 'as they were'.

They all tried next day, with no better luck. But the Company-sergeant-major did not send the two friends to England unwashed. He got his batman to put a portable bath in a tent, where they scrubbed themselves clean. Young Wills had returned from his ten days' leave.[8] He was happy. His girl friends had made a fuss of him. He had gone places; been to the theatre – "George Robey was there,[9] a hairy cave-man dancing about". He said "I don't care what happens now; I've had a bon time".

Rumour was spreading that things were building up for an attack on Cambrai.[10] The battalion was relieved one night during a cold dark storm, and made its way back to an encampment of Nissen huts near Fremicourt. It was there that the men learned of their comrades' coming great attack; preparations for which had been cunningly screened.[11] Zero hour struck at 6.20 next morning, (November 20th), when all the guns for miles around burst into a sudden thunder of noise.[12] Thousands of deafening drums beating a terrific tattoo. The Germans were completely taken unawares; there had been no preliminary bombardment to arouse suspicion. Suddenly great flights of aeroplanes appeared as it were from the void, like startled birds, hastening to the battle.[13] The battalion remained at this camp four days, standing by.[14] During that period other battalions of the Division did valuable work, fighting in the Hindenburg Line, as well as capturing a most important position near Moeuvres.

The order to move came one evening: the battalion left at nine o'clock. Battalions of the Guards were going the same road. After a long march, Doignes was reached. It was a village no longer. At that moment the furious Boche was laying it waste. The platoon spent the remainder of the night carrying material to the trenches, under constant shell fire, during which Baines was slightly wounded. On the following morning, Gawkey Rudd climbed on to a heap of debris to watch the fine trees of Bourlon Wood[15] being transformed into flaming torches. Pushing back an unruly quiff[16] of hair from his forehead, he adjusted a pair of Jerry field glasses. As he looked, the chorus of a cockney ballad Snipe had sung to the men a few nights before kept jingling through his head:

> 'Wot cheer' all the neighbours cried,
> Who're yer going to meet Bill;
> 'ave yer bought in the street Bill?"
> Knocked 'em in the ol' Kent Road.[17]

Suddenly Gawkey's eyes were blinded by a violent force that hurled him to the ground; the earth erupted all about him, shooting up swarms of stones and brickbats mingled with vile smoke. Blood gushed from an ugly wound in the lad's shoulder. Two stretcher-bearers came, bound a tourniquet to his broken arm, and carried him away. A sergeant and a rifleman lay dead a few paces away.[18]

All day long columns of fresh troops passed by. The battalion moved off in the evening, by companies, independently.[19] At length the platoon got into a trench, which they afterwards learnt was the reserve line, behind the front line, at a place called Tadpole Copse, west of Moeuvres. Here the men took their places under the unseeing eyes of the dead who were laid out in a row on top for removal. The troops in front were not in full possession of their trench; some of the enemy on the other side of the barricade were fighting a fierce onslaught to bomb them out. An officer climbed out of the British section, ran along the top and threw bombs down amongst the Germans until one of them shot him. Whilst all this was going on, the sun darkened and snow fell. What a pleasant Sunday afternoon for civilised men! With every hour, the casualties mounted higher and higher. Harry Russel was hit and borne away half dead with an ugly gaping wound in his side. He was the lad who tantalised the boys at the battalion concert in Simencourt when, made up as a pink blonde-bewigged flapper, he minced on to the stage and sang his falsetto songs. The toll grew so heavy that all reserve personnel were called up, together with the men lately returned from hospitals in France and Britain; among whom were Skinner, Davey and Drew.

The Boche made the hours of darkness a nightmare, dropping his shells all around the platoon. Once a five-nine[20] dropped within five yards of a Lewis gun (luckily outside the trench).[21] The trenches were in an execrable state, abounding with mud, knee-deep in places. The nights were cold and wet. The men were on battle rations, i.e. bully and army biscuits, and not much of that. How eagerly, therefore, they looked forward to their dram of rum after a long night of exposure and peril. Mr. White, the newly made platoon officer, evidently thought the stuff was detrimental to his men, so arrogated to himself the right to deprive them of their legitimate measure (which was small enough in all conscience). After having made fools of their mouths he invariably had a goodly surplus, which he would carry back to company headquarters dugout, where certain people received more than was good for themselves. One morning Knight determined to have his full whack; so, after taking his meagre thimbleful of rum, he contrived to get farther along the trench next to the last man to be served. When that time came, Knight proffered his mess-tin lid; and the officer – all-unsuspecting – poured out the second dose.

The Germans sent hundreds of gas shells over their heads all the night long, in an attempt to disable the artillery; a furious prelude to the awaited counter-attack. The British had, since November the twentieth, swept forward in a series of splendid successes. Now, thought the Germans, their day had come.[22] More than 100,000 were hurled against the British in an attempt to re-capture the Hindenburg Line. The battalion stood waiting to advance. It came quickly. Sergeant Jonah led his platoon along the trench, out over the stretch of country that led to the fighting line. As each rifleman and bomber passed a dump en route, he was handed a box of 12 bombs[23] to carry up. The Lewis gunners were carrying their magazines of ammunition. Swarms of enemy aeroplanes circled and hovered above like great evil birds. The barrage was savage; casualties piled up. Reinforcements from other battalions of the division were hurrying forward. One particular spot the Boche shelled furiously. It was where the open ground gave way to a communication trench leading to the front line. The Germans knew that reinforcing troops were compelled to enter that spot, so made it a veritable shambles. Each man rushing across the place ran through the teeth of death – and he knew it before he took the plunge.

With his Lewis gun upon his shoulder, Knight took his chance. As he shot across his glance fell upon some of those who had been stricken down. Little Wills lay upon his side: so swift and sure had been the touch of death that he appeared to be in a peaceful slumber. Nearby lay Sergeant Jonah – that fine 1914-star man[24] – mortally wounded. One of his feet was almost severed, but, with his indomitable spirit, he was trying to raise himself to a stretcher while he urged "Carry on!". All this Knight saw as he ran that bloody gauntlet and cheated death. Farther along he passed another of the platoon being borne on an improvised stretcher: a trench duckboard; a simple working man, who reckoned not of the grievous hurt, but shouted to his pals his quaint battle-cry "Lloyd George says 'carry on'".[25]

The shelling was tempestuous: Knight thought "Surely I must be hit soon!" The communication trench was but a shallow ditch, barely reaching to the knees; thick slime lay all along it, several inches deep. Boche snipers and machine-gunners potted at the exposed men as they ran. Their artillery, too, was enfilading the trench. Panting and choking, Knight stumbled against the fallen men; some stilled forever, others wounded but endeavouring to crawl through the slime and bloody waters: here a tough man, cursing his fate and the Huns; there a sensitive lad with agonised face imploring the hurrying men not to kick his poor broken body. The gunner reached the fire trench, which was deeper. It had need to be, for it was being strafed murderously. Drew was leaning against the side shaking violently, his eyes protruding wildly. The Germans came over in mass formation, and into their midst the British poured their fire with rifle and machine-gun. The sweating bombers chucked their deadly eggs, whilst somewhere on the left a Stokes mortar was hurling damnation against the advancing host. Streams of lead belched from the machine-guns; the artillery wrought fearful havoc. Half-way across, most of the 'shock troops' turned and fled. Those of tougher breed who came on were either bayoneted or pulled into the trench to engage into hand-to-hand struggles. In that close melee, there was little room to use rifle or bomb. A big Hun got to Manley's throat and was forcing his fingers against the throttle when Steenie seized a bomb box and crashed it into the Jerry's face. Anything to slash about with.

The platoon was forced to give ground a little: the men tore up duckboards and threw them across the trench together with lumps of revetment, coils of barbed wire and bits of battle debris, making a barrier to bomb and shoot across. The ding–dong battle went on for hours: 'the sun stood still in the midst of heaven'. Heriot was shot while attempting to pull Savage caught in the barbed wire. With the coming of darkness the shelling slackened and things quietened down. Beyond question, the Boche had received a terrific thrashing. Nonetheless, the platoon and the rest of the battalion continued to receive grievous casualties.[26] The R.A.M.C. men were untiring in their work of burden bearing. All night long, they passed by, carrying the wounded and the dead. At length the battalion was relieved, after almost twenty-four hours of fighting, and got back to the third line.[27]

Notes

1. 'Cantonment' – military quarters.
2. These are the hutted camps at Fremicourt referred to in note 17 in the previous chapter.
3. The grave marker referred to by Steward is that of Captain Percy Herbert Cherry VC, 26 Infantry Battalion, Australian Army. Captain Cherry was killed in action on

27 March 1917 during his company's attack on the village of Lagnicourt. Wounded early in the day, he continued to lead his men in clearing the village and in defeating a number of enemy counter-attacks. He was killed by shellfire at about 4.30pm and was subsequently buried outside his command dugout. He was posthumously awarded the VC. His grave was subsequently marked by a grave marker, which included his VC award. According to the CWGC records Captain Cherry is now buried in Queant Road Cemetery (Plot VIII, C, 10).

4. This is a quote from Major C.H. Dudley Ward, *The Fifty-Sixth Division, 1st London Territorial Division 1914–1918* (Naval & Military Press, repr. edn, 1921), p. 160, and indicates that the author must have been using this book while writing his account.

5. The BWD continues through September and October with the battalion alternating between periods in the line near Lagnicourt and at rest in Fremicourt.

6. The reference to the use of one of the officially sanctioned brothels by members of the platoon may indicate that this account was not written for the author's family.

7. This reference to distance in kilometres is an indication of how familiar British soldiers had become with the continental European unit of measurement. The author and his comrades would naturally have worked in yards and miles, as metrication was far in the future.

8. The reference to ten days' leave for 'Young Wills' is revealing. In reality, the person on leave was the author. Steward's service record shows him on leave to the UK between 7 and 17 October 1917. One consequence of this is that there is no mention in the account of an incident that occurred on 13 October 1917 while the battalion was in the line. This relates to the rescue by members of the battalion of a Royal Flying Corps [RFC] officer who had crash-landed in no man's land. Despite attempts by the enemy to shell the aircraft and pilot several times, he was eventually recovered by Captain Heath, Sergeant Manzi and Corporal Leigh. A BWD entry on 25 October1917 records that Captain Heath was awarded a bar to his MC and both NCOs received the MM. During the course of the rescue attempts both Captain Heath and the CO, Acting Lieutenant Colonel Shaw, were wounded. T. Henshaw, *The Sky Their Battlefield. Air Fighting and the Complete List of Allied Air Casualties from Enemy Action during the First World War* (London, Grub Street, 1995), p. 238 identifies the aircraft concerned as DH5 serial number A9277, piloted by Lieutenant D.G. Morrison, 68 (Australian) Squadron RFC, who was shot down while engaged on a close operation patrol. The aircraft was subsequently destroyed by shellfire later the same day. Lieutenant Douglas George Morrison subsequently died of his wounds on 29 October 1917 and is buried in Grevillers British Cemetery (Plot VII,C,19). We are left with the distinct impression that whatever is in the account was seen by the author. There can be no doubt that his comrades would have told him about the event of 13 October 1917, but he did not feel that it was appropriate to use the information at third hand. This reinforces the eyewitness quality of the account.

9. George Edward Wade (20 September 1869–29 November 1954), known by his stage name George Robey, was a music hall 'star' of the period. He gave his full backing to the war, supporting recruiting campaigns and raising money for charities. He was performing in London in the autumn of 1917, probably in the hit show 'The Bing Boys Are Here'.

10. The Battle of Cambrai was the third assault made on the German positions since the beginning of the year. The plan included the mass use of tanks, extensive use of the RFC in direct support to ground forces and the employment of two cavalry divisions to exploit the expected breakthrough. The attack was launched at dawn on the

morning of 20 November 1917, with all available tanks advancing across a ten kilo-
metre front. No fewer than 476 tanks were accompanied by six infantry divisions.

11. The deception plan for the battle included using low-flying aircraft to provide noise
    to cover the tanks moving into position and the lack of any form of preliminary
    bombardment.

12. A thousand artillery pieces were used in the bombardment.

13. Fourteen RFC squadrons took part.

14. According to the BWD the battalion moved to Fremicourt and remained in the
    sector until 18 November 1917, when it was moved out of the line, returning to
    Middlesex Camp. On 23 November 1917 the battalion received orders to move
    forward to Cinema Camp at Lebucquire. At the time the strength was quoted as
    twenty-one officers and 502 other ranks. D Company was commanded at this time
    by Captain N.J. Inns. The battalion moved into the line on 24 November 1917 with
    D Company in reserve.

15. Both editors were involved in battlefield archaeology in Bourlon Wood and
    witnessed at first hand the destruction caused by the fighting over ninety years
    before.

16. The military fashion of 1917 consisted of short back and sides worn with long hair
    at the front which could be hidden under a cap or helmet during inspection.

17. From 'Knocked 'em in the Old Kent Road' by Albert Chevalier, the chorus of which
    gives a good idea of the sort of language that was used in London of the time. The
    style is typically a 'Coster's' song using cockney slang throughout.

    > 'Wot cher!' all the neighbours cried
    > 'Oo yer gonna meet, Bill?,
    > 'Ave yer bought the street, Bill?,
    > Laugh? – I fort I should've died,
    > Knocked 'em in the Old Kent Road!

    See http://thelondonnobodysings.blogspot.com/2009/07/knocked-em-in-old-
    kent-road.html

18. In reference to the sergeant lying dead nearby, SDGW details only one sergeant and
    three men killed on 27 November 1917. The sergeant is identified as 490065
    Sergeant A.E. Shelley, who is now recorded on the Cambrai Memorial to the
    Missing (CWGC). Tadpole Copse, referred to in the narrative, is located west of
    Mouevres (Trench map sheet 57cNE1 Queant).

19. The BWD details the battalion being relieved on 29 November 1917 by the 8th
    (Service) Battalion, Middlesex Regiment [8 Middlesex].

20. 'Five-Nine' – 5.9 or 150mm German shell.

21. The BWD identifies 27 November 1917 as the day on which the battalion was
    subjected to very heavy shelling all morning. Under cover of this fire, the enemy
    subjected the bombing blocks to determined attacks, which were repulsed by the
    battalion and the neighbouring 12 London.

22. The BWD reports that the German counter-attack at Cambrai occurred on 30
    November 1917 and was preceded by a very heavy bombardment and massed
    aircraft employed in the ground attack role. According to the BWD D Company was
    moved forward in support of 14 London at about 11.15am.

23. The standard bomb box was made of wood with rope handles at each end and
    contained twelve bombs with detonators. The boxes are heavy and cumbersome.

24. The reference to the '1914 Star' indicates that the soldier had served on the Western
    Front as a member of the original BEF between 4 August 1914 and 22 November
    1914. Given that 13 London arrived in France on 4 November 1914, survivors of the

original battalion would have qualified for the 1914 Star. By late 1917 this man would have been one of the very few pre-war members of the battalion to be still serving.

25. 'Lloyd George' – the Prime Minister, previously Minister of Munitions.

26. SDGW identifies two possible candidates for the men named as killed. Wills and Jonah may be 493743 Private Mills, killed in action on 30 November 1917, and 490276 Sergeant L.W. Jones, who died of wounds on 3 December 1917. CWGC records show that Private Mills is recorded on the Cambrai Memorial to the Missing at Louverval and Sergeant Jones is buried at Achiet Le Grand Communal Cemetery Extension (Plot II, A, 10). SDGW records three officers and eight other ranks as being killed on 30 November 1917. The BWD in contrast only records two officers and sixty-eight other ranks as casualties and is not specific as to fatalities versus wounded.

27. According to the BWD the battalion was relieved at 5.00am on 2 December 1917 and moved back to Fremicourt, where it arrived at 8.30pm that evening.

Chapter Thirteen
Vimy and Oppy Wood

A sudden surprise came later, when the 51st Scottish Division took over. The troops wore jerkins of grey fur.[1] As they filed up the dark shell-holed road they cautioned their followers 'watch your feet', which tickled the cockneys, so different from the warning 'mind the hole'. Then the Division got away, down the long tree-lined Bapaume–Cambrai road, each step taking them far from that horrid land where foul devils danced and weltered in the sweat and blood of men. A tramp of several miles brought the battalion to a field at Fremicourt where, after a meal of stew, then tea, then rum, those fortunate enough to be free of duties turned into the nearby sheds, were given blankets, and slept soundly for hours. On the following morning, before the battalion moved off again, the C.O. read a telegram of congratulations from Sir Douglas Haig stating how valuable had been the stand made by the division, which resulted in saving the left flank against the attack on the Cambrai sector on November the 30th. Fighting with the 2nd Division and the 47th (London) Division, they had withstood a tremendous onslaught. At the conclusion of the speech the battalion left the camp, travelled by train to Beaumetz Riviere, then marched to Simencourt.[2] The men thought they were there for a rest; but two mornings later were marched to Roclincourt, a village on the north of Arras. The Division had now moved into the XIII Corps' area and taken up its headquarters at Roclincourt.

The line taken over from the 31st Division was situated at the bottom of the Vimy Ridge slope, on a plain between the two villages of Gavrelle and Oppy.[3] Gavrelle was held by the British; the latter by the Germans. The battalion sent three companies into the firing line; the fourth (the platoon's) remained in reserve. This reserve was a system of old trenches containing small built-in bivvies covered with sheets of corrugated iron. On the afternoon after their arrival the company was paraded in the open and had physical jerks followed by arms drill with fixed bayonets. A German observation balloon hung high in the air. Shrapnel began to burst overhead, so the men were dismissed to their bivvies. The mess-orderlies fetched the tea under fire; two were wounded. Half the platoon sat in their shelter having tea when a vicious discharge of shrapnel burst right overhead. Savage was kneeling next to Knight, spreading some margarine on a piece of bread, when he suddenly rolled over with a cry of "Oh, my God". For a few seconds he choked for breath, thick blood oozed from his nostrils and ran into a mess tin at Knight's feet; there was a quivering struggle then silence. A stretcher-bearer who was one of the party unfastened Savage's tunic then, looking up, said "He's gone". A shrapnel ball had burst through the iron roof and buried itself in the victim's back.[4] The dead man was placed on a stretcher with a ground-sheet for a pall, and laid outside the doorway. The heavens darkened and the rain poured down. The stricken lads looked out upon the still covered shape that a few minutes before had sat amongst them pulsing with warm life and taking an interest in the little worries and pleasures of existence. The storm raged; he heeded it not – for him the Great War[5] had no appeal. Here was a life sacrificed by military stupidity and the mania for ceremonial drill whenever possible. No wonder Jerry strafed them – he didn't mind Tommy's fighting; but presenting arms to him! Men of the Labour Corps nearby said they had worked there a long time but had never been shelled. They blamed the officers. Savage was taken back to a British cemetery and left in charge of an N.C.O. who said the dead man would be buried when a chaplain turned up. Thus ended Private Savage, veteran of the Somme, Ypres and Cambrai, volunteer soldier.[6]

The rain continued, so further plans for giving free exhibitions to the Boche in the balloon basket did not mature. Two days later it was the company's turn to relieve their comrades in the firing line, to approach which the men walked in single file down a communication trench three miles long, named Ouse Alley. The platoon's position, Oppy Wood Post,[7] was a big circular entrenchment, behind which the enemy could steal if sentries were not vigilant. It was said that a previous division had been slack; that Jerry was in the habit of occasionally pouncing on an unsuspecting man; remarking "Oh, the ......s are still here", then taking him away for evidence of the fact before his careless companions were aware that anything untoward had happened. That story may have been the creation of an inventive cockney's brain. A small patrol did pay the platoon a visit soon after its arrival, but they were rumbled and fired upon, and one was caught.

It was now well into December. Patrolling at night afforded some change from the narrow confines of the post; and was warmer work. The men were allowed to go out wearing soft caps, and with no equipment save a bandolier, rifle and a couple of bombs; the chief gunner having in lieu thereof his loaded Lewis gun on the shoulder and his revolver in his pocket. The weather was very bitter. There were many deaths from cold among the French civilians. Snow and ice lay thick. The barbed wires out in front were covered in sparkling frost, laid on by St. Nicholas to celebrate his festival. But Christmas time made no difference to the platoon in their outpost – although Blake did endeavour to entertain the chaps by playing seasonal tunes on a tin whistle that had been sent to him for a Yuletide present.[8] They were very near the enemy; so near that they had been ordered to keep their voices low; so near that the German's Verey-lights dropped on their ramparts and behind. Wire entanglements had first to be constructed in the post and stealthily put out at night. When the time came for the platoon to be relieved, it made its way up the long communication trench, to a light railway, then joined the rest of the battalion. The little train, fitted with small open trucks, carried the troops merrily on through fields and people's gardens, and even a house, until they reached a small-inhabited town named Maroeuil, boasting a few shops and estaminets.

The whole battalion billeted in a big factory and slept on wire beds; hundreds of them, tier on tier. But it was off again next morning, to the railway station, where it had to wait for the arrival of trains carrying more troops of the division that had relieved them in the line. Exchanging places with these men, the battalion went farther back until it reached Tincques, on the Arras–St. Pol road. Then a march of about five miles to the village of Magnicourt-en-Comte. The battalion stayed in this place three weeks.[9] Although the Division was supposed to be 'at rest', the men worked very hard preparing the terrain for the expected counter-attack.[10]

But it was not all work. There were shows in the brigade cinema, and rides to see 'Bow Belles', the Divisional concert party. Once the battalion, led by the band, marched to an adjacent village and watched a football match between its team and that of another brigade. Refresher courses were held at brigade schools, where officers and sergeants, drawn from the battalions, gave instruction in the warlike arts. Edgley was sent to one, on a Lewis gun course.[11] The Divisional rest finished on February the first.[12] The battalion packed up, marched to Tincques and went on by train to Ecurie, then marched to Roclincourt, an hour's journey. Arras was within walking distance of this town.

When the time came for the company to take over its share of the Gavrelle–Oppy sector, Mr. White's platoon went again into the Oppy Wood Post, the circular breastwork, and fire trench running completely round it, with extended arm, so making the outpost banjo-shaped. The arm of the banjo was about twenty-five feet long, and was protected on both sides and the end by breastworks. The Germans were continually strafing the post with minenwerfers. Tommy hated the things; they rushed down through the air with the voice of doom – 'For you, for you, for you, for you!' then crashed. One morning Singen and Davey took their turn at the end of the sap, where a periscope had been fixed. A box of bombs was inlaid in the wall of the trench. By its side stood the men's rifles with bayonets fixed. While Singen's eyes were glued on the periscope, his companion paid more attention to the cleaning of his false teeth than watching for Huns. He had the set in his hand and, after operating upon it with a match stalk, proceeded to polish it with a scrap of flannelette known as 'four by two', which had been issued to him for the sole purpose of cleaning out the barrel of his rifle; the while he expatiated on the instability of human aggrandisement. Suddenly there was a sharp crash; bits of glass, tin and wood rattled down about Singen's ears. Jerry had scored a bull on the small portion of periscope exposed above the sap. Thus deprived of their trench eyes, the two had to stand on guard with rifles ready in hand, in case this trick was the prelude to a raid. But nothing exceptional happened, so the two fixed up a temporary bit of mirror. They had a very good idea where one of the snipers was lying, some two hundred yards away to the left. They fixed Mills grenades on rifles and whizzed them over to his lair.[13]

Oppy Wood, a ghostly copse, overlooked the position.[14] An eerie atmosphere hung about the place. Shots were fired from mysterious quarters. In the listening post, if one stamped one's foot a little to ease the pain of the cold, and so swayed the body, making the moonshine dance on one's tin hat, a hissing bullet would come from the rear. When Knight and Burril went out one night to work in No Man's Land, they left their equipment behind save the gas respirators worn high up on their chests. Knight carried his loaded revolver tucked in the sachet of his mask for instant use. They had to work at the wiring on their knees and on their backs, keeping an ear for the click of a Verey light pistol. Whilst they were at their task, great translucent curtains slowly stretched, like magic silk, adown the sky, and a roseate light gleamed behind them. It was the Aurora Borealis. Some nights later, they were out in No Man's Land again, this time with the gun. During the day, an airman had dropped a bomb on the Boche wire to make a big gap, in preparation for a raid that the British intended to make.[15] So now (the night before the raid) the two gunners were detailed to take turns, with the gun, relieving each other hourly. Their job was to prevent German working parties from mending that gap. It was dark, so one had to peer closely and listen for sounds. When he thought he descried figures moving in the gloom, he opened fire through a piece of wet sacking placed on the mouth of the gun, then shifted his position to perplex Jerry. The gun had a stoppage once, when Knight was forced to half strip it and put it right wholly by the sense of touch (an operation he had learned at the brigade school).

The raid was artfully carried out. Stand-to came and went as usual. The raiders waited until it was quite light and judged that the weary enemy men opposite had stood down and most of them retired to their couches. To further mislead them, their brethren down on the left were shelled by artillery as well as being treated to a smoke barrage and a trench-mortar strafe. Then the raiding party (who had been practising behind the lines and were now waiting in the post) wearing no equip-ment – not even a gas helmet – having all evidence of identification removed, but with rifles, fixed bayonets and bombs jumped over the platoon's parapet and rushed into the enemy trench. A machine-gunner was quickly dispatched as were others offering resistance. One of the raiders lifted the covering of a funk hole in which two sons of the father-land were sleeping. "Hi", he shouted. They awoke and gazed at him with sleepy unbelieving eyes. "Come out!" he commanded, pointing his rifle at them. They stared at him stupidly, but would not obey. He shot them … others were taken captive. Then the bugler in attendance blew a blast upon his horn and the boys hopped back – except one who had been killed.[16] The whole show was over in a few minutes, and broke the time record for a raid. The prisoners were taken farther back, given cigarettes, a tot of rum, and interrogated.[17]

Knight and Burril afterwards learned that their Lewis gun tactics the previous night had persistently broken up the wiring parties sent to mend the gap. One of the raiders told them that he had seen a pile of steel body-belts lying on the German fire-step. The brass hats were very pleased, especially was the Brigadier-general. Later, the following brief report appeared in the press: 'Another successful raid was carried out this morning by London troops in the neighbourhood of Oppy. Several of the enemy were killed and a few prisoners were taken by us'. Having completed their task, the raiders left the Post and went back to the transport lines. As they neared the latter the boys of the battalion that was 'out' lined the road and welcomed the victors with the soldiers' substitute for sackbut and psaltery, to wit, biscuit tins and bugles. As for the platoon, who of course remained to guard their Post, they in due time received from the Boche artillery the angry retaliatory strafe inflicted with all the fury of stung pride.

When the platoon's turns of duty were over the men went to Roclincourt, which they reached at midnight. Early next morning they marched to Ecurie, some distance away, to do a sort of initiation barrage stunt, with flags. It was now early March; the weather conditions were ideal for attack, but still the Germans delayed the expected offensive. Long before dawn each morning the British troops stood to arms, waiting; remaining thus until the sky paled and the brilliant star that graced it disappeared. The trenches were doubly manned all day.[18]

Notes

1. This reference is curious. Fur jackets or jerkins had been issued in the winter of 1914/15 but by the end of the war were quite rare.
2. According to the BWD the battalion arrived at Simencourt on the evening of 3 December 1917 and on the following day then men were engaged in refitting and baths.
3. According to the BWD, when the battalion moved forward into the line on 7 December 1917 A, B and C Companies moved into the line and D Company was placed in reserve at 'Daylight Railhead'. This is further proof that 'the platoon' was in D Company.
4. The BWD records one other rank killed and one wounded on this day.
   SDGW does not record any casualties on 7 December 1917, but does record eight other ranks killed on 8 December 1917. However, 493629 Lance Corporal Albert Savage was killed in action on 28 November 1917. This may refer to the same individual and perhaps indicates a lapse of memory on the author's part in respect of dates and names.
5. The term 'Great War' was initially applied to the conflict with Revolutionary and Napoleonic France, which ended at the Battle of Waterloo in 1815. By 1915 the name was being applied to the current conflict.
6. CWGC references show that Lance Corporal Savage is buried at Hermieres Hill British Cemetery (Plot I, H, 29).
7. References to Ouse Alley and Oppy Wood Post do not appear in the BWD but Ouse Alley and Oppy Post both appear on Trench map sheet 51bNW2 Oppy.
8. The BWD fails to record any change of reserve company before the battalion's relief by 14 London on 13 December 1917, when the battalion moved into brigade

support. Between 13 and 18 December 1917 the battalion was engaged in supplying working parties. This pattern continued through December with the battalion in the line between 18 and 22 December 1917. From 23 to 28 December 1917 the battalion was out of the line in billets at Roclincourt. This clearly contradicts the narrative as far as the festive season is concerned.

9. The BWD for 1 January 1918 places the battalion still in divisional reserve at Wakefield Camp and engaged in training. On 3 January 1918 it moved forward and took over the front in the Mill Post sector near Oppy (Trench map sheet 51bNW2 Oppy). The battalion was relieved on the morning of 6 January 1918 and, as per the narrative, moved back to Magnicourt via Maroueil and Tincques, arriving in billets at 3.20pm on 7 January 1918.

10. One of the ironies of the pattern of trench warfare was that there was often more work for the men who were not in the trenches than those that were. The idea that men who were out of the line were 'resting' is illustrated here.

11. Throughout the war an increasing number of military schools offering courses in everything from weapons training to scouting and the suppression of rats sprang up behind the lines. The syllabus could be extensive and offered the participants an opportunity to learn news skills, potentially receiving specialist pay and the opportunity to rest away from the front.

12. According to the BWD the battalion remained at Magnicourt until 1 February 1918. During this period the men were engaged in battalion and company training. A series of inter-company competitions was held during the period. No. 14 Platoon, D Company, under the command of Second Lieutenant Thorpe, was selected to represent the brigade in the corps inter-platoon competition. There is, however, no mention of the battalion being engaged in preparing defensive positions during this period.

13. One of the improvements made to the use of grenades was the development of various forms of rifle grenade from 1915 onwards. This allowed the bomb to be projected far further than could be achieved by hand. Importantly the bomb's trajectory followed a steep arc which meant that it could drop into a trench or shell hole that an opponent was using for cover.

14. The BWD details the battalion's move forward to Roclincourt West Camp on the night of 10 February 1918. The battalion returned to the line in the Oppy sector on 19 February 1918 and the operation order dated 17 February 1918 indicates that D Company did assume responsibility for Oppy Post. This again clearly corroborates the narrative and identifies 'the platoon' as belonging to D Company. The battalion was relieved again on 23 February 1918 and returned to Roclincourt West Camp. On 27 February 1918 it moved into support of 14 London. During this period D Company was located at a railway embankment near Bailleul.

15. The BWD confirms that the battalion returned to the line on 5 March 1918 and that a raid on the enemy was ordered on 6 March 1918. The raid itself took place on the morning of 9 March 1918. Commanded by Second Lieutenant R. Lester, the raiding party, consisting of Second Lieutenant W. Smith and forty-two other ranks left the saphead at Oppy Post at 6.45am. Dividing into two parties, they made their way into the enemy lines, proceeded to bomb a number of dugouts, and engaged the enemy within the trenches. The party completed the raid and returned via the saphead at Oppy Post only twelve minutes after leaving.

16. According to the BWD British casualties are recorded as one man killed and two wounded. According to SDGW only one man was killed on 9 March 1918, 495596

Private A.E. Payne. According to the CWGC Private Payne is listed among the missing on the regimental panel on the Arras Memorial to the Missing.

17. The BWD account of the raid also claims fourteen Germans killed and four missing.

18. The battalion was relieved on 11 March 1918 and returned to Roclincourt West Camp, where it remained until 17 March 1918. During this period it was engaged on training and the provision of working parties in support of the Royal Engineers. At this point there was certainly anticipation of a German attack and references to the preparation of the Green line as a defensive position. On 17 March 1918 the battalion moved into support and on the morning of 21 March 1918 took over the front line in the Oppy sector. Battalion dispositions indicate that D Company was positioned in battalion reserve at Bailleul East Post (Trench map sheet 51bNW2 Oppy).

Chapter Fourteen
The Kaiser's Battle

The great onslaught came at 4 a.m. on March 21st, when sixty-eight German divisions attacked on a forty-four mile front between Croiselles and La Fere.[1] For a week, the main fighting centered round the armies south of Arras, towards Albert and the Somme. The 56th Division had spread out east of the Vimy Ridge area, between Arleux and Gavrelle.[2] On March 28th, at 3 a.m., torrents of gas and high-explosive shells rained down upon their front line. Trench mortars bombarded the system of forward posts to wipe them out. As the storm troops advanced, shoulder-to-shoulder, they were met by rapid rifle and Lewis gunfire. A bloody battle for the posts ensued. Oppy and the others were overwhelmed; the enemy pushing forward over open ground, to be shot down by riflemen and machine gunners manning communication trenches, shell holes and other spots of vantage. The grey masses, picking their way through rows of their wounded and dead, bombing as they advanced, forced the defenders back; but the stubborn men of London's regiments disputed every post, every Alley, despite their dire losses, fought their way back to the Bailleul–Willerval Line, where they joined up with the remainder of the Division. The Germans dragged their batteries forward behind a screen of smoke,[3] to fire point-blank at the Bailleul Line, while their airmen flew low and shot at the men in the trenches. But the British artillery shattered them then laid down a protective barrage. As the day wore on the Germans tried again; but their force was spent and zeal had gone out of them.[4] By evening comparative quiet prevailed. Next night the 4th Canadian Division started to relieve the 56th, when the three brigades moved back individually to Villers au Bois, Mount St. Eloi, and Ecoivres.[5] The battle had cost the Division fifteen hundred casualties.[6] But it had, for the second time, mastered a disastrous situation. The Germans had hoped to breach the Bailleul–Willerval Line, and then bring up three strong divisions to capture Vimy Ridge. Eleven divisions attacked four British north and south of the river Scarpe, in an endeavour to take Arras, then press on to capture Amiens.

The overriding ambition of the 'great offensive' had been to cut the allied armies apart then drive the left wing of the British towards the channel ports. In the end it was the fighting efficiency, high morale and dogged bravery of the British troops that forced Ludendorff to admit defeat – 'One of the bloodiest defeats of the whole war', said The Times. Men of the Canadian Division that relieved the 56th found such an orderly, matter-of-fact lot that they got the impression accounts of the battle had been exaggerated. But when they patrolled No Man's Land, they found it thick with enemy corpses. The platoon, now in billets back at Ecoivres, was poorer by the loss of three men dead and four wounded.[7] Tubby Steel had received his last, his fatal blow at Oppy Post during the minenwerfer strafe. The C.O. had the battalion on parade and told the men (after warning them to be prepared for more battles), that the King, on visiting First Army Headquarters, had sent for the Divisional Commander to personally congratulate and thank him and the Division. The Corps Commander's thanks, too, were read out in orders of the day. All had good reason to be pleased, for twice in four months the division had, fighting with the 4th, the 15th and the 32nd Divisions, met the fierce onslaughts of the foe and smashed them. To cover up the defeat in the eyes of their countrymen, the German government circulated a statement to the press to the effect that the 56th Division had been annihilated! North of Arras the Germans had re-taken Messines which the British had mined and captured the previous summer.[8] Then Armentieres fell. On that same day, April 11th, 1918, Sir Douglas Haig sent a vital message to all ranks:- 'There is no other course open to us but to fight it out. Every position must be held to the last man. There must be no retirement. With our backs to the wall and believing in the justice of our cause each man of us must fight on to the end'.[9] Whilst working together at their digging, Knight talked to Manley about this:

"That'll put the wind up the people in Blighty, especially those who've got used to the war. I noticed it when I was on leave: theatres producing farce after farce; society girls in their 'dinky' uniforms posing before photographers, miniature shows on the water in Trafalgar Square to persuade people to buy war-loan, and so on".[10]

The Division took over a new front, astride the Arras–Cambrai road.[11] Since the Germans' decisive defeat in this area on March 28th they had restricted their activities to patrolling No Man's Land at night. Sometimes the British were out there too, where-upon a bloody clash followed. For weeks, officers and men of the three London Brigades made systematic raids. One dark morning, before stand-to, the platoon staged a raid on a German machine-gun outpost.[12] Mr. White, Steenie and a few others stole out into No Man's Land and laid low. When it grew light and the raiders calculated that the Germans had stood down, they stealthily crawled to the flanks of their post then pounced upon the occupants. Some of the Jerrys were found sitting on a fire step peacefully smoking ... A dixie containing some fishy concoction, probably intended for breakfast, stood in the trench. The machine gunner swung his weapon round and wounded two of the raiders, but himself was immediately bayoneted and shot, as well as one of his companions; the other two being taken prisoner. Their machine gun was firmly fastened down; and as Mr. White did not think it good policy to stay there too long, he blew it up with a bomb.

The battalion was relieved to go into support, i.e. St. Sauveur Caves, the ancient workings spread underneath Arras, where the Engineers had installed electricity, wire beds and other amenities.[13] The platoon was lodged in a cellar near an underground casualty clearing station.[14] One afternoon Edgley took a stroll above ground. Climbing through a hole that a shell had torn in a wall, he found himself in a convent garden. The pious nuns had long since departed, driven away by the screeching demons of destruction which had smashed down the walls of prayer and desecrated the quiet paths of peace. But the trees and flowers, neglected by those gentle hands, had put on a wilder beauty: orange flower blossomed on the untended branch, like the bridal gown of a gipsy queen. Roses, red, yellow, pink, white studded the green bushes and sent their fragrance to the soldier. Small wild flowers of divers hues peeped from the ground, intermingled with the grass. The swaying trees seemed to speak some language of joy. A cave had been carved in the side of a mound and seats placed in a semi-circle around its inner wall. Outside, a fountain had once played; but now it was dried up; stagnant water lay along the tiny canal that stretched its way about the garden. Edgley pictured the nuns taking their breviaries to the secluded shelter of that nook built among the trees and watching the fountain send high its clear waters. On the top of the mound – that is to say the roof of the cave – a large crucifix stood, sequestered by trees and accessible by two flights of steps that stretched up the sides of the mound from the garden.

The platoon moved from Arras to an encampment of wooden huts near the village of Berneville.[15] The weather at this period was glorious. At a church parade, the Divisional General presented medal ribbons won at Cambrai the previous November and since. He shook hands with each recipient, then spoke a few encouraging words to the battalion. Sec. Lt. White received the Military cross, and Steenie the Military medal.[16] Then the battalion sang the hymn, which was supposed to have been Kitchener's favourite:

> 'And when the strife is fierce, the warfare long
> Steals on the ear the distant triumph song;
> And hearts are brave again and arms are strong.'[17]

Twenty-four hours later, the troops were stuffing greatcoats and unnecessary impedimenta into their valises, dumping them and parading in battle order. Then they marched to Arras – a four-hour journey – without a halt. They left at 10 p.m. and went to the front line by the nearest way, over the top, to the left of Neuville Vitasse.[18]

Private Godfrey had been promoted to lance corporal. One of his duties was to distribute rations to his section. After morning stand-down he would go to Sergeant Champion, who had received the platoon's from the quarter-bloke. So, this morning the corporal issued from the sergeant's presence with his arms full of food, which he tumbled upon a piece of newspaper on the floor of the trench. The eyes of his section were watching.

"How many in a loaf?" asked Singen.

"Four, and a bit of buckshee".[19]

The corporal cut up the bread and handed each man his portion, putting aside his own. Occasionally there were some bits of army biscuit that the corporal would carefully count and divide amongst the men. Or perchance the cooks had taken the biscuit ration and raisins which were issued last Friday in lieu of jam and, with the assistance of a little water, made a nice, heavy, warranted-to-fill pudding. The duff had been made more palatable by the adhesion of many a hair from its erstwhile conveyance, the sandbag.[20] The corporal took this mass in his hands and let it fall upon a sheet of Family Journal,[21] obliterating the words: 'Send this to your hero on active service'. Brandishing his table knife, he said: "I suppose you all want a bit of puddin?"

"I don't want yer Christmas pudden" exclaimed a shrill voice in the wings.

Then the corporal spread out and counted little bits of cold meat and handed them to his 'scholars', some receiving the scraps on their grimy palms; others in their mess-tin lids. A cold potato each followed. There was one tin of bully between the section; but there was no competition, so Godfrey kicked it against the wall: "Nobody want bully? Right: I'll leave it here and you can help yourselves – if that pudding doesn't satisfy you", he added.

Next, he held up a partly filled tin of jam in one hand and his spoon in the other. "Now roll up for your possy".[22] All the men but one placed small heterogeneous jam tins on the floor in front of him, to which he added his own.

"Now, Baines, what about your tin?"

"Leave my share in the tin, corporal".

"When the devil are you going to get a tin of your own? Too bloody lazy to carry it, I suppose. I've told you about it before: no tin, no jam next time – got me?"

"I'm entitled to me ration".

"Then have the jam in your blooming hand".

Godfrey started to place a spoonful of possy into each tin, then stopped with suspended spoon over one:

"About time you washed your tin, isn't it?"

"Aint got no water sarg – er corporal" stuttered the slothful one; a 1918 conscript.[23]

"Then clean it with dirt and spittle".

"Here you are, Baines, here's your share left in the tin. You'll be unlucky next time.' Baines took the tin and peered into it, sarcastic-like. He put his finger in and licked it. Then he cut a slice of bread, spread the jam upon it, chucked the tin over the top and said "There's my tea gone west and it's not dinner time yet".

Unusual quiet now obtained on the two Fronts. Canadian troops held the line on the right flank of the Division. The gun section was standing-to one morning when two sergeants of Princess Pat's Canadian Light Infantry came into the fire bay with a bunch of beautiful pink roses which they had scrounged somewhere in the rear in honour of Dominion Day.[24] For all the fine weather and comparative quiet, Death never deserted the platoon; remorselessly he exacted his dread due. In the middle of July the 56th was relieved by the Second Canadian Division; and moved to the neighbourhood of Dainville.[25] Then followed a series of day marches, ending at La Haie in the north-west. Here the time was spent in intensive training and rehearsals for attacks. Then, back into the trenches again; this time to Blangy on the Arras front.[26]

Bobby Thomas had returned from a fortnight's seaside holiday at the First Army Rest-Camp for War-worn Soldiers at Audressilles near Wimereux. Burril was the first to welcome him back, and set about pursuing him with questions.

"We were only three minutes walk from the sea; and slept in tents on the sands".

"What about routine?"

"There was hardly any. After a wash and breakfast, we cleared away the rubbish, tied up the brailings[27] and stood outside the tents with our kits for the Camp Commandant to inspect the lines. With the exception of the brief morning parade, we were left to spend our time as we liked; sprint to the beach, undress on the sands and splash into the sea in our birthday suits".

"Sounds fine!"

"There was a village about a mile distant, with estaminets, a big Y.M.C.A. canteen, lending library and concert hall. At the other end of the village, on the cliffs, old sweats ran a housey housey racket. Some of the chaps gambled there all day until dark. I preferred to swim in the sea and play water polo. The Canadian troops in the camp played baseball, very fast and exciting. I got a pass to Boulogne one day and saw the cathedral. It had been badly knocked about. I went in with one of the chaps who wanted to see if the altar was O.K."

"And was it?"

"Yes. There were figures of the Madonna and child looking down from a little boat, where people had hung a lot of bits of jewellery along the side".

"A boat – that's a funny idea".

"Well, Boulogne is a seaport".

"We had a special sports day in the camp; nurses from a hospital near were invited and took part in some of the competitions. And the Canadians got together a fine brass band. Before I left there was a massed church parade, called Remembrance Day. Hundreds of men from camps nearby, and a contingent of nurses came. It was conducted by clergymen of three denominations".

"Well, back to the warpath. I feel great now. We all had plenty of grub, beaucoup sleep — and no sergeant-majors to worry us".

Notes

1. The battle of March–April 1918 was the consequence of the Treaty of Brest-Litovsk, which had been signed with Russia in early March 1918. The treaty formally ended the war between Russia and Germany, which had resulted in the collapse of the Tsarist regime and the communist take-over. With a treaty in place, Imperial Germany could transfer thousands of men and guns from the Eastern Front to the West. The plan was to deliver a knock-out blow on the Allies before the United States could effectively mobilise. Features of the German attack were a centralised artillery plan, the extensive use of gas and the employment of storm-troops to spearhead the assault. The operation was referred to by the Germans as 'the Kaiser's Battle'.

2. According to the BWD on 26 March 1918 D Company relieved A Company in the line at Bradford Post (Trench map sheet 51bNW2 Oppy). On 27 March 1918 the 56th Division was ordered to extend its frontage and the battalion, having been relieved by two companies of 5 London, moved to the Arleux sector and relieved elements of the 2 Canadian Mounted Rifles. D Company was placed in battalion reserve between Willerval South Post and the Red Line north to Tired Alley (Trench map sheet 51bNW2 Oppy).

3. The 'smokescreen' was largely fog, which masked the German attack.

4. The BWD records that on the morning of 28 March 1918 there was considerable hostile activity, including shelling and gas. During 28 and 29 March 1918 the enemy made several attempts to break through the line but were held by the battalion and its neighbouring units. It appears that D Company remained in battalion reserve during this period. This would certainly explain why there is no description of the German attacks, as the author was well away from the main action.

5. The battalion was relieved at 2am on 30 March 1918 and withdrew to Mont St Eloi, south of Vimy Ridge.

6. According to the BWD during this period the battalion had suffered two officers wounded, eight other ranks killed, twenty-four wounded and eleven missing.

7. According to the BWD the wounded officers included Captain N. Inns of D Company, who was wounded by shellfire on 23 March 1918. SDGW records six fatalities, including a Corporal S.J. Love, who is recorded on the Arras Memorial to the Missing (CWGC).

8. The Battle of Messines commenced on 7 June 1917 when twenty-two mines loaded with high explosives were detonated under the German lines on the high ground near the village of Messines. The explosions, which it is claimed could be heard in England, killed or entombed hundreds of the German defenders and the attack by the British Second Army was a success. News that places that had been so hard-won were now falling to the enemy was a demoralising blow.

9. This order from Sir Douglas Haig, which was read to all units, was generally well received by the BEF and with their 'backs to the wall' they fought on and stemmed the German assault.

10. This reference to the increasing distance between attitudes at home and those at the front are typical for the period. Soldiers were not happy to see women in uniform, were worried about women potentially taking their jobs and thought that miniature sea battles and other 'stunts' did not reflect the reality of their experience. In these circumstances home leave could be a bad experience for a returning soldier who found civilians earning vastly more than men at the front and propaganda that did not reflect the 'real' war.

11. The BWD for April 1918 places the battalion in reserve near Mont St Eloi and

moving to Duissans on 7 April 1918. It then moved through Berneville into reserve in the Telegraph Hill sector (Trench map sheet 51bSW1, Neuville Vitasse) taking over on 8 April 1918. During this period they provided working parties assisting the Royal Engineers in deepening communication trenches and cable runs. On 14 April 1918 the battalion moved into support but continued to provide working parties reinforcing defensive lines. On 18 April 1918 D Company was sent forward to take over support trenches from 14 London. This was only for a short period and on 20 April 1918 the entire battalion and brigade were relieved and moved back to Dainville.

12. According to the BWD at 2am on 31 May 1917 a raid led by Second Lieutenant A.D. James was carried out on an enemy machine-gun position that resulted in the death of one of the enemy and the capture of two prisoners. It is known that Second Lieutenant James was serving in D Company and therefore likely that this raid is the one referred to in the narrative. According to the Regimental History, Second Lieutenant James was awarded the Military Cross for his action in the raid and his second-in-command, Sergeant Brownjohn, received the Military Medal. A larger-scale raid was carried out by C Company and one platoon of A Company under the command of Lieutenant Smith on 1 June 1918.

13. On 23 April 1918 the battalion again moved to St Saveur Caves, where it remained until 29 April 1918. Throughout this period the battalion supplied working parties to assist the Royal Engineers. On 21 April 1918, for example, the BWD records that 500 men were engaged in maintenance work. The diary also refers to specialist classes for Lewis gun sections and snipers during this period. A small section of these caves has been preserved and is open as a tourist attraction. *La Carriere Wellington* is located at Rue Delétoille 62000 Arras, Tél : +33 (0)3 21 51 26 95.

14. This dressing station was called 'Thompson Cave'. Andrew Robertshaw had the opportunity to be shown round the remarkable site by Alain Jacques, the Arras-based archaeologist and expert on the Great War. It is not open to the public.

15. The BWD records that for the remainder of May the battalion alternated between periods in the line and support in the Arras area. The men also spent time out of the line in the area of Dainville, where they continued training in practice attacks and on the ranges. The battalion returned to the line on 22 May 1918, taking over trenches in the Observation Ridge sector.

16. The battalion remained in the line until 10 June 1918, when it moved back to Berneville, remaining there until 17 June 1918. On 16 June 1918 a Church Parade did take place, following which gallantry medals were awarded to members of the battalion for earlier acts. This may be the medal parade referred to in the narrative.

17. The Anglican Bishop William Walsham How wrote 'For All the Saints' as a processional hymn.

18. The BWD records that on 17 June 1918 the battalion returned to the front in the Arras area, taking over the line at Telegraph Hill, remaining there until 29 June 1918, when it moved into support at Blangy Switch.

19. This indicates that the loaf should be divided into four ration portions and that there would be some left over. 'Buckshee' indicates something that is free or surplus. The word is derived from Hindustani.

20. 'Duff' – pudding, usually boiled.

21. Not all reading matter sent to soldiers was acceptable and the fate of this copy of the *Family Journal* indicates the ways in which magazines, newspapers and books were actually used.

22. This is unusually specific as, although jam was known in the army as Pozzy, there

was a type of condensed milk called 'Posy Brand', which was sold in camps early in the war. When jam was in short supply this was used instead of jam.

23. The arrival of conscripts into the platoon is clearly seen as detrimental by the author. It is, perhaps, not surprising that the volunteers in the unit should have a low opinion of men who had been forced to do 'their duty'.

24. Dominion Day is 1 July.

25. The BWD records that during the first half of July 1918 the battalion remained in the Arras area, acting in support of the Telegraph Hill sector, providing working parties and being given the opportunity for baths and periods of training. While at Dainville the battalion engaged in sports and training until 11 June 1918, when it moved to Wagonlieu. Over the next few days the battalion was relocated via Lattre St Quentin, Grand Rullecourt and Ballieul, and on 18 July 1918 arrived at Canada Camp, Chateau de la Haie. During the battalion's stay here the men underwent further range training, sports and platoon and company training.

26. The battalion received orders to move on 31 July 1918 and moved via light railway to St Aubin. From there the men marched back into the line in the Tilloy sector.

27. Brailings are the cords that allow the sides of the tent to be lifted up to air the tent during the day.

Chapter Fifteen

The Last Hundred Days

When the Division was relieved by the 15th Scottish Division, it marched from the Tilloy–Vitasse sector to Arras, then beyond.[1]

The platoon reached Berneville, a quiet village, in the early hours. After a hasty breakfast, the men were pushed into light-railway trucks and carried several miles westward to Liencourt, then marched to Gouy-en-Ternois. The battalion arrived there at half past six. The platoon were banking on having a rest from their exertions after tea; but they had hardly finished when the order to 'pack up F.S.M.O. at once' reached them. The troops moved off at nine, as twilight melted into dark. Then, followed a long night march, hot and thirst creating, the hours relieved only by the all-too-brief rests of ten minutes duration. The foot-sloggers[2] went through strange country: they were in the dark in more ways than one. Rumours were rife. Many fell behind. The journey's end – St. Amand, near Souastre – was reached at 2.15 next morning.[3] There was a hut for each platoon. Knight approached his treading on two beautiful water blisters. There would have been training for an hour next day, but the order was washed out,[4] the men were told to get battle order ready. For an hour or two, they sat outside huts with equipment ready to sling upon shoulders. Field cards were written; for no one knew when he would get another posted.[5]

The battalion had now become aware that it was to take part in the fighting which had been gradually, stubbornly developing in favour of the Allies since the middle of July, and had, as August advanced, become decisive.[6] That was all: the job was to be patient and obey. At a quarter to five the order 'On parade' came. The battalion marched off by platoons, keeping an interval of one hundred yards between each.[7] The way led across open country, affording no cover from the scorching sun. In the course of the journey a village was reached where some of the Guards were quartered. Rumour said there was going to be a big attack by the British: several divisions had passed through on their way to the line. The summer sun went down and the stars came out; and still the column plodded on. Men had been dropping out – no, not men, but boys just of age, not hardened to such a life. Sometimes they suddenly fell on their faces in the thick dust. At length the company halted on a field and remained there whilst the officers went away for a pow-wow. Some of the men took their groundsheets from their belts, covered themselves and fell fast asleep on the ground. But it was not for long; they had to move on again.

The Germans were getting spiteful; their screeching shells making the way hideous. Gas reeked all around, compelling the men to fix their respirators; but they could not see clearly through the eyepieces so were forced to drop them and suffer their eyes to smart[8] as there was no halting.

"We're going over the top in the morning, boy", said Singen.

"If they send us over in this state they're mad", answered Knight.

The Germans were gassing the artillerymen heavily – they had rumbled the coming attack.[9]

The battalion tramped high roads and fields, down steep banks, along sunken paths, through old trenches and across railways whose heavy metals had been smashed and curled up. It was sunrise when the platoon reached what was thought to be its destination; but the men had to shift again. The artillery barrage for the attack had commenced before they got into their trench. They had been marching twelve hours; and now knew their objective — the town of Boyelles lay before them.[10]

"I'm glad I'm not a German this morning" said Mr. Blest, the platoon commander, as the thunder of the barrage increased and the swift destructive tide tore over their heads. It was quite light now. Enemy shells were dropping out in front and in the trench. The platoon climbed out to the top and immediately opened into blob formation. There were bits of wire to dodge, half hidden in the grass and weeds, old shell holes to avoid and new ones being made as some men met their death. The survivors pressed on and reached their objective. Here they were met by men quivering and half-crazed by the incessant shellfire.[11] When Knight reached the enemy trench a ghastly spectacle confronted him. An entire British machine-gun team lay in a gruesome heap, completely blocking the way. A shell had exploded and torn them to pieces. The officer's revolver lay like a broken toy. After taking some bullets from the pouch to replenish his loss, he took some groundsheets and covered the awful heap from men's eyes and to keep away the swarm of filthy flies that buzzed in the sunshine.[12] He went away round the traverse and stood solitary on the fire step. A few minutes later, an elderly German, bare-headed and defenceless, emerged from the shambles and, looking up, nodded to Knight (as a neighbour might greet another in peace-time). And the gunner suffered him to pass by. The captors clung to their gains as the morning wore on. Parties were sent out to wipe up machine-gun posts. A battered crew was found in one; some were dead, others wounded. The film of death was glazing the eyes of one, who pointed with slow finger to his throat and said 'fini', as if to ask leave to die.

In the afternoon, the platoon went over the top again without artillery barrage for support. The Boche had retired a long distance, but his observation balloon kept him informed. It was strange ground; there had been no time for reconnaissance. The men extended out in sectional blobs and came under machine-gun fire.[13] Still advancing, they eventually spotted the enemy who were ensconced on a big railway embankment and firing from the permanent way. From that eminence (called Bank Copse) they could rake the ground with lead. A small party of Coldstream Guards was advancing on the platoon's right. When the attackers neared the embankment all the sections closed up level for the charge and ran across the remaining ground to the foot of the slope. But the Jerrys did not wait to kill with their murderous little guns. They got up, scooted down the farther side of the embankment and scampered like hares across the field beyond. Meanwhile the London men and the Coldstreamers had climbed the stiff bank. Knight placed his gun upon the railway lines and fired upon the retreating foe, in company with the other gunners, the riflemen joining in the chorus with their 'bondooks'. Mr. Blest and the officer in charge of the Guards decided to remain at this position; the latter remarking that the men had done very well, had advanced a long way over rough ground, so it would not be right to take advantage of their goodwill. The Boche artillery strafed the embankment savagely. A heavy shell splinter fell in front of Knight's face onto the gun, denting the casing down upon the radiator. It did not put the weapon out of action; it came within an ace of putting its keeper out, however. Having failed to drive enemy back, Jerry sent gas, horrible stuff. It drove Ford out of his senses; the poor fellow raved and gesticulated wildly in his choking agony. Few of the company had been able to penetrate the subsequent barrage, so, with the exception of the small party of Guardsmen on the right, both flanks were exposed. At this time Mr. Blest was wounded and put out of action. As dusk fell the survivors redoubled their vigilance, suspecting to see the grey-clad men creeping upon them in the shadows. But the fortunes of war had swung in their favour; there was no counter-attack. The bluff of a few isolated men had succeeded.[14]

Late at night, a battalion of the rear Brigade came to the relief. The men of the platoon made their way back over the three miles of that strange ground, hastened by enemy shells, until they reached at daybreak an old German trench, then rejoined their Company and rested. A little later, they made their way back to Brigade Headquarters. A halt was made when the column met the limbers containing rations. Some dry tea was issued; wood was scrounged from adjacent ruins, fires got going and tea made in double quick time. Such a space was afforded to talk with comrades in other platoons and hear of casualties. The battalion, spread along that country road, presented a curious spectacle; faces grimed with sweat and dirt; chins covered with stubble growth. While some smoked and talked together, others strolled up the road to enquire after their chums in other companies. A group was competing together for captured German revolvers and showing each other their souvenirs – Jerry soft caps, bayonets, and belts bearing the motto 'Got mit uns', N.C.O.'s coloured tassels. Some, unable to stand the torment any longer, were 'chatting' by the way. Here and there a far-sighted soul was cleaning his rifle to save himself the job when he reached the other end and so gain more sleep; whilst another, unwilling to keep his loved ones in suspense an hour longer, was writing field cards, glad to be able to leave clear the first familiar sentence: 'I am quite well'.

The brief rest and meal over, the last stage of the journey was reached, a system of trenches at Blairville, back west. Here, the Medical Officer contrived a trench aid-post. Men with all kind of complaints gathered in a big group on top of the parapet. The M.O. swiftly examined each, prescribed for his ailment, or sent him to hospital. Knight became so tired of waiting that he left, and attended to his feet himself. He slept until 5.30 next morning – the first good long sleep for many days and nights. At seven o'clock, the platoon stood on parade with the rest of the company, ready to return to the front line. The O.C. had been offered another command. Before taking his leave, he said he wanted to thank them 'from the bottom of my heart' for their work in the recent attack. He spoke of his admiration of the way the company went to the assault again in the afternoon, 'with the eyes of the remainder of the battalion upon it'. Then another captain assumed command of the company, and the platoon was given a fresh officer. Within four days, both made the supreme sacrifice.[15] A three hours march brought the battalion to the very ground it had captured two days before. It was now a back area, so swiftly had the enemy evacuated.

The Division attacked again on the following day.[16] The platoon's battalion was in reserve, so went forward in artillery formation and at length was ordered to man the trenches from which the attack had been launched earlier that morning. Later that evening the order went along: 'Get ready to move'; but the men were kept waiting in complete ignorance for an hour or more. Then they shifted again. Darkness had fallen: they appeared to be progressing a long way to the left. Like sheep, like soldiers, they followed the leaders, over stretches of wasteland slashed with deserted trenches, which they blindly jumped in the gloom. A final halt came at 4 a.m. Rations were served out very early, with the order to eat and then prepare for the attack. Operations did not commence, however, until the afternoon. Then it seemed that hell had broken loose. The British guns burst out with deafening clamour, like frenzied demons thumping gigantic drums, sending the screeching shells to destroy and kill. The attackers followed the barrage and took the first line of defence. The platoon was in the thick of it, chasing the Germans up the communication trench, both sides bombing each other as they ran. Their commander was killed here; shot through the head.[17] He had come to them three days before.

It was another of those days when there was nothing to mark the progress of time; for the men's eyes were so intent on the ground that they did not regard the sun in the heavens. As they passed through the German positions they saw many signs of Jerry's hopes to stay put. There were large wooden huts containing stores of clothing and boots. Singen passed by a cook's rough fireplace upon which three large cauldrons stood, containing water and some green stuff cut into small pieces. But the fire was out; likewise the cook.

General Hull's strategy in moving his division the previous evening by a mysterious forced march to the left and for today's attack, was now manifest: having failed in the morning's assault, by reason of the intensity of enemy machine-gun fire, the division had quietly gone round in the night and, before the enemy realised it, executed a flanking movement. This was reported in the press:- "The village of Croiselles, where the enemy has maintained an obstinate resistance, was gradually outflanked by London troops and is now in our hands". The pursuit was stayed at dusk, and sentries placed. There was little sleep that night; only a fitful doze under a groundsheet. While Blake and Manley watched together, they spoke of early days. Manley had put in for a commission and had been accepted.

"How did you come to join up in the first place?" asked Blake.

"Well, it was sort of accidental in a way. I was walking along the Westminster Bridge Road when I saw a recruiting-sergeant shouting to the crowd at the corner of a side street. There was a young V.C.[18] home on leave. The lad was standing on the tailboard of a lorry appealing for recruits. Well, to cut a long story short, the sergeant came up to me and roped me in". Blake grinned.

"What about you?" asked Manley.

"You'll laugh when I tell you; it was a poem that did it".

"What; not that doggerel of old Bottomley's?"[19]

"Good lord, no. It was a book I picked up at home one evening and what I read made me feel ashamed".

"How?"

"Because of my complacency. The only contribution I was making towards winning the war was to pin little allied flags in a map stuck on my wall. Then I read the challenge: 'Our England is a garden, and such gardens are not made by singing "O how beautiful" and sitting in the shade, while better men than we go out ...'"

"And you decided to do something", interrupted Manley.

"Yes, I went to the recruiting depot first thing next morning".

The Germans did not counter-attack that night: they could not. With daylight, the troops moved forward, leaving their trenches and going across the open. They passed deserted gun positions and a light-railway siding, which had been used for the transport of shells and was camou-flaged with sheets of netting sprinkled with bits of green cloth. The platoon halted against a tall green bank leading to a sunken road, and rested. No food had come up, so the men were given permission to eat their iron ration. A Boche airman with a machine-gun, however, disturbed the meal. At first, his fire was ineffectual, but he gradually worked around in the open until he could fire directly at the whole bank with its living targets. A fearful scene followed, blood flowed and men rolled over. Godfrey saw the grey death-shadow overspread Steenie's face; that hardened old warrior who had fought with him for three arduous years. He lay on the ground, leaning on one arm, wistful, as though he were loath to leave this world – for all its hardships and dis-illusionments – and stumble into the darkness beyond. Godfrey loved this man; who had carried right through with such Spartan cheerfulness. The two had oft times trodden the verge of the grave together when grim Death had sought to make a trio.

After this blunder had become apparent in so tragic a manner, the platoon was ordered to leave that spot and obtain cover in the sunken road. The men then learnt that they would have to make another attack at one o'clock. Meagre details were given. The platoon had no officer, so Sergeant Champion[20] passed what particulars he had to section leaders, who hurriedly gathered their men around them and told them what they had to do. The artillery barrage opened – a somewhat weak affair. The first blobs of men left the sunken road, climbed on to the top and went forward to face the rat-tat-tat of the machine guns. The platoon attacked across the plain in short sharp rushes:[21] a Lewis gunner would run with his weapon and dive into a shell hole, then a man behind with a pannier of ammo would take his place as he ran forward. The new company commander's responsibility sat heavily upon him. His handsome face looked worn and serious, as though he felt a foreboding of death. He moved about on that fatal field fulfilling his duty manfully. He wore on his tunic the ribbon of the military cross, earned in previous attacks. A few minutes sufficed to lay him low and smooth the pain and anxiety from his features.[22]

Enemy marksmen were singling out officers, N.C.O.s and men carrying Lewis guns. The platoon had lost its commander the previous day; and now Sergeant Champion went out wounded. Lance corporal Godfrey found himself platoon commander; and the two gun teams came under Knight's charge. The men went forward until they reached a redoubt[23] on top of which machine gunners were peppering a belt of wire down below. The barbs tore puttees, trousers, and sometimes the flesh beneath. But the Germans could not stop the onslaught. Leaving their dead entangled in that vicious fence, the maddened men climbed up the embankment to fight. In a few moments, there was not an armed German left; those not killed were wounded and taken prisoner; the rest had got away. Godfrey and his men looked over the parapet and saw the next Boche position – Station Redoubt – two hundred yards away across a field towards which Jerry was retreating. Knight placed his gun on top of the bank, adjusted the sights, and fired several bursts. In his eagerness to get a good shooting position he exposed his body and heard the sound of a bullet bury itself two or three inches from his face. A Fritz had taken careful aim, with Knight's face as 'bull's eye', but had, fortunately for him, only scored an 'inner'. A little later a sharp crack sounded by his side. He looked down and saw the rifleman who was lying firing on the bank beside him, slip down and silently expire. The man had been shot in the back of his head by a sniper lurking out there on the exposed flank. All were told to conserve their ammunition, as the enemy were on three sides and might attack in force. At dusk, the company was ordered to retire a short distance; but Godfrey and a few others were left to guard the trench junctions. They anticipated a counter-attack, for shrapnel crashed over their heads, and they heard the ominous plop-plop of gas shells during the dark hours. At last, they were ordered to rejoin the company.[24] The battalion was relieved by fresh troops just as dawn was breaking. Later, at five a.m. the enemy stormed and captured Bullicourt, including the Station Redoubt. Twenty-four hours later, the division counter-attacked and drove them out again.[25] At night, the 52nd Division went up and relieved the 56th. So the division marched back to Boyelles to rest for a few days. It was the last day of August. On their way back the troops passed through Croiselles. It was a pile of debris, nothing more. Over its desolation hung the nauseous stench of unburied horses. The survivors of the platoon were met by the company-quarter-master-sergeant, who took them in Indian file to a gaping shallow trench. The exhausted men lay down and slept until morning; after which they bestirred themselves to remove as much of their dirt as was possible and shave off unwanted whiskers. As the cookers had arrived, it was good to have a hot dinner again – even though it was the familiar army stew.

Notes

1. According to the BWD for the month of August 1918 the battalion started the month in trenches in the Tilloy sector. They were relieved on 4 August 1918 and moved back into support near Blangy. Between 4 and 12 August 1918 the battalion was engaged in providing working parties and the men were able to take baths at Schramm Barracks.
2. 'Foot sloggers' – infantry.
3. On 12 August 1918 the battalion moved back into the line and newly arrived Second Lieutenant E.S. Osborn (killed in action on 5 November 1918) was posted to D Company, positioned south of the Cambrai Road. At 10.30pm on 15 August 1918 a twenty-strong party of the enemy raided a D Company post at the southern corner of Bois des Boeufs.
4. 'Washed out' – abandoned. The phrase is derived from the practice of coating targets on firing ranges with whitewash so that bullet strikes could be seen. Firing had to be suspended while the target was repainted, or 'washed out'.
5. The BWD records that the battalion was relieved on 17 August 1918 and it is at this

point that the narrative resumes. After leaving the front the battalion moved to Berneville, where it camped on the football field.

6. On 18 July 1918 the French Army under Marshal Foch launched its offensive on the Western Front. This was followed by the assault by the BEF which began on 8 August 1918. Surprise and the use of new technology contributed to what General Ludendorff called the 'Blackest Day of the German Army'. From then until the end of the war, at the conclusion of 'the Hundred Days', the Germany Army was in retreat. This does not mean that it did not resist, however, and casualties mounted on both sides during this final decisive campaign.

7. According to the BWD the battalion then travelled via Gouy to Liencourt, arriving on 20 August 1918. On 21 August 1918 the battalion was ordered to St Amand in preparation for an attack planned for 23 August 1918. Note the distance between platoons described in the account; this was intended to reduce casualties from shelling.

8. Although we tend to think in terms of Great War gas being deadly (and indeed in high concentrations it was), it could also be used to make conditions difficult, though not intolerable, for soldiers. Tear gas, which is used for riot control today, causes similar difficulties to those described here, making it difficult to see and breathe. It is easy to see how this would inhibit military activity, although the effects would, ultimately, wear off.

9. Gas was especially effective against artillerymen as their work is very physical and loading guns or moving them was greatly impeded by being forced to wear a respirator.

10. The BWD records that the battalion moved forward into the assembly trenches near Boyelles on the night of 22 August 1918, with A and B Companies in front and C and D Companies in support.

11. The attack, preceded by a very effective barrage, was led by supporting tanks, which cleared the way for the infantry. D Company initially moved forward into the British front line and remained in reserve.

12. The retrieval of the dead officer's revolver ammunition provides further support for the editors' conclusion that the author was a member of a Lewis gun team and was armed with a revolver and not the standard issue rifle. The observation by the author, and his concerns for the dignity of the dead, is borne out by both contemporary photographs and archaeological finds. Both editors were present when a member of the 10th (Service) Battalion, Argyll and Sutherland Highlanders [10 A&SH], killed in 1915 at the Battle of Loos, was discovered on the battlefield in 2008. His kilt had ridden-up as his body had been moved to a place of burial, and an unknown soldier had covered his lower half with a ground sheet.

13. 'Sectional blobs' consisted of groups of nine to twelve men moving together but spread out to reduce potential casualties. Such formations were a common part of the training from 1917.

14. The BWD details the actions of the battalion during the engagement; later in the morning, because of machine-gun fire from the battalion's left flank, two platoons of D Company were sent forward to support the attack. This corroborates the narrative, with the two platoons being sent via Station Trench (Trench map sheet 51bSW3 Boisleux) to Boyelles and then assisting in clearing the village. At 1.20pm, D Company moved forward on the right of the battalion front with the Guards Brigade on the right. Two platoons of D Company in conjunction with the Guards successfully rushed the railway embankment at grid T.20.d (Trench map sheet 51bSW3 Boisleux) forcing the enemy to withdraw to Boyelles Reserve. These two

platoons then rejoined the remainder of their company on the right of the battalion line in grid square T.19. The enemy shelled this area heavily during the afternoon. The BWD records that at about 5pm, while visiting his men in the line, the CO, Acting Lieutenant Colonel R.E.F. Shaw, was sniped and killed. He was originally buried in Blairville Cemetery and subsequently reinterred in Cabaret Rouge British Cemetery (Plot VIII, N, 11). In the BWD is a telegram addressed to all in the battalion from Her Royal Highness Princess Louise in which she expresses her sympathy for the loss of Acting Lieutenant Colonel R.E.F. Shaw, whom she describes as 'your gallant beloved young Colonel'. Contained within the document archive of the Imperial War Museum are the papers of Sergeant Stanley Lane MM, who according to his account acted as a pall-bearer at the funeral of this very popular CO. In addition to the CO, two officers and twelve other ranks were killed and five officers and ninety-one other ranks wounded. Of the officers wounded in this action, it is known from previous entries in the war diary that Lieutenant A.D. James was serving with D Company. It is therefore likely that he is the platoon officer named as Lieutenant Blest in the narrative. The battalion was relieved at 4.00am on 24 August 1918 and moved back to Hendecourt near Blairville.

15. According to the narrative the new platoon commander was killed on 28 August 1918. In support of this the BWD records the death of Lieutenant J.F. Baker as the only commissioned fatality. However, SDGW also records the death of Second Lieutenant J.C. Goadby. It is therefore possible that one of these refers to the subaltern. The CWGC records show that Second Lieutenants Baker and Goadby are both buried in HAC Cemetery, Ecoust St Main (Plots VI, B, 6 and Special Memorial II respectively).

16. The BWD records that on 25 August 1918 the battalion returned to the line, taking over reserve trenches south of Boyelles. They moved forward again on the morning of 27 August 1918 into Summit Trench overlooking Croiselles. From here, the battalion moved forward on the morning of 28 August 1918 into assembly positions and then moved south down the Hindenburg Line in support of 4 London. At this point D Company was in support. During 28 August 1918 the advance continued across the valley of the Sensee River. As the battalion moved south, it encountered a number of enemy positions, which delayed the advance. Where possible, these were engaged with light trench mortars and then mopped up by the infantry. By the end of the day the battalion was located in assembly trenches identified as Pelican Avenue opposite Bullecourt (Trench map sheet 51bSW4 Bullecourt) in preparation for an attack on the village the next day.

17. This entry refers to the death of the new platoon officer previously identified as either Second Lieutenant J.C. Goadby or Second Lieutenant J.F. Baker. It describes in detail the confusion of trench fighting and relates the way in which the officer was killed.

18. 'V.C.' – a Victoria Cross winner.

19. 'Bottomley' – Horatio Bottomley was a journalist and later politician who strongly supported the war. He gave a large number of highly patriotic speeches encouraging men to volunteer.

20. With casualties mounting, NCOs increasingly had to take over the responsibilities of officers and it says much for the training and experience of the men that they could take over these tasks so successfully.

21. Short rushes would today be called 'bounds' and are the hallmark of well-trained soldiers. Only some of the men are moving at one time, while the remainder provide covering fire.

22. The narrative refers to the death of the recently appointed OC, the holder of the Military Cross. This man is confirmed as Lieutenant W.E. Smith, who had been awarded his MC for his part during the raid on 1 June 1918 while serving with A Company. His name is recorded on the Vis en Artois Memorial to the Missing (CWGC) but appears on the Middlesex Regiment panels. Prior to his death, Lieutenant Smith had been granted a Regular commission in the Middlesex Regiment but had elected to remain with the 13 London for the duration of the war.

23. 'Redoubt' – a defensive position or strongpoint.

24. On 29 August 1918 the battalion was again involved in the advances around Bullecourt when just after midday it formed the right flank of the brigade, with 14 London on the left and 4 London in support. The attack commenced with A and B Companies leading, C Company in support and D Company in reserve. C Company became committed immediately but the battalion was still held up by heavy machine-gun fire from an area known as Station Redoubt (Trench map sheet 51bSW4 Bullecourt). As a result of this, one platoon of D Company was ordered forward in an attempt to silence the machine guns; the advance was, however, still held up and the situation was not improved until approximately 7.00pm, when flanking attacks by the neighbouring brigade (76th Infantry Brigade) forced the enemy to withdraw from Station Redoubt. At about 8.00pm the battalion received orders that it would be relieved during the night. The relief was completed by 5.00am on 30 August 1918.

25. The battalion remained in support on 31 August 1918, during which time Station Redoubt and Bullecourt were captured. Despite the requirement to provide support, the War Diary gives no indication of D Company being utilised.

Chapter Sixteen
Rest Eternal

The day had gone very well with the comrades elsewhere. There had been a big battle astride the Arras–Cambrai road, resulting in a breach of the much-vaunted Drocourt–Queant Line and the capture of 10,000 Germans. The village of Queant, opposite Bullicourt, was captured. Next day Drocourt fell. From that time the British, French and Americans never looked back, but swept on triumphantly, whilst the broken, demoralised enemy retreated in undisguised haste.[1]

Whilst walking alone about the open fields, Knight saw a small cavalcade approaching. As it drew near, he saw a tiny union flag fluttering on a trooper's lance behind which rode the Commander-in-Chief. Knight's appearance looked regimental as he stood to attention and saluted. The Field Marshal looked down from his horse as they flashed by and returned with all gravity the solitary soldier's salute.[2] Sir Douglas was on his way to Divisional Headquarters at Boisleux St. Marc to congratulate General Hull on the good work done recently by all ranks.[3] Later that evening Singen mentioned to Edgley that he had written to his cousin in the House of Lords to ask him to use his influence to get more food for the troops. Edgley laughed: "As if that would make any difference!"

"Well, somebody here's got the wind up about it, because I'm to be transferred to another unit", replied Singen.

Next day the Brigadier-General went to the Battalion to convey the Field Marshal's message. He was very friendly; making the men sit on the grass whilst he talked to them of war.[4] He spoke of the good fighting record of the battalion, and how, since the enemy had retired farther back. He had gone over the ground that had been won at so great a cost and seen men with the regimental badge on their tunics lying dead on the field or stretched lifeless on the barbed wire or in the German strongholds. All this and the many piles of empty cartridge cases that had been vomited from enemy machine-guns were silent testimony to him of the strong opposition, which had been encountered.

He went on: "Generals and their staffs could organise and plan a battle up to a pitch, but after that it is you fellows who do the job and gain the day; you are the men who get the job done; and without your efforts our preparations would be in vain".

Of course, his hearers knew he was leading up to something, and it came at last:

"There is a lot more hard work for you to do, probably in the near future; but I am sure you will carry on with the same cheerfulness ...". At which there were a few whispers of 'Soft soap!'.

Sure enough, reveille roused all ranks as early as 4.30 next morning. Finishing a hasty breakfast, the platoon got on parade at 5 o'clock. That is to say, all but Private Baines. Called in the darkness, he at last turned up, his cap all awry, his equipment in a tangle, his rifle dangling over his forearm with the sling out to its fullest extent; whilst in his hands he carried some odds and ends which should have been tucked into his haversack. Sleepily, he fell in on the wrong side of the platoon.

"Put your hand out to see whether you're awake" snapped Corporal Godfrey.

"He's like a big girl with her stocking down", commented Blake.

The battalion marched all day, going by way of Cherisy and Vis-en-Artois until it reached Boiry-Notre Dame in the evening.[5] The troops had come to a land of marshes, ponds and rivers. The Sensee flowed nearby, which tempted some of the men to bathe their feet in the cool waters. Next evening the platoon made its way to the line. It grew very dark, as the long tramp took the men to a great waste of flat ground pocked with shell holes, at the rear of Etaing.[6] Into one of these holes slid a Lewis gun team. The men found that previous occupants had cut a flat platform inside it upon which they could sit in a circle. Their orders were to patrol at night, but to lie doggo in the daylight, to keep the enemy guessing. There was to be no fighting – for the time being. Shellfire was spasmodic. The hole was about four feet deep and eighteen in circumference: and they lived in it four days and four nights. They soon set about a shelter, scrounging under cover of the night lengths of wood that they placed above them for protection against rain. They were a happy party, the five of them. In the daytime they yarned, sang, or prepared their simple meals. Each put his bit of cold meat, potato and beans into his mess tin and fried the whole over a Tommy's cooker. At tea time the comforting properties of the char usually had the effect of loosening the tongue of an ex-carman named Hook who had recently joined the battalion. On such occasions, he was wont to entertain his pals with stories of his 'adventures'. He told them that on one Christmas Eve he 'pinched' a prime turkey, drove it to his domestic domicile, flung open the street door (which invariably stood ajar), pushed the carcass into the passage, shouted "'ere y'are, missus" to his spouse and quickly departed to finish his round.

"One day I 'ad to go to a repository to shift some furniture. There was a big armchair standing outside, so I 'lifted' it, and when I got the chance I took it 'ome. It's in our front room now – if the missus 'asn't pawned it".

Yet he was the type of man who would not rob a comrade. Oddly enough, too, he was fond of getting the team to sing in harmony with himself hymns ancient and modern. What would his missus have thought if she could have seen him seated there, facing the others, in that hole in a dreary waste, unwashed, unshaven, softly, albeit hoarsely, singing 'Abide with me'?[7]

Strict army orders would have made the team take turns of sentry all the day, looking over the ground; but they knew no Jerrys would be walking about there in broad daylight; so they squatted in their hole in the middle of No Man's Land, regardless of everyone. The sky cleared and the men had a lovely sunny day – had they not been pestered by a swarm of wasps which flew from miles around, attracted by their bread and jam. Caught unawares, they set about the invaders with their flat knives as they gulped the food down profane throats.

"The buggers know we're in a trap" swore Hook. But his quick resource came to the rescue: he slung his jam tin over the top, and the yellow horde went after it.

Two mornings later Blake crawled out to pick some wild flowers he had seen growing in the sides of an old shell hole: with thoughts to send them to his girl when he got back to Every Man's Land. Back now; he sat quietly with a pad on his knee.

"Who are you writing to?" Hook enquired. Blake regarded the lad's quizzical face.

"To my love and my lady" he said.[8]

"Cor; aint you satisfied with one, then?"

"I was merely quoting poetry". Returning to his pad, he wrote: 'My darling, here are some ....'

A tremendous crash rent the air outside the hole; a shard of fierce metal flew down, split open the lover's temple, and scattered the little flowers at his feet.[9]

When its six days rest was past,[10] the battalion moved up to Rumaucourt close to the Canal du Nord. The 56th Division's line ran from marshy Palleul down to Marquion.[11] The platoon took up its new position in a trench so shallow that the men were all night working to deepen it. Two stormy nights later, they dug from ten o'clock to stand-to making shell hole outposts in No Man's Land. It was arranged that at the first hint of dawn the men in the outposts would withdraw and join the others in the assembly trench; there to wait until the hour of attack struck, when all would take part in operations by which Cambrai would be outflanked from north and south. It was the morning of September 27th. The platoon's new commander and the sergeant, both fresh from England, went unprepared for the battle, being their first time in the line.[12]

Just before dawn, the platoon stood ready for the jump-off;[13] but the order was delayed. When the men did get on the move, the two 'leaders' halted them in the middle of No Man's Land whilst they roamed around seeking the goal. Then the thunder of the British guns told them that the attack had begun. Before long the enemy was laying down his barrage of shells, some of which fell perilously near the waiting men. At length the platoon was got to the assembly trench; to wait until the afternoon, for the attack was being made on the right. At 3.15, the men climbed out and went forward.[14] The officer led them some distance, across fields and through roads whose stone cobbles had been shattered by shells. They sprinted across hot spots covered by the fire of hidden machine-guns and lurking snipers – but immune from the old horror, shellfire. Reaching the vicinity of the Canal du Nord – a sodden meadow bristling with thick belts of barbed wire – they found the defence ensconced, commanding from that vantage ground all the area. Men were sent with rifle grenades to try to see what they could do; but that proved ineffective, so they resorted to flanking tactics. They came upon a cobbled road, the greater part of which was under water. Wading through, the men found themselves on a path that led straight to the canal. The platoon then re-joined the rest of the company, which stretched right along the road.[15]

Night had fallen. The enemy shot up star shells from various close points. Patrols crept forward to reconnoitre, but were held up by deep belts of wire and other obstacles, as well as point-blank machine-gun fire which did murderous execution. Finally, everyone was ordered to dig himself in the waterlogged side of the road.[16] The entrenching tool, which infantrymen carried, had to be used. Knight did not possess one, so he had to wait patiently until someone could oblige him. He said it was a judgment on him; for the last time he had to use one for this purpose was two years before, at Leuze Wood during the Somme offensive in July 1916. Since then he had carried the heavy tool everywhere when on duty. Nine days before this attack, with the object of lightening his heavy load, he drew the iron from its sheath and the wooden helve from its carrier and dumped them. The men were furiously digging in; he waited with what philosophy he had. "Leuze Wood" he mused, "so much had happened since then". One by one, his chums had cruelly been snatched away. When at last Knight was able to get the tool, he had a swift race with time to dig his shallow grave-like trench. He was doing fairly well, when he was called to go out at once with a small patrol. They were to reconnoitre the impenetrable places, which the darkness of the night had hidden.

He took with him six others. They went up the edge of the road, which had been enfiladed a few hours before.[17] A field of long grass stretched on either side, called Mill Copse. The road sloped to a path leading to the canal. The ground was covered with barbed wire, but, aided by the light, the men found a way round. Knight left the patrol, crept forward and climbed the canal bank towards an iron bridge, the first small arch of which faced a towpath. Taking care not to get in the way of a possible machine-gun, he crawled in front with revolver in hand ready to shoot. There he faced a breastwork of sandbags topped by a pile of cartridge cases; but the gun had gone – likewise the gunners. They had left behind a rifle and a steel helmet. A straw bed lay in a corner. The Germans had used their murderous weapon to fire right down the towpath of the canal. Knight turned and went back to the waiting lads. "There's nobody up there", he said. "We'll go along the towpath and cross by that wooden bridge farther up". So they went and crossed the bridge, turned left and walked along the other towpath towards the second arch. They were a cheerful bunch, young (except Peter Knight, now a veteran in his thirties) and emboldened because their side was winning.

"It's all quiet: I reckon the Jerrys have hopped it", said one.

But unseen crafty eyes were watching up there. As the small party drew closer, a thick finger pressed the trigger of a machine-gun and fired the fatal shots that sent the unsuspecting souls into eternity.[18]

Notes

1. The collapse of the Imperial German Army was gradual but dramatic. By 8 November 1918 it is estimated that the Germans had more than a million deserters, and losses of men and material were mounting. With the men of the High Seas Fleet in mutiny and a fraction of the men available to hold off the advancing Allies, the Kaiser abdicated and the High Command sought an armistice, which came into effect at 11am on 11 November 1918.

2. To the soldiers of the BEF Sir Douglas Haig was 'DH' or 'The Chief', a remote and lofty figure who was admired by many as the architect of victory. This reference to the Commander-in-Chief returning the salute of a single soldier indicates that the author held his commander in high regard when he wrote this book.

3. The history of the 13 London confirms that the Commander-in-Chief did, indeed, visit the divisional commander on 3 September 1918. This history was published in 1936, after the editors believe that Steward's account was completed, and it thus appears that this reference is from memory rather than another source.

4. The idea that a divisional commander would talk to the other ranks whilst they sat informally on the grass does not fit commonly held beliefs about the Great War. This talk to the men clearly happened, and it seems, from the lack of emphasis placed by the author on the event, it was not uncommon. Well trained and experienced soldiers do not respond well to 'bull', as the author has made clear.

5. The BWD commences September 1918 with the battalion in reserve in the Boyelles area; in the evening of 6 September 1918 it moved to Vis-en-Artois.

6. According to the BWD during this period in the line the battalion was engaged in active patrolling of the flooded areas of the Sensee Valley. At this point the front line consisted of an outpost line of slit trenches and shell holes. This certainly supports the narrative account of the Lewis gun section being deployed in a shell hole.

7. 'Abide with Me' is the hymn supposedly played by the *Titanic*'s small orchestra, which continued to play as the ship sank beneath them in 1912. This may be a reference to the feeling of hopelessness among some of the platoon.

8. 'To my love and my lady' – perhaps a reference to the toast common among soldiers, 'To wives and sweethearts! May they never meet!'

9. The manner of Blake's death highlights the suddenness with which a man's life could end and the way in which their comrades would have to accept the loss and continue. Such terms as 'when your number is up' epitomise the perhaps fatalistic view of the soldier by this stage of the war. One's luck could only last for so long.

10. The BWD records that the battalion was relieved on 13 September 1918 and, travelling via Vis-en-Artois, arrived at St Laurent Blangy on the morning of 15 September 1918. On this day seventeen new second lieutenants joined the battalion fresh from the reserve battalion in England.

11. The battalion remained at St Laurent Blangy until 19 September 1918, when it moved via Feuchy to Vis-en-Artois and bivouacked 1,000 yards southwest of the St Rohart Factory. At 7.00pm that evening the battalion marched via the Arras–Cambrai Road to Rumaucourt, where it moved into the support line. D Company moved forward into the right front sector. During this time in support the battalion was engaged in providing working parties and on 23–25 September 1918 in digging assembly trenches west of Sauchy-Cauchy.

12. The BWD records that of the officers who arrived on 15 September 1918, the following were allocated to D Company: A.B. Vandervord, S.A.J. Moorat, J.M.H. Wright and J. Mendes-Chumaciero. One of these officers would have been the 'new officer' referred to in the narrative.

13. 'Jump off' – the order to attack.
14. The BWD details that on the evening of 26 September 1918 the barrage commenced and the Canadian Corps began its attack south of the Arras–Cambrai Road and crossed the Canal Du Nord. Six hours after the Canadian attack the 11th Infantry Division moved forward and crossed the canal, in company with 169 Brigade, which took up a position on the east bank of the canal facing north. At about 3.28pm on 27 September 1918 the 11th Division and 169 Brigade began their advance north along the canal. At the same time the battalion moved from its assembly trenches and, on reaching the Canal du Nord, turned north and began to advance on a two-platoon frontage along the west bank with B Company leading and D Company in support.
15. According to the BWD the advancing troops encountered little opposition and the leading company reached the first objective, the Sauchy–Cauchy Road, at 4.35pm. At this point A and D Companies moved through B Company and continued the advance northwards towards the final objective at Mill Copse (Trench map sheet 51bSE2 Oisy Le Verger). At this point considerable opposition was met, with heavy machine-gun fire being aimed at the leading platoons. By 6.20pm D Company had established a line about 500 yards short of Mill Copse. They experienced particular problems from a number of enemy machine guns located near the canal bridge at Mill Copse and attempted to reach these via a flooded pave and the canal towpath, both of which were covered by machine guns. After dark the men of D Company began to work their way along the pave lane towards Mill Copse and by 2.30am on 28 September 1918 had reported that the enemy had withdrawn from Mill Copse and that they had established a line north of the location. They also reported that the machine guns on the bridge had been abandoned following a bombing attack by elements of the company. This corresponds with the position described in the narrative as that visited by Knight during his final patrol.
16. The battalion remained in position during the day and was relieved on 29 September 1918, returning to its assembly area near Rumaucourt.
17. According to the BWD casualties for the period 27–28 September 1918 were light, with only nine other ranks reported as wounded and none killed. SDGW records only one fatality for the same period, 494199 Private Albert McNally, who died of wounds on 29 September 1918. According to CWGC records he is buried in Brie British Cemetery (Plot IV, F, 4).

Time to Go Home

It is at this point on 28 September 1918 that the narrative closes, with the final patrol of Knight and his section. Why the author elected to end the narrative here is not clear. It is known, however, that he was granted leave to the UK on 20 October 1918 and returned to the battalion on 3 November 1918.

According to the BWD the battalion was relieved on the night of 11 October 1918 and returned to Rumaucourt, becoming the divisional reserve. On 14 October 1918 the battalion moved to Marquion, where it entrained and moved to Arras, arriving after delays and a twenty-two hour journey. The battalion remained in Arras until 31 October 1918, when it moved back to the line in the area of Rhonelle. According to his service record, Joseph Steward rejoined the battalion on 3 November 1918 near Famars. Between 3 and 7 November 1918 the battalion was engaged in operations pursuing a retreating enemy moving through Saultain, Sebourquiaux and Angre.

During this period battalion casualties included Captain H.B. Perry, Second Lieutenant W. Osborn and nine other ranks killed and Second Lieutenant J.H.M. Wright and thirty other ranks wounded. Captain Perry and Second Lieutenant Osborn, according to CWGC records, were both buried in Valenciennes (St Roch) Communal Cemetery (Plots III, A, 9 and 15 respectively). During 8 November 1918 the battalion moved to and was billeted in Autreppe and on 9 November 1918 moved to Erquennes. The BWD describes the welcome given to the men by the locals as they marched through en route to Rieu de Bury, where they arrived on 10 November 1918.

On 11 November 1918 all available men of the battalion were engaged on road repairs under the direction of the Royal Engineers. The work continued despite hostilities ceasing at 11.00am and the usual military precautions were maintained.

Select Bibliography and References

Original Sources
The National Archives
War Diaries
13th (Kensington) Battalion, London Regiment WO95/2955
168 Infantry Brigade, July 1916–May 1917 WO95/2951
Service Records
Joseph Johns Steward WO363/S2335
Second Lieutenant J.F. Baker, killed in action 28 August 1918 WO374/3366
Captain R.G. Barnett, survived WO374/4150
Second Lieutenant H.N. Bundle, killed in action 20 September 1917 WO374/10759
Second Lieutenant F.B. Burd, killed in action 20 September 1917 WO374/10819
Second Lieutenant R.S. Dawes, killed in action 9 September 1916 WO374/18704
Major C.C. Dickens, killed in action 9 September 1916 WO374/19553
Major V.A. Flower, killed in action 15 August 1917 WO374/24780
Second Lieutenant J.C. Goadby, killed in action 28 August 1918 WO374/27654
Captain N.J. Inns, wounded 24 March 1918 WO374/36423
Lieutenant A.D. James MC, wounded 23 August 1918 WO374/36942
Second Lieutenant A. Lester, killed in action 8 May 1918 WO374/41782
Second Lieutenant W. Mortlock, discharged unfit as result of wounds WO374/49164
Second Lieutenant W.L. Posnett, killed in action 22 June 1917 WO374/54769
Second Lieutenant C.S. Ranson, killed in action 16 August 1917 WO374/56242
Second Lieutenant W. Sanders, killed in action 9 September 1916 WO374/60260
Second Lieutenant E.R. Seabury, killed in action 21 September 1917 WO374/61118
Acting Lieutenant Colonel R.E.F. Shaw, killed in action 23 August 1918 WO374/61725
Lieutenant W.E. Smith MC, killed in action 29 August 1918 WO374/63842
Second Lieutenant A. Swift, wounded 16 August 1917 WO374/66676

Imperial War Museum
Personal papers of P.D. Mundy (13 London) Box 80/43/1

Published Sources
General Histories

Anon., *The Best 500 Cockney War Stories* (London Evening News, 1921)

Anon., *Cemeteries and Memorials in Belgium and France* (Commonwealth War Graves Commission, 2004)

Bailey, O.F. and Hollier, H.M., *The Kensingtons: 13th London Regiment* (Regimental Old Comrades Association, London, 1936)

Becke, A.F., *Order of Battle of Divisions, Part 1: The Regular British Divisions* (Naval & Military Press Ltd, 2007)

——, *Order of Battle of Divisions, Part 2a: The Territorial Force Mounted Divisions and The 1st-Line Territorial Force Divisions 42–56* (Naval & Military Press Ltd, 2007)

——, *Order of Battle of Divisions, Part 3: New Army Divisions 9–26* (Naval & Military Press Ltd, 2007)

——, *Order of Battle of Divisions, Part 4: The Army Council, GHQs, Armies and Corps, 1914–18* (Naval & Military Press Ltd, 2007)

——, *Order of Battle of Divisions, Index* (Naval & Military Press Ltd, 2007)

Beckett, I.F.W., *The Great War* (Harlow, Pearson Education, 2nd edn, 2007)

Brophy, J. and Partridge, E., *The Long Trail, What the British Soldier Sang and Said in 1914–1918* (London, Andre Deutsch Ltd, 1965)

Corns, C. and Hughes-Wilson, J., *'Blindfold and Alone'. British Military Executions in the Great War* (Cassell & Co., 2001)

Dudley Ward, Major C.H., *The Fifty-Sixth Division, 1st London Territorial Division 1914–1918* (Naval & Military Press, repr. edn, 1921)

Dymond, S., *Researching British Military Medals, A Practical Guide* (Crowood Press, n.d.)

Edmonds, J.E., *Military Operations France and Belgium, 1916, Sir Douglas Haig's Command to the 1st July 1916, Battle of the Somme* (HMSO, 1932)

——, *Military Operations France and Belgium, 1916, Sir Douglas Haig's Command to the 1st July 1916, Battle of the Somme, Appendices* (HMSO, 1932)

——, *Military Operations France and Belgium, 1916, 2nd July to the End of the Battle of the Somme* (HMSO, 1938)

——, *Military Operations France and Belgium, 1917* (HMSO, 1940)

——, *Military Operations France and Belgium, 1917 vol. II* (HMSO, 1948)

——, *Military Operations France and Belgium, 1918, vol. IV, 8th August–26th September 1918* (HMSO, 1948)

Gould, R.W., *Campaign Medals of the British Army 1815–1972, An Illustrated Reference Guide for Collectors* (London, Arms & Armour Press, 1972)

——, *Locations of British Cavalry, Infantry and Machine Gun Units, 1914–24* (Heraldene Ltd, 1977)

Hart, P., *1918, A Very British Victory* (Weidenfeld & Nicholson, 2008)

Henshaw, T., *The Sky Their Battlefield. Air Fighting and the Complete List of Allied Air Casualties from Enemy Action dDuring the First World War, British, Commonwealth, and United States Air Services 1914 to 1918* (London, Grub Street, 1995)

James, E.A., *British Regiments, 1914–1918* (Samson Books, 1978)

——, *A Record of the Battles and Engagements of the British Armies in France and Flanders, 1914–1918* (Naval & Military Press, repr. edn 1924)

Lloyd, M., *The London Scottish in the Great War* (Leo Cooper, 2001)

MacDonald, A., *Pro Patria Mori. The 56th (London) Division at Gommecourt, 1st July 1916* (Diggory Press, 2006)

Makepeace-Warne, A., *Brassey's Companion to the British Army* (Brassey's, 1995)

Middlebrook, M., *Your Country Needs You. Expansion of British Army Infantry Divisions, 1914–1918* (Pen & Sword, 2000)

Mottram, R.H., *Journey to the Western Front, Twenty Years After* (London, G. Bell & Son Ltd, 1936)

Myatt, F., *The British Infantry 1660–1945: the Evolution of a Fighting Force* (Blandford Press, 1983)

Oram, G., *Death Sentences Passed by Military Courts of the British Army 1914–1920* (Francis Boutle, 1998)

Walker, R.W., *Recipients of the DCM, 1914–1920* (Midland Records, 1981)

Westlake, R., *The Territorial Battalions, A Pictorial History 1859–1985* (Guild Publishing, 1986)

White, A.S., *A Bibliography of Regimental Histories of the British Army* (London Stamp Exchange, 1988)

Wise, T. and S., *A Guide to Military Museums and Other Places of Military Interest*, 10th edn (Imperial Press, 2001)

Training Manuals

The Pattern 1908 Web Infantry Equipment (War Office, 1913)

General Staff, *Infantry Training (4-Company Organisation)* (War Office, HMSO, 1914)

——, *SS 143 Instructions for the Training of Platoons for Offensive Action 1917* (HMSO, 1917)

——, *SS 448 Method of Instruction in the Lewis Gun* (HMSO, May 1917)

Ancestry and Research

Beckett, I.F.W., *The First World War. The Essential Guide to Sources in The National Archives* (Public Record Office, 2002)

Cantwell, J.D. *The Second World War, A Guide to Sources* (Public Record Office, 1998)

Duckers, P., *British Campaign Medals 1914–2000* (Shire Books, 2003)

——, *British Gallantry Awards 1855–2000* (Shire Books, 2001)

Fowler, S. and Spencer, W., *Army Records for Family Historians* (Public Record Office, 1999)

Fowler, S., Spencer, W. and Tamblyn, S., *Army Service Records of the First World War* (Public Record Office, 1998)

Fowler, S. *Tracing Your Army Ancestors* (Barnsley, Pen & Sword, 2006)

Golland, R., *Tracing Your Family History, Army* (Imperial War Museum, 1999)

Holding, N., *World War I Army Ancestry, Third Edition* (Federation of Family History Societies, 1997)

——, *More Sources of World War I Army Ancestry, Third Edition* (Federation of Family History Societies, 1998)

Holding, N. and Swinnerton, I., *World War I Army Ancestry, Fourth Edition* (Federation of Family History Societies, rev. edn, 2003)

——, *The Location of British Army Records 1914–18* (Federation of Family History Societies, rev. edn, n.d.)

Roper, M., *The Records of the War Office and Related Departments 1660–1964* (Public Record Office, 1998)

Spencer, W. *First World War Army Service Records, A Guide for family Historians, Fourth Edition* (The National Archives, 2008)

——, *Records of the Militia and Volunteer Forces 1757–1945* (Public Record Office, 1997)

Summers, J. *British Commonwealth War Cemeteries* (Shire Library, 2010)

Swinnerton, I., *Identifying your World War I Soldier from Badges and Photographs* (Federation of Family History Societies, 2001)

CDs/DVDs

Captured German Trench and Operations Maps from the National Archives (Naval & Military Press, 2003)

Official History of the Great War, 1914–1918, Military Operations France and Belgium. Transportation on the Western Front and Occupation of the Rhineland (Naval & Military Press, 2010)

Soldiers Died in the Great War 1914–1919 (version 2, Naval & Military Press Ltd, 2004)

The National Archive British Trench Map Atlas, The Western Front 1914–1918, 1:10,000 Regular Series (Naval & Military Press, 2008)

Useful Websites

Ancestry www.ancestry.co.uk

The Ogilby Trust, Army/Regimental Museums www.armymuseums.org.uk

British Library www.bl.uk

Commonwealth War Graves Commission www.cwgc.org.uk
Find My Past www.findmypast.co.uk
London/Edinburgh Gazettes www.gazettes-online.co.uk
Imperial War Museum www.iwm.org.uk
Ministry of Defence Veterans Agency www.veterans-uk
National Archives www.nationalarchives.gov.uk
National Army Museum www.nam.ac.uk
Naval and Military Press www.naval-military-press.com
Steve Roberts www.steverobertsmilitaryancestors.com
Andrew Robertshaw www.battlefieldpartnerships.co.uk
Western Front Association www.westernfrontassociation.com
www.military-genealogy.com

Index

General Index

Bold type indicates that entries appear in the chapter notes.

Underlining indicates fictional characters in *The Platoon*.

British Army Units: